Student Handbook

Child and Adolescent Development

Child and Adolescent Development

Second Edition

Kelvin L. Seifert
Robert J. Hoffnung

Student Handbook

Mary Ann McLaughlin
Clarion University of Pennsylvania

Robert F. Rycek
Kearney State College, Nebraska

HOUGHTON MIFFLIN COMPANY   BOSTON

DALLAS   GENEVA, ILLINOIS   PALO ALTO   PRINCETON, NEW JERSEY

Printed in the U.S.A.

ISBN: 0-395-57359-9

ABCDEFGHIJ-HS-99876543210

Contents

To the Student

This Student Handbook was prepared to help you master the information provided in the text *Child and Adolescent Development*, Second Edition, and to facilitate your study and retention of the important theories, facts, and concepts related to developmental psychology.

In developing a student handbook, we recognize that most students have devised their own ways of studying and learning new material. We encourage you to try those means you have found useful to make studying interesting and productive. At the same time, having access to a student handbook developed especially for a text may help you study more efficiently and effectively, particularly as this may be introductory material for you.

Handbook content parallels textbook content and contains the following materials for each chapter:

1. A list of *learning objectives*, drawn specifically from the textbook's coverage. They describe what you are expected to be able to do to show that you have learned the material in the chapter.

2. A detailed *chapter outline* that summarizes the main points of the chapter.

3. A brief *overview* of chapter content, along with a series of *fill-in-the-blank statements* related to the key concepts of the chapter. The answers to these questions appear at the end of each chapter of this Handbook.

4. A list of *key terms* for you to define, along with the page numbers of the textbook where they are defined. Most of these terms are also defined in the glossary for the text.

5. A set of *short-answer study questions*. The questions are in order of their coverage in the textbook. We suggest that you respond to the questions as you read the text.

6. A *multiple-choice self-test*. This test is designed to test your knowledge of chapter content and to give you practice in taking multiple-choice tests based on this content. The answers to the test, along with a detailed explanation of why the correct choice is right and the other choices are not, appear at the end of each Handbook chapter.

7. *Activities*. Each chapter of the Student Handbook also contains a set of activities designed to help you demonstrate that you understand specific course content or to provide you with practice in activities important to that understanding.

Dr. Mary Ann McLaughlin of Clarion University of Pennsylvania is the primary author of the Second Edition of this Student Handbook. Dr. McLaughlin prepared the chapter outline, created a number of new activities, and revised the overview and key concepts, key terms lists, and study questions. The learning objectives and multiple-choice self-tests and explanations were written by Dr. Robert F. Rycek of Kearney State College, Nebraska. Dr. Libby Byers of Sonoma State University, California, is the author of most of the activities appearing in this book, which were originally created for the First Edition of this Student Handbook.

We hope that this Handbook will help you to learn the material in your textbook more easily and thoroughly, and we wish you success in your study of developmental psychology.

Student Handbook

Child and Adolescent Development

CHAPTER 1
Introduction: Studying Development

Learning Objectives

1. Define what is meant by development and describe the nature of developmental change.

2. Sketch the history of the concept of childhood and indicate how certain historical situations contributed to the emergence of developmental psychology.

3. Identify and discuss the major controversial issues in developmental psychology.

4. Describe the three features of the scientific method.

5. Compare and contrast the strengths and limitations of the primary methodologies (naturalistic, experimental, cross-sectional, and longitudinal) in developmental psychology.

6. Discuss the ethical constraints on conducting research with children.

Chapter Outline

I. THE NATURE OF DEVELOPMENTAL CHANGE
   Developmental change contributes to a person's long-term growth, feelings, and patterns of thinking and can be distinguished from other kinds of change.

   A. Three Domains of Development

      1. *Physical development* involves biological development.

      2. *Cognitive development* involves changes in reasoning and thinking, and language acquisition.

3. *Psychosocial development* concerns changes in feelings and emotions.

B. An Example of Development: Aaron
The case of a child named Aaron is presented in order to amplify developmental ideas and domains and to illustrate the interrelationship of developmental changes.

II. WHY STUDY DEVELOPMENT?
Knowledge of human development can help you formulate realistic expectations for children, respond sensitively to actual behavior, recognize unusual development, and understand yourself.

III. THE HISTORY OF DEVELOPMENTAL CHANGE

A. Childhood and Adolescence as Concepts
Historically, children were accorded early adult status. Adolescence was unknown before the twentieth century.

B. Early Precursors to Developmental Study
Current notions of childhood can be traced to the work of Locke and Rousseau and to a historically emerging awareness of children's needs.

C. The Emergence of Modern Developmental Study
Modern observational studies of children emerged in the nineteenth century from *baby biographies* and led to the work of Arnold Gesell and his formulation of *norms* as well as to the influential work of Jean Piaget.

IV. CURRENT ISSUES IN DEVELOPMENTAL STUDY

A. Nature and Nurture
The importance of heredity and environment is often considered in terms of the relative importance of inborn qualities of persons (their *nature*) compared with skills and qualities they acquire through experience and environment (their *nurture*).

B. Continuity and Discontinuity
Development may be viewed as a continual process, or it may be viewed as a series of distinct stages.

1. *Continuity* views picture development as continual, rather than in a series of stages.

2. *Discontinuity* views envision qualitative developmental changes that occur rather suddenly, creating stages.

C. Universal and Context-specific Development
Traditionally, psychologists have concentrated on development that is universal or independent of specific circumstances. However, the culture in which a child grows up

affects when and how the child develops particular qualities and behaviors. As a result, some developmental psychologists have focused on the specific *context* or circumstances surrounding children's development.

1. *Universal* views emphasize experiences that all children have in their development.

2. *Context-specific* views consider experiences that are unique to specific children.

V. METHODS OF STUDYING CHILDREN AND ADOLESCENTS

A. The Scientific Method
Research studies of human development follow certain general procedures that comprise steps in the *scientific method*.

1. Formulation of research questions

2. Stating research questions more precisely or as *hypotheses*.

3. Testing the hypothesis by conducting a study

4. Interpretation and publicizing of results

B. Ways that Research Studies Vary
Each of the ways used by developmental psychologists to study children has strengths and limitations. Viewed broadly, research studies vary along four dimensions: how much to emphasize quantitative measurement, how much to intervene in children's behavior, the kind of time frame to use, and the number of children or "subjects" to observe or study at a time.

C. Quantitative Versus Qualitative Studies
Quantitative studies seek to measure behavior and to attach numerical values or quantities to observations of how children act. *Qualitative studies* observe or record features of children's behavior without primarily attaching quantities to them.

D. Naturalistic Versus Experimental Studies
Naturalistic research purposely observes behavior as it normally occurs in natural settings. *Experimental studies* try to arrange circumstances so that just one or two factors or influences vary at a time.

1. *Naturalistic studies* do not attempt to alter the natural social environment or to manipulate groups of children.

2. *Experimental studies* arrange groups of children so that *independent* and *dependent variables* can be utilized.

a. In experimental research, *random sampling* is often used to identify *populations* of children for study.

b. *Experimental groups* that receive special treatment or intervention are distinguished from *control groups*, which do not receive intervention.

c. *Validity* of experimental studies can be improved by *blind administration* in which the children do not know the purpose of the study (*single blind*) or in which neither children nor experimenters know the purpose (*double blind*).

E. Time Frames for Studying Development
Cross-sectional studies consider subjects of different ages at the same point in time. *Longitudinal studies* observe the same subjects periodically over a relatively long period, often years. Sometimes, dilemmas posed by the time frame are solved by combining elements of both these research approaches in what are called *sequential studies*.

F. Sampling Strategies
The number of persons observed or considered for data collection in a study varies in relationship to the utilization of at least three types of *sampling strategies*.

1. Large-scale *surveys* may sample hundreds or even thousands of individuals about facts or opinions.

2. *Interviews* are face-to-face directed conversations that are used when in-depth information is sought.

3. A *case study* is used when research is done on just a few individuals or even on only one subject. A case study can pull together a wide variety of information about an individual case.

VI. ETHICAL CONSTRAINTS ON STUDYING DEVELOPMENT
Considered in general, research about human beings must face at least three ethical issues.

A. *Confidentiality* refers to protecting the identity of subjects in a scientific study.

B. *Full disclosure of purposes* refers to informing children who are subjects in research and their parents of the true purposes of the study.

C. *Respect for an individual's freedom to participate* ensures that individuals will not be pressured into participation.

D. When all three ethical principles are met, researchers allow for *informed consent* and for the ethical treatment of very young subjects under the principle of *in loco parentis*, or treating children as their own parents would treat them.

Overview and Key Concepts

Chapter 1 introduces the reader to the field of child development and its parent discipline, developmental psychology. Basic concepts and ideas in human development are considered particularly in relationship to three major developmental domains—physical development, cognitive development, and psychosocial development. A brief history of developmental change is presented along with three prominent issues—nature/nurture, continuity/discontinuity, and universal/context-specific development. The scientific method is explained in conjunction with various types of studies that accrue from the scientific study of children. Ethical constraints on research are also presented.

Directions: Identify the following key concepts introduced in Chapter 1.

1. Child and adolescent study deal with change that is _developmental_ in nature, meaning that it contributes to a person's long-term growth, feelings, and patterns of thinking.

2. Human development can take many forms. For convenience, this book distinguishes among three major types or _domains_ of development: _physical_ development, _cogn._ development, and _psychosocial_ development.

3. In response to the question "Why study development?" identify four major ways in which knowing about human development can help you.
   know what to expect
   know yourself
   guidance in responding to behav.
   seeing abnormality

4. Childhood and adolescence are historically recent concepts. Until a few hundred years ago, children in Western society were not really perceived as full members of society. They graduated to _adult status_ in life—around age seven or eight—by taking on adultlike tasks in the community.

5. Because children took on adult responsibilities so soon, the period we call _adolescence_ was absolutely unknown. Lack of awareness of unique periods in life was possibly related to _infant mortality_, the fact that relatively large proportions of children died early in life.

6. At the end of the seventeenth century, certain philosophers began arguing that childhood was a special period of life. Two of the most influential of these were _Locke_ and _Rousseau_.

7. Modern observational studies of children emerged in the nineteenth century from ___baby biegry___, detailed diaries of particular children.

8. Later psychologists added both specificity and generality to earlier methods of studying children. After studying more than five hundred children, Arnold Gesell generalized standards of normal development or ___stages___.

9. Jean Piaget, one of the most influential observers of children in the twentieth century, focused on children's behaviors that illustrated their _____ or _____.

10. As child development has evolved as a discipline, several issues about the nature of human development have emerged and endured. Three foremost issues are _____, _____, and _____.

11. Research studies of human development follow general procedures called the _____. These procedures make developmental psychology a science and lead to various ways of studying children. Whereas _____ studies seek to measure behavior, _____ studies observe and record features or qualities of children's behavior.

12. At one extreme, _____ purposely observes behavior as it normally occurs in natural settings. _____ try to arrange circumstances so that just one or two factors vary at a time. In the latter type of research, a distinction is made between _____ and _____ variables.

13. Experimental studies have a number of precautions to ensure that their findings have _____, meaning that they measure or observe what they intend to measure. One way to improve validity is by observing not one but two sample groups, the _____ group and the _____ group.

14. Because human development by nature occurs gradually over a long period, developmental psychologists have essentially two choices: _____ studies, which compare groups of children who are similar in every way except age, and _____ studies, which observe the same subjects periodically over a relatively long period.

15. Sometimes ethical concerns influence the methods that can be used to study a particular question about development, for example, punishment. Considered in general, research about human beings must face at least three ethical issues: _____, _____, and _____.

Key Terms

Directions: Provide a definition for each of the following key terms. Check your answers against the Glossary or the text page number that follows each term.

Blind administration (p. 23) _____

_____

_____

Case study (p. 28) _____

_____

_____

Cognitive development (p. 5) _____

_____

_____

Cohort (p. 25) _____

_____

_____

Context (p. 16) _____

_____

_____

Control group (p. 23) _____

_____

_____

Cross-sectional study (p. 24) _____

_____

_____

Dependent variable (p. 22) _____

_____

_____

Developmental (p. 4) _____

_____

_____

Domain (p. 5) _____

_____

_____

Experimental group (p. 23) _____

_____

_____

Experimental study (p. 21) _____

_____

_____

Hypothesis (p. 18) _____

_____

_____

Independent variable (p. 22) _____

_____

_____

Informed consent (p. 30) _____

_____

_____

In loco parentis (p. 31) _____

_____

_____

Interview (p. 27) _____

_____

_____

Longitudinal study (p. 24) _____

_____

_____

Naturalistic research (p. 21) _____

_____

_____

Nature (p. 14) _____

_____

_____

Nurture (p. 14) _____

_____

_____

Population (p. 22) _____

_____

_____

Physical development (p. 5) _____

_____

_____

Psychosocial development (p. 5) _____

_____

_____

Qualitative study (p. 21) _____

_____

_____

Quantitative study (p. 20) _____

_____

_____

Quasi-experimental research (p. 24) _____

_____

_____

Random sample (p. 22) _____

_____

_____

Scientific method (p. 18) _____

_____

_____

Survey (p. 26) _____

_____

_____

Validity (p. 22) _____

_____

_____

Study Questions

1. How does developmental change differ from other kinds of change? (pp. 4–5)

_____

_____

_____

_____

2. What are the three major domains of development discussed in Chapter 1? Briefly define each one. (p. 5)

_____

_____

_____

_____

3. How does the case of Aaron illustrate the interrelationship of developmental changes? (p. 8)

_____

_____

_____

_____

4. What are four major ways in which knowing about human development can help you? (pp. 8–9)

_____

_____

_____

_____

5. How has the status of children in Western society changed over the past few hundred years? (pp. 9–10)

_____

_____

_____

_____

6. How did the work of Locke and Rousseau and the authors of baby biographies prepare the way for more modern methods of studying children in the twentieth century? (pp. 10–13)

_____

_____

_____

_____

7. What is one way in which "growing up" in India is understood differently from "growing up" in the West? (pp. 12–13)

_____

_____

_____

_____

8. What are three very important and current issues in developmental study today? Comment briefly on each. (pp. 13–17)

_____

_____

_____

_____

9. What do you think is the major implication of the famous "wolf children" studies for the issue of critical periods in development? (pp. 14–15)

_____

_____

_____

_____

10. What are the four overlapping "ecological contexts" described by Urie Bronfenbrenner in his contextual view of child development? (p. 19)

_____

_____

_____

_____

11. What are four procedures generally followed in implementing the scientific method in psychology and child study? (pp. 18–19)

_____

_____

_____

_____

12. Why do researchers implement the steps in the scientific method in many different ways and through many types of studies? (pp. 19–20)

_____

_____

_____

_____

13. Basically, how do qualitative studies differ from quantitative studies? (pp. 20–21)

_____

_____

_____

_____

14. How does naturalistic research differ from experimental research? (p. 21)

_____

_____

_____

_____

15. What are some of the major concepts and strategies involved in experimental studies? (pp. 21–24)

_____

_____

_____

_____

16. What time frames may be used in studying development? (pp. 24–26)

_____

_____

_____

_____

17. What three major sampling strategies are described in Chapter 1? Comment briefly on the design of each one. (pp. 26–29)

_____

_____

_____

_____

18. How does confidentiality relate to ethical constraints on studying development? (pp. 29–30)

_____

_____

_____

_____

19. Briefly, what is meant by full disclosure of purposes and informed consent? (p. 30)

_____

_____

_____

_____

20. What is meant by the principle of in loco parentis? (p. 31)

_____

_____

_____

_____

Multiple-Choice Self-Test

1. The science that examines how various abilities evolve as an individual grows older is called
   a. biology.
   b. developmental psychology.
   c. psychobiology.
   d. psychology.

2. Two-year-old Sara now realizes that when her mother goes to the closet to get her coat, she is going to leave. Sara's knowledge of her mother's behavior can best be described in terms of
   a. development.
   b. inborn reflexes.
   c. learning.
   d. maturation.

3. Children in medieval times were
   a. pampered during childhood because not many survived.
   b. raised in large group homes or sold into slavery.
   c. treated quite harshly as compared with modern children.
   d. very much like modern children in their daily activities.

4. The idea that a child's mind is like a blank slate was introduced by
   a. Jean Itard.
   b. Jean-Jacques Rousseau.
   c. Jean Piaget.
   d. John Locke.

5. A psychologist studying language argues that cooing, babbling, and first words are qualitatively different and represent a step-wise progression in development. This psychologist probably holds a _____ view of language development.
   a. universal
   b. discontinuity
   c. genetic
   d. nurture

6. The ecological view of development
   a. examines behavior and behavior change as part of an entire system at various levels.
   b. indicates that change comes about through a series of stages.
   c. is based on inborn tendencies to find commonalities.
   d. all of the above.

7. Because developmental psychology utilizes procedures that formulate research questions, state hypotheses, and test hypotheses, it is considered
   a. an art.
   b. a discipline.
   c. a science.
   d. a theory.

8. Which of the following types of studies typically has the fewest controls?
   a. cross-sectional research
   b. experimental research
   c. longitudinal research
   d. naturalistic research

9. A psychologist looking at the effects of TV violence on aggression sets up a situation in which he measures aggression after a group of children watch either violent TV or nonviolent TV. In this study, the measure of aggression is the
   a. dependent variable.
   b. hypothesis.
   c. independent variable.
   d. natural variable.

10. Peter is participating in a single-blind experiment. This means that
    a. Peter is blindfolded during the study.
    b. Peter is not aware that an experiment is taking place.
    c. Peter is not aware of the true nature of the experiment at this time.
    d. The experimenter is not aware of the true nature of the experiment.

11. Which of the following is true of a cross-sectional study?
    a. It always involves the manipulation of several independent variables.
    b. It compares age groups rather than individuals.
    c. It is expensive and time consuming.
    d. It tests the same subjects repeatedly.

12. A study that tests the same subjects periodically across several years is best termed
    a. a cross-sectional study.
    b. an experimental study.
    c. a longitudinal study.
    d. a naturalistic study.

13. Which of the following is a major limitation of the interview method?
    a. Too much data that can't be quantified may be collected.
    b. Subjects must be able to read and write.
    c. Responses may be affected by personal qualities of the interviewer or subject.
    d. Distinguishing between important and trivial behaviors is difficult.

14. Informed consent involves
    a. ensuring confidentiality of the subject's identity.
    b. allowing a subject the choice of whether or not to participate.
    c. informing the subject of the true purpose of the study.
    d. all of the above.

Activities

Activity 1.1

Objective: To identify the unique and the universal characteristics coexisting in one individual.

Recall when you were in the primary grades. Indicate those characteristics you shared with your age mates at school, in the neighborhood, in your country, and throughout the world. There is, of course, at least one characteristic that was neither unique nor shared by everyone: your gender.

Age chosen: _____

Characteristic	Unique?	Universal?	Shared by Some?
Size for age			
Body build			
Face			
Preferred language			
Pronunciation			
Choice of words			
School performance			
Language arts			
Math			
Graphic arts			
Music			
Drama			
Science/nature			
Behavior			
Study habits			
Use of spare time			
Fears			
Health			
Aspirations			
Friends			
Expertise			
Weaknesses			
Favorite TV and radio programs			
Responsibilities			
Personality			
Temperament			
Getting along with adults			
Teachers			
Family			
Strangers			
Other characteristics			

Activity 1.2

> **Objective:** To compare the degree of adult responsibility given to children at the turn of the century with the adultlike expectations of today's children.

This activity has two parts: (1) an interview with your grandparents or their contemporaries and (2) observation and reflection about today's children.

1. Ask your grandparents to look back on their childhood and adolescence to answer the following:

   a. Number of years of schooling:
   b. Responsibilities at home

      Supervising younger children or being supervised by a slightly older sibling

      Household or housekeeping responsibilities

      If in a rural home, home or farm chores

      Other family responsibilities

   c. Responsibilities away from home

      Age for first paid work away from home:

      Length of training period for long-term occupation:

      (For women) Did you earn a wage when you were an adolescent?

      Later?

      At what age did you begin to assume household and child-care responsibilities?

      What were they?

d. Other indicators of adult responsibility

Adult privileges:

Age at which infant dress was no longer used:

Age at which young women wore adult hair styles:

Age at which young men and women wore adult clothing:

2. We know that today's children and adolescents spend more years in school. They are economically dependent on their families for more years than in the past. On the other hand, consider and comment on the following aspects of their lives that they may share with adults.

a. Access to information from media (worldwide events, such as the threat of war, nuclear holocaust, terrorism)

b. Opportunity to take part in current technology (e.g., use of computers)

c. Access to substances that alter moods

d. Opportunities to become sexually active

e. Risks of physical, sexual, and psychological abuse
Do you think the incidence of abuse and neglect is a modern trend or discovery?

f. General mobility (e.g., use of automobiles)

g. Pressures to achieve academically

h. Other

Activity 1.3

Objective: To become familiar with terms commonly used in developmental study.

Match each term with the most appropriate statement(s).

Piaget's carefully written observations of his own children from birth through the first few years

Effect of a new instructional technique on children's arithmetic test scores

Effects of preschool educational programs on academic performance in high school

Degree to which elementary school boys and girls play separately during recess

College library use six weeks after classes begin and during final exam week

Variations in number of high school graduates who enlist in the military

Inborn characteristics compared with those that result from environmental influences

Formulating a hypothesis, conducting a study, reporting and interpreting results

longitudinal study

macrosystem

cross-sectional study

observational study

experimental method

scientific method

study in context

Activity 1.4

Objective: To give examples of cases to which stage theories of development do not necessarily apply.

Stage theories of development are sometimes criticized because they do not take into account individual variations. Think about your own development and what you have noticed about others. Identify one or more people you know of who fit into the general population quite well but whose inner "time clocks" appear to differ from the usual expectations in the following ways. (You need not use real names.)

Did not walk until two years old

Read alone, and with pleasure, at three years

Ten-year-old who could swim (or run) faster than most adults

Read and wrote with much more fluency than in spoken communication

Fourteen-year-old who could not sleep without favorite blanket

Ten-year-old who regularly beat parents at checkers

Thirty-year-old who looks fourteen

Eight-year-old beginning to show secondary sexual characteristics

Other

Activity 1.5

> **Objective:** To analyze yourself or someone whom you know well from the stand-point of the three domains of development discussed in Chapter 1.

List or briefly describe some of your foremost mental or intellectual (cognitive) traits, socioemotional and personality (psychosocial) traits, and health-nutrition, physique, or athletic ability (physical) traits within the appropriate domains.

Cognitive Domain

Psychosocial Domain

Physical Domain

Activity 1.6

Objective: To enrich your view of child development from a multicultural or cross-cultural perspective.

Along with reading "Growing Up in India" (p. 12) in Chapter 1, interview a fellow student or someone you know from a country in the Eastern Hemisphere. Or, if you are from the Eastern Hemisphere, interview someone from the United States or a Western Hemisphere nation and complete the comparative chart below.

	Eastern Nations	Western Nations
View of childhood		
Protection and nuturance of children		
Structure of family and division of labor		

Activity 1.7

Objective: To speculate on the relative contributions of heredity and environment (nature/nurture) to some of your own personal traits.

Mentally compare yourself and some of your major traits to the traits of your parents, siblings, and other close relatives. Formulate some opinions about whether heredity or environment has been more significant in your development of traits in the major categories listed below. *Note:* If you are an adoptive child or do not know many of your blood relatives, write about someone you know whose family you also know well and speculate about the hereditary continuity of traits in that family.

Personality Traits

Traits of Intelligence

Physical Traits

Activity 1.8

Objective: To become more familiar with young children and to have the opportunity to engage in naturalistic observation of young children.

Most universities operate at least one preschool program for young children. Many have enrichment programs that they offer through child development centers, and others operate both enrichment programs (meeting for 2- or 3-hour sessions) and full-time day-care centers. If such a center is operated on your campus, ask your instructor or the director of one of the programs about opportunities to observe and interact with the children. After visiting the center, write some of your impressions below.

Answer Key

Overview and Key Concepts

1. developmental (p. 4)

2. domains; physical; cognitive; psychosocial (p. 5)

3. knowledge of normal development; guidance in responding to actual behavior; recognition of unusual development; self-understanding (pp. 8–9)

4. early adult status (p. 9)

5. adolescence; early mortality (p. 10)

6. John Locke; Jean-Jacques Rousseau (p. 10)

7. baby biographies (p. 12)

8. norms (p. 12)

9. growing cognitive skills; ability to think (p. 13)

10. nature and nurture; continuity and discontinuity; context and universality in development (pp. 13–16)

11. scientific method; quantitative; qualitative (pp. 18–21)

12. naturalistic research; experimental studies; dependent; independent (pp. 21–22)

13. validity; experimental; control (pp. 22–23)

14. cross-sectional; longitudinal (pp. 24–25)

15. confidentiality; full disclosure of purposes; respect for the individual's freedom to participate (pp. 29–31)

Multiple-Choice Self-Test

1. Choice (b) is correct; developmental psychology focuses on changes in long-term growth, feelings, and patterns of thinking. (p. 4)
   Choice (a) is the study of living organisms and life processes; (c) focuses on the biological basis of behavior; and (d) is the study of behavior and mental processes. Although some of

these overlap with developmental psychology, none exclusively examines changes associated with age.

2. Choice (c) is the best answer because learning looks at the acquisition of routine information. (p. 5)
   The best answer is not choice (a) because the example does not imply that normal growth would result in this information (although the abilities to gain this kind of insight might be developmental). Choices (b) and (d) both imply underlying biological/genetic processes that are not involved in this specific example.

3. Choice (c) is correct. In medieval times very young children were viewed as "talented pets" and were given adultlike responsibilities when they reached age seven or eight. (p. 9)
   It is true that many children did not survive, as indicated in choice (a), but those who did were not pampered. Instead, parents sought not to get too fond of them. Children were not raised in group homes or enslaved—choice (b). Nor were they viewed as children today are viewed—choice (d).

4. John Locke, choice (d), introduced the term *tabula rasa*, which means "blank slate." Locke believed that a child must acquire all ideas from experience. (p. 10)
   Itard, choice (a), studied the "wild boy" found in the woods of France. Rousseau, choice (b), was noted for developing special methods of education that emphasized the emerging needs of the child. Piaget, choice (c), developed a major theory of cognitive development.

5. Choice (b) is the best answer. The discontinuity view holds that change occurs in qualitatively different steps or stages. (p. 15)
   Although choice (a) could be correct because it is not inconsistent with a discontinuity view, universality of development simply implies that everyone develops in a similar fashion. This development, however, does not necessarily involve stages. Choices (c) and (d) refer to mechanisms of development being based either on heredity or on environment.

6. Choice (a) is correct. The ecological view is based on the notion that development occurs within naturally occurring environmental contexts. These contexts can be described at different levels—microsystems, mesosystems, and so on. (p. 19)
   Choices (b) and (c) are not necessarily part of the ecological point of view because the underlying assertion is the interaction between levels, not stages or genetics. Choice (d), therefore, is also not correct.

7. Choice (c) is correct. The items in the question outline the scientific method; a science is defined not by what it studies but how it studies it. (p. 18)
   Choice (a) does not imply a systematic approach, and (b) is an area of study that may or may not be scientific. Theories, choice (d), are part of the scientific process and are used to organize information, but simply having a theory does not mean that the theory is scientific.

8. Choice (d) is correct. Naturalistic studies study behavior by observing its natural occurrence; thus there is no control. (p. 21)
   Choices (a) and (c) are research methods used in developmental psychology to look at age differences and age changes. They vary in the degree of control. Choice (b) is the most controlled: an experimenter manipulates certain variables and observes their effect on other variables.

9. Choice (a) is correct. A dependent variable depends on the subject's behavior; level of aggression is the measure. (p. 22)
   Choice (c) is the variable manipulated by the experimenter; in this example, it is the type of TV watched. Choice (b) is the idea being tested; in this case, the hypothesis might be that children who watch violent TV will be more aggressive than those who watch nonviolent TV. Choice (d) is not a meaningful term used in psychology.

10. Choice (c) is correct. In a single-blind experiment, the subject is not told the purpose of the study because that information might affect his performance; however, the subject would be told the study's purpose at its conclusion. (p. 23)
    Choice (a): "Single blind" has nothing to do with being blindfolded. Choice (b): Some naturalistic studies are single blind; however, in a single-blind experiment the subject may or may not be aware that an experiment is being conducted. Choice (d): If neither the subject nor the experimenter knows the true nature of the study, then it is a double-blind study.

11. Choice (b) is correct. A cross-sectional study compares groups of individuals of different ages and does not directly compare one individual with another. (p. 24)
    Choices (c) and (d) are characteristics of a longitudinal study. Choice (a) could be included in a cross-sectional study to make it a more complex design. The variable of focus in a cross-sectional study, however, is always age.

12. Choice (c) is correct. By definition, a longitudinal study examines the same individuals repeatedly across time. (p. 25)
    Choice (a) looks at different people of different ages; (b) involves the manipulation of certain variables to see their effect on other variables; and (d) involves observation with minimal interference or manipulation.

13. Choice (c) is correct. Characteristics of the interviewer and subject may interact in positive or negative ways. (p. 27)
    Choice (a) is not necessarily a problem. You can never collect too much data. At times, quantification may be troublesome, but it is not viewed as an inherent problem with interviews. Choice (b) is a limitation of surveys, and (d) is a limitation of the case study approach.

14. Choice (d) is correct. All of the items, (a), (b), and (c), make up informed consent. The subject understands the nature of the research, feels his or her rights are protected, and feels free to refuse participation. (p. 30)

CHAPTER 2
Theories of Development

Learning Objectives

1. Define what is meant by a theory, a developmental theory, and a stage theory. Describe the characteristics of each.

2. Discuss the basic ideas in Sigmund Freud's psychosexual theory of development, including the id, ego, and superego. Be able to describe each stage.

3. Discuss the basic ideas in Erik Erikson's psychosocial theory of development and compare it to Freud's theory. Be able to describe each stage.

4. Discuss the basic ideas behind the behavioral approaches to development. Describe classical and operant conditioning and define the key concepts involved in each.

5. Compare and contrast social learning theory with the traditional learning approaches. Identify what key concepts this approach adds to learning theory.

6. Discuss the basic ideas in Jean Piaget's theory of development, including the processes of assimilation and accommodation. Describe the characteristics of each stage of development.

7. Describe the basic features of the information-processing approach. Identify and describe the various components of memory.

8. Compare and contrast the major approaches and theories covered in the chapter. Be able to indicate how each accounts for development.

Chapter Outline

I. THE NATURE OF DEVELOPMENTAL THEORIES

    A. What Is a Developmental Theory?

        1. Theories help us understand the world.

            a. A good theory systematically *organizes* what is known about a subject.

            b. It *explains* what is going on in terms of helpful principles and mechanisms.

            c. A good theory is *generative*.

            d. It is *testable* and can be studied through research.

        2. Developmental theories describe changes in human development by discovering principles that underlie *the process of change*.

    B. Stage Theories of Development
       Many developmental theories focus on developmental stages and are called *stage theories*.

        1. Intact organisms follow the same sequence of stages.

        2. Each stage is qualitatively different from other stages.

        3. The stages represent a logical progression in development.

    C. Differences Among Developmental Theories

        1. Theories differ in how much they emphasize *maturation versus learning*.

        2. They differ in the degree to which they focus on *activity versus passivity* in the learner.

        3. They differ in how much they emphasize *conscious versus unconscious* processes in development.

        4. They differ with regard to *breadth versus depth* in various areas of development.

II. PSYCHODYNAMIC THEORIES OF DEVELOPMENT

Psychodynamic theorists believe development is an active process that is most strongly influenced by social and emotional experiences.

A. Freudian Theory

1. Sigmund Freud developed the method of *psychoanalysis*, which he used to develop his psychosexual theory of development.

2. Freud found it useful to think of the individual's personality as consisting of three parts.

   a. The *id*, which contains the *libido* and operates on the *pleasure principle*

   b. The *ego* or rational part of personality

   c. The *superego* or moral part of personality

3. Freud believed that development occurs through a series of psychosexual stages.

   a. During the *oral stage* in infancy, physical and emotional pleasure is sought through the mouth.

   b. By toddlerhood, the infant enters the *anal stage*, in which pleasure shifts to the anus and activities related to elimination.

   c. As the child's libidinal interest shifts to the genitals, the child enters the *phallic stage* at about age three.

   d. Next, the child enters the *latency period*, during which psychosexual development is largely suspended.

   e. Finally, the *genital stage* emerges with the onset of puberty and continues throughout life.

4. Freud believed that the ego manages conflict among the components of personality through the use of *defense mechanisms*, or unconscious ways of reducing anxiety. In *regression*, for example, a person reverts to an earlier, immature way of handling a problem.

5. Freud's theory has been criticized for being vague and culture-bound; however, its appreciation of the inner, emotional lives of children has led to emphasis on qualitative aspects of early childhood experiences.

B. Erikson's Psychosocial Theory

1. Erikson, who studied with Freud, developed a set of *psychosocial stages of development*.

2. Erikson's stages, unlike Freud's, cover the entire lifetime and are based on a series of social, rather than sexual, conflicts.

a. Trust versus mistrust (birth to 1 year)

b. Autonomy versus shame and doubt (1 to 3 years)

c. Initiative versus guilt (3 to 6 years)

d. Industry versus inferiority (6 to 12 years)

e. Identity versus role confusion (12 to 19 years)

f. Intimacy versus isolation (19 to 25 years)

g. Generativity versus stagnation (25 to 50 years)

h. Ego integrity versus despair (50 and older)

3. According to Erikson, three interrelated forces influence personality development.

a. Biological and physical strengths and limitations

b. Unique life circumstances and developmental history

c. Social, cultural, and historical forces at work during a person's lifetime

4. Psychosocial conflicts are never fully resolved; rather, more or less favorable ratios are achieved between, for example, trust and mistrust.

5. Erikson's theory, like Freud's, is difficult to test scientifically; however, two important strengths it has are its understandability and its generativity.

III. BEHAVIORAL AND SOCIAL LEARNING THEORIES OF DEVELOPMENT

A. Behavioral Theory

1. Behavioral theorists focus on learning as relatively permanent changes in observable behavior and on learning experiences as sources of developmental change.

2. Ivan Pavlov (1849–1936) developed his behavioral theory of *classical conditioning* while studying digestion in dogs.

3. Later B. F. Skinner developed a learning theory known as *operant conditioning*.

4. Classical conditioning involves involuntary behaviors. Operant conditioning involves voluntary behaviors.

5. The main strengths of behavioral theories are the simplicity of the basic ideas and the ease with which behavioral techniques can be applied. Weaknesses are related to the fact that behavioral theories may lose sight of children's humanity by reducing their activities to simple patterns of behavior.

B. Social Learning Theory

1. Social learning theorists build on classical and operant models by focusing on social influences in learning, on learning by observing models, and on the mutual interaction of individual and stimulus environment (*reciprocal determinism*).

2. In comparison with behavioral theories, social learning theory provides greater flexibility in defining learning; however, like other learning theories, it lacks an overall theoretical explanation for development and underestimates unobservable thoughts and feelings.

IV. COGNITIVE THEORIES OF DEVELOPMENT
The two theories discussed in this section share a strong interest in how children's thinking and problem solving develop.

A. Piaget's Theory

1. Jean Piaget (1896–1980) was a very influential figure in developmental psychology, and his views have changed our understanding of human *cognition*.

2. Piaget's theory of cognitive development views thinking as a conscious process and places major emphasis on stages that are tied to maturation.

3. Piaget outlined stages that are increasingly complex and in which each stage incorporates and revises the stages that precede it. Piaget's theory incorporates several *key principles*.

   a. He described preschool children as being characterized by *egocentrism:* not being able to take another person's perspective.

   b. In part, children move from stage to stage by responding to new experiences on the basis of concepts they already know. Piaget called this process *assimilation*.

c. In *accommodation*, a child modifies existing schemes to better fit new ideas or experiences.

d. Piaget believed that development occurs because of the interplay between assimilation and accommodation, resulting in a process called *adaptation*.

e. Cognitive *disequilibrium* occurs when the child encounters new experiences and must seek harmony and *equilibrium*. This leads to greater development through a process that Piaget called *equilibration*.

4. Piaget described four major cognitive stages.

a. In the *sensorimotor stage* an infant's understanding of the world is based on simple unlearned reflexes, or *innate schemes*, which rapidly change to fit experiences.

b. During the *preoperational stage* (2 to 7 years) there is a major shift from action-oriented schemes to schemes based on language and other forms of symbolic representation.

c. Children enter the *concrete operational stage* (7 to 11 years) when they begin to coordinate ideas logically. *Operations* are logical relationships among concepts or schemes.

d. Children enter the *formal operational stage* when they begin to think logically, abstractly, and scientifically.

5. In terms of strengths, Piaget's theory provides a clear and thorough framework for looking at the process by which children develop. Also, it integrates a wide range of information about cognitive change. On the other hand, the theory is weakened by the fact that it narrowly focuses on cognition at the expense of social and emotional development.

B. Information-Processing Theory
An alternative view to Piaget's cognitive theory is *information-processing theory*, which focuses on the precise, detailed features or steps involved in mental activities.

1. Key principles of information-processing theory are related to such memory stores as *sensory register, short-term memory*, and *long-term memory*.

2. Developmental changes in information processing are related to acquisition of *control processes* and the development of *metacognition*, which is an awareness and understanding of how thinking and learning work.

3. In terms of strengths and weaknesses, information-processing theory describes the complexity of human thinking as it occurs during specific tasks. It has an advantage

over Piaget's theory in that it describes the actual performance of mental tasks. However, unlike Piaget's theory, information-processing theory does not fully explain processes involved in cognitive development.

Overview and Key Concepts

The purpose of any theory is to help us understand the world and guide our future actions. Developmental theories specifically offer understanding about development, maturation, and learning, and they seek to explain and describe developmental processes in ways that suggest new ideas and in ways that can be scientifically tested. Psychodynamic theories focus on emotions and personality as well as on stages of development. Behavioral and social learning theories focus on observable behaviors of modeling and learning without much regard for stages. Jean Piaget's influential cognitive theory has dominated our view of thinking and problem solving in children. Information-processing theory presents a useful alternative to Piaget's theory. There is no one true theory; rather, each one provides a different perspective on development.

Directions: Identify the following concepts introduced in Chapter 2.

1. The purpose of any theory is to help us _____ the world and guide our future actions.

2. Many developmental theories focus on the concept of developmental stages, and for that reason they are known as _____ .

3. According to psychodynamic theories, the personality is the product of the pleasure-seeking _____ , the rational _____ , and the moral-ethical _____ .

4. Social and emotional experiences associated with the mouth are said to occur during the _____ stage of development. Subsequent stages, according to Freud, are the _____ , _____ , and _____ .

5. The period of little psychosexual activity, almost a nonstage, during the middle childhood years, is called _____ .

6. Erikson's theory describes _____ stages that span a person's _____ .

7. In Pavlov's behavioral theory, the process by which the dog learned to respond is called _____ . In Skinner's behavioral theory the emphasis is on reinforcing behavior through _____ .

8. _____ , while accepting the importance of classical and operant conditioning, focuses on ways in which social influences and children's cognitive activity influence development.

9. Social learning theorists emphasize a process called _____ , which is very similar to the psychodynamic concept of identification.

10. The influential theory of Jean Piaget has radically changed our understanding of _____ or _____ .

11. Several key principles in Piaget's cognitive theory are _____ , _____ , _____ , _____ , and _____ .

12. According to Piaget, development occurs because of the interplay between _____ and _____ , a process he called _____ .

13. The four stages described in Piaget's series of increasingly complex stages are _____ , _____ , _____ , and _____ .

14. _____ theory has gained attention in recent years as an alternative to Piaget's cognitive theory.

15. Three major memory stores, _____ , _____ , and _____ , are emphasized in information-processing theory; so too are control processes and _____ , which is an understanding of how thinking and learning work.

Key Terms

Directions: Provide a definition for each of the following key terms. Check your answers against the Glossary or the text page number that follows each term.

Accommodation (p. 58) _____

_____

_____

Adaptation (p. 58) _____

_____

_____

Anal stage (p. 40) _____

_____

_____

Autonomy versus shame and doubt (p. 46) _____

_____

_____

Assimilation (p. 57) _____

_____

_____

Classical conditioning (p. 50) _____

_____

_____

Cognition (p. 56) _____

_____

_____

_____

Concrete operational stage (p. 60) _____

_____

_____

Conditioned response (p. 50) _____

_____

_____

Conditioned stimulus (p. 50) _____

_____

_____

Conservation (p. 60) _____

_____

_____

Control processes (p. 64) _____

_____

_____

Defense mechanism (p. 42) _____

_____

_____

Deferred imitation (p. 60) _____

_____

_____

Developmental stages (p. 37) _____

_____

_____

Dramatic play (p. 60) _____

_____

_____

Ego (p. 39) _____

_____

_____

Ego integrity versus despair (p. 48) _____

_____

_____

Electra conflict (p. 41) _____

_____

_____

Equilibration (p. 58) _____

_____

_____

Extinction (p. 54) _____

_____

_____

Formal operational stage (p. 61) _____

_____

_____

Generativity versus stagnation (p. 48) _____

_____

_____

Genital stage (p. 42) _____

_____

_____

Id (p. 39) _____

_____

_____

Identification (p. 41) _____

_____

_____

Identity versus role confusion (p. 47) _____

_____

_____

Industry versus inferiority (p. 47) _____

_____

_____

Information-processing theory (p. 63) _____

_____

_____

Initiative versus guilt (p. 46) _____

_____

_____

Internalization (p. 42) _____

_____

_____

Intimacy versus isolation (p. 48) _____

_____

_____

Latency period (p. 42) _____

_____

_____

Libido (p. 39) _____

_____

_____

Long-term memory (LTM) (p. 63) _____

_____

_____

Metacognition (p. 64) _____

_____

_____

Modeling (p. 55) _____

_____

_____

Negative reinforcement (p. 52) _____

_____

_____

Object permanence (p. 59) _____

_____

_____

Oedipal conflict (p. 41) _____

_____

_____

Operant conditioning (p. 50) _____

_____

_____

Oral stage (p. 40) _____

_____

_____

Partial reinforcement (p. 52) _____

_____

_____

Phallic stage (p. 41) _____

_____

_____

Pleasure principle (p. 39) _____

_____

_____

Positive reinforcement (p. 52) _____

_____

_____

Preoperational stage (p. 60) _____

_____

_____

Psychoanalysis (p. 39) _____

_____

_____

Punishment (p. 52) _____

_____

_____

Reality principle (p. 39) _____

_____

_____

Regression (p. 42) _____

_____

_____

Reinforcement (p. 52) _____

_____

_____

Repression (p. 42) _____

_____

_____

Scheme (p. 57) _____

_____

_____

Sensorimotor stage (p. 58) _____

_____

_____

Sensory register (SR) (p. 63) _____

_____

_____

Short-term memory (STM) (p. 63) _____

_____

_____

Social transmission (p. 58) _____

_____

_____

Stage theory (p. 37) _____

_____

_____

Sublimation (p. 42) _____

_____

_____

Superego (p. 39) _____

_____

_____

Trust versus mistrust (p. 45) _____

_____

_____

Unconditioned reflex (p. 50) _____

_____

_____

Unconditioned response (p. 50) _____

_____

_____

Unconditioned stimulus (p. 50) _____

_____

_____

Study Questions

1. What four things characterize a good theory? (p. 37)

   _____

   _____

   _____

   _____

2. How do developmental theories try to describe and understand long-term patterns of change during a person's lifetime? (p. 37)

   _____

   _____

   _____

   _____

3. What are three common characteristics of stage theories? (p. 37)

   _____

   _____

   _____

   _____

4. What are the three components in Freud's view of human personality? Briefly define each component. (pp. 39–40)

_____

_____

_____

_____

5. What is the major occurrence in each of Freud's four psychosexual stages of development? (pp. 40–42)

_____

_____

_____

_____

6. Briefly, what are the strengths and weaknesses of Freudian theory? (p. 44)

_____

_____

_____

_____

7. What were the circumstances of Erikson's life that led him to formulate the concept of identity crisis? (pp. 46–47)

_____

_____

_____

_____

8. What are the salient points of the Eriksonian stages of development from infancy through the middle years of childhood? (pp. 45–47)

_____

_____

_____

_____

9. Why are Erikson's stages called *psychosocial stages* in contrast to Freud's psychosexual stages? (p. 45)

_____

_____

_____

_____

10. What are the strengths and weaknesses of Erikson's theory? (p. 49)

_____

_____

_____

_____

11. How do behavioral theories differ from psychodynamic theories? (p. 49)

_____

_____

_____

_____

12. What is the difference between the classical conditioning associated with Pavlov and the operant conditioning associated with Skinner? (pp. 50–52)

_____

_____

_____

_____

13. What are two or three of the major concepts on which operant conditioning is based? (pp. 52–54)

_____

_____

_____

_____

14. What are the strengths and weaknesses of behavioral theories? (pp. 54–55)

_____

_____

_____

_____

15. How does social learning theory build on the concepts of classical and operant conditioning? (p. 55)

_____

_____

_____

_____

16. What are the strengths and weaknesses of social learning theory? (p. 56)

_____

_____

_____

_____

17. What is Piaget's *méthode clinique*? (p. 57)

_____

_____

_____

_____

18. How is adaptation accomplished through the interplay of assimilation and accommodation? (p. 58)

_____

_____

_____

_____

19. What is the major occurrence in each of Piaget's four major stages of cognitive development? (pp. 58–61)

_____

_____

_____

_____

20. What are three key principles and three major developmental changes in information-processing theory? (pp. 63–65)

_____

_____

_____

_____

Multiple-Choice Self-Test

1. A theory that explains the process of behavior change as a sequence of structurally different steps that follow a logical pattern, systematically organize known facts, and are testable is
   a. a developmental theory.
   b. a good theory.
   c. a stage theory.
   d. all of the above.

2. Developmental theories that view an individual as progressing by resolving conflicts or by solving problems tend to view change as
   a. an active process.
   b. a conscious process.
   c. a learning process.
   d. a maturational process.

3. Freud viewed development as progressing through a series of
   a. maturational stages.
   b. psychosexual stages.
   c. psychosocial stages.
   d. unconscious stages.

4. Whereas the id follows the _____ principle, the ego follows the _____ principle.
   a. pleasure; conscious
   b. pleasure; reality
   c. reality; logical
   d. unconscious; conscious

5. Which of the following is the correct ordering of Freud's stages of development?
   a. anal; oral; latency; phallic; genital
   b. anal; oral; genital; latency; phallic
   c. oral; anal; genital; latency; phallic
   d. oral; anal; phallic; latency; genital

6. Unconsciously Valerie is sexually frustrated, but she uses the energy generated by her frustration to be a great concert violinist. Freud would say that Valerie is using the defense mechanism of
   a. identification.
   b. sublimation.
   c. regression.
   d. repression.

7. Erikson's first stage of development is concerned with the development of
   a. autonomy.
   b. intimacy.
   c. integrity.
   d. trust.

8. During which of Erikson's stages does an individual deal with the development of close relationships while risking the loss of identity?
   a. autonomy versus shame and doubt
   b. identity versus role confusion
   c. intimacy versus isolation
   d. trust versus mistrust

9. Immediately before breast-feeding her three-month-old, Cathy turns on the light next to the rocker she is sitting on. After a while, Cathy noticed that her infant begins to suck as soon as the light is turned on even if the breast is not present. Her infant's response to the light can best be described in terms of
   a. operant conditioning.
   b. classical conditioning.
   c. a reflex mechanism.
   d. unconscious conflict.

10. In classical conditioning, the conditioned stimulus
    a. is always a bell.
    b. is initially neutral.
    c. produces the unconditioned response.
    d. is identical to the unconditioned stimulus.

11. In operant conditioning, any stimulus that temporarily suppresses the response that it follows is known as
    a. a conditioned stimulus.
    b. a negative reinforcer.
    c. a punishment.
    d. an unconditioned stimulus.

12. Social learning theory goes beyond learning theory by adding the concept of
    a. assimilation.
    b. libido.
    c. reciprocal determinism.
    d. unconditioned responses.

13. Which of the following is *not* true of Piaget's theory?
    a. Piaget's stages are closely tied to maturation.
    b. Early sensorimotor development is based on reflexes.
    c. The ability to use symbolic representation and rules in thinking does not appear until the formal operational stage.
    d. The theory's primary focus is cognitive change.

14. The concrete operational person is capable of all of the following *except*
    a. conservation.
    b. deferred imitation.
    c. hypothetical reasoning.
    d. rule mastery.

15. Short-term memory
    a. can hold about seven items.
    b. lasts approximately five minutes.
    c. replicates all information from the sensory register.
    d. contains strategies for learning information effectively.

16. In general, the use of developmental theories may predispose scientists to
    a. draw conclusions that are consistent with the theory.
    b. focus on certain aspects of development and not on others.
    c. make assumptions about development that may not be accurate.
    d. all of the above.

Activities

Activity 2.1

> **Objective:** To recognize that the effective application of theory may depend on the meaning of the behavior.

Three prekindergarten children are disturbing others in the class by throwing blocks. Each of them has a different reason for being disruptive.

1. Consider each circumstance and recommend a strategy for helping the children to play more constructively.

2. Identify your theoretical position.

Child 1: Usually attracts attention when being disruptive. Often, mother attempts to distract him with a cookie, whereas teacher invites him to engage in a favorite activity. In both cases, the child temporarily stops throwing blocks, until the next day.

a. What do you recommend to change the pattern of disruption to more acceptable behavior?

b. What is your theoretical position?

Child 2: This child can also be redirected with an interesting activity—again, temporarily. But child 2, unlike the others, is in a chronic state of anxiety from having witnessed repeated violent quarrels between his parents. He suspects that the source of their anger is his naughty behavior and that they may "send him away" at any time. A program of behavior modification works, but the child continues to be upset, crying easily and clinging to adults.

a. What do you recommend to help this child?

b. What is your theoretical position?

*Adapted from Lillian G. Katz, "Condition with Caution," *Young Children* 27, no. 5 (June 1972): 277–280. Reprinted in National Association for the Education of Young Children, *Talks with Teachers*, 1977.

Child 3: This block-thrower is an only child who lives in a rural area. The prekindergarten program is his first experience with other children and with materials other than those at home.

a. What would be your strategy to help the child play with blocks in a more acceptable way?

b. What is your theoretical position?

Activity 2.2

Objective: To define certain basic concepts of Freud's theory of psychosexual development.

Imagine that it is 1909 and that you are Sigmund Freud one week after you have given your first lecture in the United States, at Clark University. You have granted an interview to a newspaper reporter. The following questions are included in the interview. Write your answers in the spaces below.

INTERVIEWER: Dr. Freud, your theory is quite different from what we have always thought to be the nature of children and adults. Some of our readers may be a bit shocked by the details. How did you first come to be interested in development?

FREUD:

INTERVIEWER: What do you actually do when you treat your patients?

FREUD:

INTERVIEWER: This "id," what is it?

FREUD:

INTERVIEWER: How, then, do we keep it under control?

FREUD:

INTERVIEWER: Does the innocent baby even have a libido?

FREUD:

INTERVIEWER: What evidence do you have for the libido in infancy?

FREUD:

INTERVIEWER: How do little boys and girls resolve their Oedipal conflicts without being driven to violence?

FREUD:

INTERVIEWER: Things do quiet down when children are going to school? Why is that?

FREUD:

INTERVIEWER: But, after all, young men and women do become attracted to each other and marry. When does that happen?

FREUD:

INTERVIEWER: During this enlightened era, the end of the first decade of the twentieth century, we are at last able to protect our wives and the mothers of our children by keeping them safe at home. They have become the guardians of our children, and yet you consider the moral fiber of men to be stronger than that of women? How, then, can we raise our children to the highest moral standards?

FREUD:

INTERVIEWER: [What would *you* like to ask?]

FREUD:

Activity 2.3

Objective: Using the identity crisis as an example, to recognize that Erikson's crises repeat themselves in the course of human development.

Erikson's description of the identity crisis during adolescence views it as so acute that there is a tendency to assume that, once it is resolved, it never arises again. Describe the following identity crises that occur during other life transitions.

Event	Age and Description
Physical changes	
Gender roles	
Responsibility for others	
Career changes	
Legal definitions (driving, drinking)	
Graduations	
Health/illness	
Hopes fulfilled	
Hopes disappointed	

Activity 2.4

Objective: To be able to distinguish between assimilation and accommodation.

We have many schemas about the nature of our world. For example, we have a schema for domestic animals, into which we fit dogs, cats, and canaries. In order to include domestic *farm* animals, however, we must change our existing schema to include other animals that are raised with pets but used as sources of food or clothing, to be used at home or sold commercially. This change is called accommodation. We accommodate our existing schema to include farm animals, and we enter a new state of equilibrium.

Give at least one example of assimilation and accommodation for each of the following schemas:

Schema	Assimilation	Accommodation
Driving an automobile		
Theories of learning and development		
Tying knots		
The fine arts		
Music		
Mathematics		
Family		
Vocabulary		
Plants		
Dancing		

Activity 2.5

Objective: To recognize theories discussed in this chapter, out of context, as set forth in original quotations.

Match the following quotations with their authors.

"In its beginnings, assimilation is essentially the utilization of the external environment by the subject to nourish his heredity or acquired schemata. It goes without saying that schemata such as those of sucking, sight, prehension, etc., constantly need to be accommodated to things . . . ."

"The finding that subjects exposed to the quiet models were more inhibited and unresponsive than subjects in the aggressive condition, together with the obtained difference on the aggression measures, suggests that exposure to inhibited models not only decreases the probability of occurrence of aggressive behavior but also generally restricts the range of behavior emitted by the subjects."

"The infant's first social achievement, then, is his willingness to let the mother out of sight without undue anxiety or rage, because she has become an inner certainty as well as an outer predictability."

"A person escapes from aversive treatment by behaving in ways which reinforce those who treated him aversively until he did so."

"From about the sixth or eighth year onwards a standstill or retrogression is observed in the sexual development, which in those cases reaching a high cultural standard deserves to be called a *latency period.*"

Skinner

Bandura

Erikson

Freud

Piaget

Activity 2.6

Objective: To reflect on the format of stage theories and the mechanisms that they incorporate to explain progress from one stage to the next.

Brainstorm a developmental theory of your own in which you formulate four stages (e.g., "the baby years," "the nursery years," "the elementary school years"). Be creative! Explain at least one mechanism or process that advances the individual from one stage to another (e.g., learning, maturation, nature, nurture).

Stage I

Stage II

Stage III

Stage IV

Mechanisms of Development

Activity 2.7

Objective: To assess the cross-cultural implications of Freud's theory as tested in the research of Whiting and Child and to determine why the findings are tentative.

Carefully analyze the material in "A Multicultural View: A Cross-cultural Test of Freudian Theory" (p. 43). Cross-cultural research is interesting and valuable but imposes special difficulties for researchers. Analyze Whiting and Child's research (1953) on the basis of what you learned about the *scientific method* and research methodology in Chapter 1. Answer the following questions.

What hypothesis did Whiting and Child formulate on the basis of Freudian theory?

How did they go about collecting data to either support or disprove their hypothesis?

What conclusions did they reach?

Activity 2.8

> **Objective:** To distinguish between *domains* and *theories*.

It is easy to confuse the names of the three major domains of development with the names of developmental theories—they are similar or sometimes identical. For example, Erikson's psychosocial stages address facets of development that are contained in the psychosocial domain. Answering the following questions will help you make this important distinction.

The cognitive domain deals with intellectual development and ways in which children think. What two theories explained in Chapter 2 address the cognitive domain of development?

The psychosocial domain deals with emotional and personality development. What are two theories that attempt to describe and explain development within the psychosocial domain?

Do behavioral theories generally address a specific domain?

Answer Key

Overview and Key Concepts

1. understand (p. 37)

2. stage theories (p. 37)

3. id; ego; superego (p. 39)

4. oral; anal; phallic; genital (pp. 40–42)

5. latency period (p. 42)

6. psychosocial; lifetime (p. 45)

7. classical conditioning; operant conditioning (pp. 50–51)

8. social learning theory (p. 55)

9. modeling (p. 55)

10. the development of human thinking; cognition (p. 56)

11. egocentrism; assimilation; accommodation; social transmission; and equilibration (pp. 56–58)

12. assimilation; accommodation; adaptation (p. 58)

13. sensorimotor stage; preoperational stage; concrete operational stage; formal operational stage (pp. 58–61)

14. information-processing (p. 63)

15. SR; STM; LTM; metacognition (pp. 63–64)

Multiple-Choice Self-Test

1. Choice (d), all of the above, is correct: (a) is correct because a primary characteristic of developmental theories is a focus on behavior change; (b) is correct because one characteristic of a good theory is that it systematically organizes known facts and is testable; and (c) is correct because a stage theory is defined as having a sequence of structurally different steps that logically progress. (p. 37)

2. Choice (a) is correct. Active processes involve internal resolution or movements that bring about change; conflict situations and problem solving (as found in Freud's and Piaget's theories, respectively) illustrate an active process. (p. 38)
   Choice (b) involves the question of whether a person is aware of the changes; (c) and (d) address the issue of whether change is environmentally or biologically motivated.

3. Choice (b) is correct. Freud referred to his theory as a theory of psychosexual development. (p. 39)
   Freud does acknowledge maturational processes, choice (a), and unconscious processes, choice (d); but he does not refer to his stages in this way. Choice (c) is Erikson's term for his developmental stages.

4. Choice (b) is correct. The id seeks immediate gratification through the pleasure principle. The ego places some restraints on the id based on the reality principle. (p. 39)
   Choice (a) is incorrect. The id does follow the pleasure principle, but there is no such thing as the "conscious principle," although the ego is represented at the conscious level. Choice (c) is incorrect. The reality principle is associated with the ego, not with the id. In Freudian psychology, there is nothing called the logical principle. Choice (d), unconscious and conscious, names parts of the mind, not personality.

5. Choice (d) is correct. Oral stage is from birth to about one year, anal from one to three years, phallic from three to six years, latency from six to adolescence, and genital from adolescence and beyond. (p. 40)

6. Choice (b) is correct. Sublimation is a defense mechanism that redirects sexual and aggressive energies into safe outlets. (p. 42)
   Choice (a) is involved in the resolution of the Oedipal conflict. Choice (c) is a defense mechanism involving a return to previous immature behaviors. Choice (d) is a defense mechanism involving forgetting an experience.

7. Choice (d) is correct. Erikson's first stage involves the crisis of trust versus mistrust. (p. 45)
   Choice (a) is a focus of Erikson's second stage; (b), his sixth stage, during early adulthood; and (c), his last stage, in later adulthood.

8. Choice (c) is correct. In early adulthood, during the stage of intimacy versus isolation an individual, having established an identity, risks that identity by developing interpersonal relationships. (p. 48)
   Choices (a) and (d) are earlier stages of development that do not deal with the issue of identity or the voluntary development of close relationships. Choice (b) precedes the intimacy stage and involves the development of identity, which is a prerequisite for intimacy.

9. Choice (b) is correct. The situation involves an initially neutral stimulus (the light) that elicits an already established stimulus-response pair (breast and sucking). (pp. 50–51)
   Choice (a) involves a response followed by a reinforcer, not the case here; and (c) is

descriptive of the stimulus-response pair (breast and sucking), not the light. There is no conflict, so choice (d) is not appropriate.

10. Choice (b) is correct. An initially neutral stimulus is paired with the unconditioned stimulus, which produces the unconditioned response. The neutral stimulus becomes a conditioned stimulus when it produces the conditioned response (a response similar to the unconditioned response). (p. 50)
    Choice (a): Almost any stimulus could serve as a conditioned stimulus; Pavlov just happened to use a bell. Choice (c): The conditioned stimulus produces the conditioned response. Choice (d): The conditioned stimulus and unconditioned stimulus are different. For example, Pavlov used a bell and meat.

11. Choice (c) is correct. In operant conditioning, a punishment always decreases the probability of a response. (p. 52)
    Choices (a) and (d) are involved in classical conditioning; (b), which is often confused with punishment, increases the probability of a response by turning off an aversive situation.

12. Choice (c) is correct. A major difference between learning theory and social learning theory involves the mutual interaction of the individual and the stimulus environment, known as reciprocal determinism. (p. 55)
    Choice (a) is a concept from Piaget's theory; (b) is a concept from Freud's theory; and (d) is part of learning theory.

13. Choice (c) is correct. The first use of symbolic representation and use of certain predictable rules are found in the preoperational stage; therefore, (c) is not accurate. (p. 60)
    Choices (a), (b), and (d) all represent true statements about Piaget's theory.

14. Choice (c) is a formal operational skill. (p. 61)
    Choices (a), (b), and (d) are skills within the concrete operational person's ability.

15. Choice (a) is correct; the short-term memory holds about seven bits of information. (p. 62)
    Choice (b) is incorrect because short-term memory lasts about 20 seconds, not five minutes. Only information that is attended to is passed from the sensory register to short-term memory; thus (c) is incorrect. The control processes, not the short-term memory, contain strategies for learning; thus (d) is incorrect.

16. Choice (d) is correct. Each of these is a potential disadvantage of using theories. (pp. 66–68)

CHAPTER 3
Genetics

Learning Objectives

1. Identify and describe the mechanisms and means through which genetic information is transferred.

2. Distinguish between genotype and phenotype, dominant and recessive genes. Describe polygenic transmission of traits.

3. Describe the major chromosomal abnormalities and their resulting disorders.

4. Describe the major gene-based abnormalities and their resulting disorders.

5. Describe the methods used for detecting genetic disorders during the prenatal period.

6. Discuss the heredity-environment issue and the key concepts involved in behavioral genetics. Indicate how this issue is studied in both humans and animals.

7. Discuss the genetic basis of temperament, personality, and mental illness.

Chapter Outline

I. MECHANISMS OF GENETIC TRANSMISSION
   Genetic information is transferred through *genes* and *chromosomes* when *ovum* and *sperm* (*gametes*) unite.

   A. The Role of DNA

      1. Genes are made of *deoxyribonucleic acid*, or *DNA*.

2. All DNA molecules have a particular chemical structure, a double helix or spiral, that allows them to divide and duplicate.

3. DNA makes its genetic contribution when a *zygote* is formed at fertilization when egg and sperm unite.

B. Mitosis and Meiosis
Human beings develop from the original single cell, or zygote, by two types of cell division.

1. Most body cells are formed by *mitosis*, in which the chromosomes duplicate and divide into two sets for the two new cells formed.

2. In *meiosis* reproductive cells, or gametes, are formed by additional steps in which the chromosome number is reduced from 46 to 23.

3. When gametes from parents unite, each contributes 23 chromosomes to form the complement of 46 chromosomes.

II. INDIVIDUAL GENETIC EXPRESSION
Genetic information does not translate directly into a particular trait because its transmission is governed by a number of mechanisms.

A. Genotype and Phenotype

1. *Genotype* refers to the set of genetic traits inherited by an individual.

2. *Phenotype* refers to the traits that a person actually displays during his or her life.

3. The phenotype is really a combination of the inborn genotypic potential and the life experiences that modify inborn potential.

B. Dominant and Recessive Genes

1. Genes are inherited in pairs in which one gene may have more influence than the other.

2. Genes that have greater influence are called *dominant genes*.

3. Genes that have less influence are called *recessive genes*.

C. Transmission of Multiple Variations

1. Genes for eye color and other traits may take on a variety of forms called *alleles*.

2. A person is *homozygous* for a trait if alleles in the inherited gene pair for a trait are identical.

3. A person is *heterozygous* if two different alleles form the pair of genes for a trait.

D. Polygenic Transmission
Many traits result from the combined influence of many genes and are said to be *polygenic*.

E. The Determination of Sex

1. One pair of chromosomes, among the usual 23 pairs of chromosomes, determines the sex of the child.

   a. Genetically normal men have the combination XY, in which the Y chromosome is shorter than the X chromosome.

   b. Normal women always have an XX combination.

   c. The Y chromosome makes men more genetically vulnerable than women.

   d. Numerous genetic abnormalities, like *hemophilia,* are called *sex-linked recessive traits* because they are linked to recessive genes on the X chromosome.

III. GENETIC ABNORMALITIES

A. Variations in the Number of Chromosomes

1. People with *Down syndrome* have several distinctive physical traits and some degree of mental retardation.

   a. In the *nondisjunction type*, gametes have an extra twenty-first chromosome.

   b. In the *balanced translocation type,* the chromosomal number is normal but chromosomal damage is present.

2. A person with *Turner's syndrome,* which affects only women, has a single X in the sex chromosome instead of the normal XX.

3. *Klinefelter's syndrome* produces at least one extra sex chromosome, usually an X, to produce an XXY pattern, which is phenotypically a male.

B. Abnormal Genes
Even when the chromosomal number is normal, abnormal genes may contribute to serious medical problems.

1. In *Rh disease*, a substance in the blood called *Rh factor* causes antibodies to develop in the mother's blood that attack red corpuscles in the fetus's blood.

2. In *fragile-X syndrome* a chromosome is compressed or separated in two or more places, typically causing mental retardation.

3. *Tourette's syndrome* appears to be related to a single abnormal allele.

4. *Phenylketonuria (PKU)* severely diminishes the child's ability to utilize an amino acid called phenylalanine that is found in milk.

5. *Sickle-cell anemia*, caused by a single recessive allele, produces a curved, sickle shape in some red blood cells, often clogging circulation.

6. *Huntington's chorea* is a disease of the nervous system carried by a dominant gene.

7. *Tay-Sachs disease* disturbs the chemical balance in an infant's nerve cells.

IV. GENETIC COUNSELING
Some genetic problems can be reduced or avoided by sensitive counseling for couples who may carry disorders.

A. Prenatal Diagnosis
Through several *diagnostic techniques*, sometimes genetic disorders can be detected before birth.

1. Blood tests can determine an infant's risk for Rh disease or Tay-Sachs disease.

2. *Amniocentesis* is a method used to detect abnormalities in the fetus's chromosomes through analysis of amniotic fluid.

3. *Chorionic villus sampling* (CVS) involves collecting and analyzing tissue by inserting a thin, hollow tube into the uterus.

4. *Ultrasound* allows viewing of the fetus through use of television imaging.

B. Early Medical Treatments

V. RELATIVE INFLUENCE OF HEREDITY AND ENVIRONMENT

A. Key Concepts of Behavioral Genetics

1. *Behavioral genetics* focuses on untangling the effects of heredity from the effects of environment.

2. *Canalization* and *range of reaction* are two concepts used by behavioral geneticists to shed light on how genes influence development.

3. In an *active relationship* between genes and the environment, the child chooses or helps to create the environment. In a *passive relationship,* the child has little or no control.

4. Geneticists have devised ways to study *heritability*—the contribution heredity makes to such traits as intelligence and personality.

B. Observations of Specieswide Behavior

1. *Imprinting* is a specieswide behavior that occurs in geese only during a well-defined *critical period* after birth.

2. A broad range of animals, including humans, exhibit specieswide behaviors for which there may be a genetic predisposition.

C. Lessons from Animal Breeding
Studies of animal breeding suggest the combined effects of heredity and environment.

1. Geneticists can breed for specific traits, demonstrating a genetic bias in some traits.

2. Experiments have also suggested that proper environment can make animals more "competent," suggesting environmental influence.

3. Studies of the genetics of animal behavior have the advantage of speed, but they run the risk of *anthropomorphism,* the tendency to imagine that animals think, feel, and behave in ways that human beings do.

D. Studies of Twins and Adopted Children

1. *Identical twins* provide a "natural experiment" for comparing heredity and environment.

2. Studies of twins reared apart and of adopted children have been done through two research methods: *twin design* and *adoption design*.

3. *Intelligence* as measured by IQ tests shows both hereditary and environmental components.

4. Comparisons of twins reared apart suggest that many *personal traits* are partially hereditary.

5. Because differences in *temperament* are present at birth and because patterns of temperament remain stable, they are probably genetically influenced.

6. Features of *personality* also show genetic influences that may be direct or indirect.

7. Mental illnesses and disturbances reveal genetic influences.

   a. *Concordance*, the tendency for pairs of close relatives to become mentally ill, suggests that *manic-depression* is genetically based.

   b. *Schizophrenia* also shows hereditary patterns, and strong concordance is found among schizophrenic relatives.

E. Cautions and Conclusions About the Influence of Heredity and Environment

1. Even though genetic influence is strong, nongenetic factors contribute more than one-half to the development of most complex traits.

2. When environmental factors are influential, they tend to operate on an individual basis rather than on a family basis.

3. We should cautiously view the strong current trend to minimize environmental factors and to simplistically reduce developmental behaviors to genetic causes.

Overview and Key Concepts

The molecular structure of DNA is described along with mechanisms for genetic transmission. Individual genetic expression is defined in terms of the phenotype in relationship to the inherited traits of the genotype. Genetic abnormalities are traced to deviations in the chromosomal number or to defective alleles in gene pairs. Genetic counseling is discussed as an important preventive measure in the case of abnormality, and the complex relationship between heredity and environment is presented from the standpoint of research and several points of view.

Directions: Identify the following concepts introduced in Chapter 3.

1. Genetic information for all living organisms is carried in a molecule called
   _____ , usually referred to as _____ .

2. Except for reproductive cells called _____ , all cells in the body divide by the process of _____ .

3. The process by which reproductive cells divide is called _____ . In this process there is a second division in which the _____ do not duplicate. As a result, each new cell has only _____ chromosomes.

4. Biologists distinguish between the _____ , the set of genetic traits an individual inherits, and the _____ , the set of traits a person actually displays during her or his life.

5. Genes are inherited in pairs and often exert unequal influence. Genes that have greater influence are called _____ . Genes whose influence is less powerful because they are blocked by the gene with which they are paired are called _____ .

6. Genes responsible for various traits often take on a variety of different forms called _____ . Because genes responsible for specific traits are inherited in pairs, a person who inherits identical alleles for a trait is said to be _____ for that trait. A person who inherits two different alleles for a trait is said to be _____ for that particular trait.

7. Gender is determined by the _____ and _____ chromosomes. Genetically normal men always have a mixed combination, _____ ; normal women always have an _____ combination.

8. The most common abnormalities that result from an incorrect number of chromosomes are _____ syndrome, _____ syndrome, and _____ syndrome.

9. Even when a zygote has the proper number of chromosomes, _____ can create serious medical problems, such as _____ disease, _____ anemia, and _____ chorea.

10. _____ should be thoroughly trained in genetics and in working with other professionals because the counselor must have complete access to parents' medical and genetic history to help them estimate risk factors in having a baby.

11. _____ and _____ are prenatal diagnostic techniques that extract fluid or tissue from the uterus.

12. Untangling the effects of heredity from the effects of environment has become the special focus of _____ , the scientific study of how genetic inheritance (_____) and environmental experience jointly influence behavioral development (_____).

13. _____ provide one sort of natural experiment for comparing the effects of heredity and environment. The major research methods for studying twins reared apart and adopted children are the _____ and the _____ .

14. A strong genetic component in the complex trait of intelligence is revealed by the fact that _____ have similar IQs. Likewise, a genetic component in serious mental illnesses like manic-depression is revealed in _____ toward similar illnesses and in the _____ among schizophrenic relatives.

15. Both _____ (which refers to an individual's consistent style of responding to the broad range of environmental events) and _____ (as expressed in extroversion and other traits) show genetic and environmental influences.

Key Terms

Directions: Provide a definition for each of the following key terms. Check your answers against the Glossary or the text page number that follows each term.

Alleles (p. 81) _____

_____

_____

Amniocentesis (p. 90) _____

_____

_____

Behavior genetics (p. 94) _____

_____

_____

Chorionic villus sampling (CVS) (p. 91) _____

_____

_____

Chromosomes (p. 76) _____

_____

_____

Concordance (p. 102) _____

_____

_____

Critical period (p. 95) _____

_____

_____

Deoxyribonucleic acid (DNA) (p. 76) _____

_____

_____

Dominant genes (p. 80) _____

_____

_____

Down syndrome (p. 85) _____

_____

_____

Fragile-X syndrome (p. 87) _____

_____

_____

Gametes (p. 76) _____

_____

_____

Genes (p. 76) _____

_____

_____

Gene therapy (p. 90) _____

_____

_____

Genotype (p. 79) _____

_____

_____

Hemophilia (p. 84) _____

_____

_____

Heterozygous (p. 82) _____

_____

_____

Homozygous (p. 82) _____

_____

_____

Huntington's chorea (p. 88) _____

_____

_____

Imprinting (p. 95) _____

_____

_____

Klinefelter's syndrome (p. 86) _____

_____

_____

Meiosis (p. 78) _____

_____

_____

Mitosis (p. 78) _____

_____

_____

Ovum (p. 76) _____

_____

_____

Phenotype (p. 79) _____

_____

_____

Phenylketonuria (PKU) (p. 87) _____

_____

_____

Polygenic traits (p. 82) _____

_____

_____

Recessive genes (p. 80) _____

_____

_____

Rh disease (p. 87) _____

_____

_____

Sex-linked recessive traits (p. 84) _____

_____

_____

Sickle-cell anemia (p. 88) _____

_____

_____

Sperm (p. 76) _____

_____

_____

Tay-Sachs disease (p. 89) _____

_____

_____

Tourette's syndrome (p. 87) _____

_____

_____

Turner's syndrome (p. 86) _____

_____

_____

Ultrasound (p. 91) _____

_____

_____

Zygote (p. 77) _____

_____

Study Questions

1. In what two ways does DNA contribute to genetic reproduction? (p. 77)

_____

_____

_____

_____

2. How does meiosis differ from mitosis? (p. 78)

_____

_____

_____

_____

3. What distinction do biologists make between genotype and phenotype? (p. 79)

_____

_____

_____

_____

4. Why are recessive genes less powerful in their influence than dominant genes? (p. 80)

_____

_____

_____

_____

5. How does a homozygous genetic condition for a particular trait differ from a heterozygous condition? (pp. 81–82)

_____

_____

_____

_____

6. What is meant by polygenic transmission? (pp. 82–83)

_____

_____

_____

_____

7. What events at conception determine the sex of the child? (p. 83)

_____

_____

_____

_____

8. What are three genetic abnormalities (and their symptoms) related to variations in the number of chromosomes? (pp. 85–86)

_____

_____

_____

_____

9. What are several diseases or syndromes that are related to abnormal genes? (pp. 86–90)

_____

_____

_____

_____

10. What are three prenatal diagnostic techniques that can be utilized in genetic counseling? (pp. 90–92)

_____

_____

_____

_____

11. What is the special focus of behavioral genetics? (p. 94)

_____

_____

_____

_____

12. What are two concepts on which behavioral geneticists have relied in order to shed light on how genes influence development? (pp. 94–95)

_____

_____

_____

_____

13. Why do animal researchers run the risk of anthropomorphism? (pp. 96–97)

_____

_____

_____

_____

14. How do studies of twins and adopted children shed light on the heredity/environment controversy? (pp. 97–98)

_____

_____

_____

_____

15. What is one line of evidence for genetic influence in the complex trait of intelligence? (p. 98)

_____

_____

_____

_____

16. How is *temperament* defined in Chapter 3, and what are some facets of temperament that may be genetically influenced? (pp. 98–99)

_____

_____

_____

_____

17. What three patterns of temperament (and their major characteristics) were described in infants by researchers Thomas and Chess? (p. 99)

_____

_____

_____

_____

18. What evidence exists for genetic influence in personality? (pp. 100–101)

_____

_____

_____

_____

19. What evidence can be cited to reveal genetic influences in such serious mental illnesses as manic-depression? (p. 102)

_____

_____

_____

_____

20. How does the phenomenon of concordance offer evidence for genetic influence in the severe mental disorder of schizophrenia? (p. 102)

_____

_____

_____

_____

Multiple-Choice Self-Test

1. A human gamete cell contains
   a. twenty-three genes.
   b. twenty-three chromosomes.
   c. forty-six chromosomes.
   d. literally thousands of chromosomes.

2. Genes are composed of more fundamental structures called
   a. chromosomes.
   b. DNA molecules.
   c. gametes.
   d. nucleic acids.

3. Most living cells divide through the process of
   a. amniosis.
   b. meiosis.
   c. mitosis.
   d. osmosis.

4. Pam has blue eyes. Given that brown eyes are dominant and blue eyes are recessive, what can be concluded about Pam?
   a. Pam has the same phenotype and genotype for eye color.
   b. Pam may have a different phenotype and genotype for eye color.
   c. Pam's phenotype is homozygous.
   d. Pam's genotype is heterozygous.

5. Traits such as height, which are determined by the action of a number of genes, are said to be
   a. heterozygous.
   b. magnagenic.
   c. polygenic.
   d. homozygous.

6. If an X-bearing sperm cell fertilizes an ovum,
   a. only a female will result.
   b. only a male will result.
   c. either a male or a female can result.
   d. the sex of the offspring cannot be determined.

7. Sex-linked recessive traits are most likely to be expressed in
   a. males.
   b. females.
   c. persons whose phenotype contains a number of recessive traits.
   d. persons whose genotype is heterozygous.

8. Inheriting too many or too few chromosomes most typically results in
   a. death of the fetus.
   b. minor abnormalities depending on which chromosomes are involved.
   c. severe abnormalities in the child at birth.
   d. no detrimental effects.

9. Most cases of Down syndrome result from
    a. an extra chromosome.
    b. a missing chromosome in the twenty-first pair.
    c. a misplaced chromosome.
    d. a sex-linked recessive gene.

10. The XXY chromosomal pattern is characteristic of
    a. Down syndrome.
    b. Klinefelter's syndrome.
    c. sickle-cell anemia.
    d. Turner's syndrome.

11. Ultrasound involves
    a. monitoring the fetus's response to loud noise through the use of an EEG.
    b. monitoring the fetus's response to loud noise through the use of an EKG.
    c. the use of high-frequency sound waves to produce an image of the child.
    d. the process of listening to the fetal heartbeat to determine relative health.

12. How strongly genes are able to direct and limit development in the face of environmental influences is termed
    a. range of reaction.
    b. genotype.
    c. canalization.
    d. heritability.

13. Animal studies have found that selective breeding of certain characteristics is
    a. successful for physical but not intellectual traits.
    b. successful for intellectual traits in rats.
    c. successful only for humans.
    d. not successful for any characteristics in humans or other animals.

14. Sid and Sam are identical twins who were raised in different environments from birth. The differences between them can be attributed to
    a. genetics primarily.
    b. environment primarily.
    c. phenotype.
    d. heredity and environment equally.

15. The evidence on infant temperament seems to suggest that
    a. genetics plays a strong role in early temperament.
    b. the role of genetics increases as age increases.
    c. genetics influences temperament at a constant level throughout development.
    d. genetics has only a minor role in temperament.

Activities

Activity 3.1

> **Objective:** To note the polygenic influences on body size and proportions.

Comment on the following for your own extended family and at least one other family.

How many of the adult children exceed the extremes of their parents' heights (shorter than the shortest parent or taller than the tallest parent)?

How many of the offspring show a tendency to the size of their parents but don't quite match (rather short or rather tall)?

How many of the adult children have body builds that are similar but not identical to their parents' (large bony frame, small-boned, long trunk but short limbs)?

Do you see familial similarities of body build?

Marked differences?

Speculate about your observations in terms of DNA, alleles, polygenic transmission, and environmental influence.

Activity 3.2

Objective: To observe the influence of genetic inheritance on appearance.

As many members of the class as possible should bring snapshots of their parents as young adults and a recent picture of themselves. Handle the photos carefully while they are mixed and set out on a table for display.

Try to match parent to son or daughter. (Inevitably, some pictures will be printed on identical paper or show other technical similarities. Try to set these considerations aside.)

On what bases did you attempt to match parents and offspring?

Was it wishful thinking, or did you see real resemblances?

In any parent-child pair, how many separate similarities did you observe?

How many correct matches did the class make?

Activity 3.3

Objective: To note that a genetically coded trait, while present, may not be observable.

Some inherited traits are said to "skip a generation." A characteristic, carried by the genes, may not appear in one's children but may be seen in grandchildren.

Identify a characteristic, such as a detail in appearance, that skipped a generation or perhaps moved horizontally. An example of the latter would be a trait that does not appear in one's own children but is clearly evident in nieces or nephews from the same biological line.

Every family has remarked that one of its members is *"just* like grandmother" or like an aunt or some other family member. This sometimes refers to a character trait or a physical characteristic. The former may be a function of the environment, but the latter may be evidence of inheritance.

Give an example of this phenomenon from your own family.

Ask your parents for another example.

It may be that certain personality characteristics are indeed inherited. Identify one such characteristic in your family.

What else, besides inheritance, can account for this?

Activity 3.4

Objective: To consider advantages and disadvantages of concentrating the genetic pool of a species.

Certain bits of folk wisdom are based on true experiences. One such rule of thumb is to avoid concentrating the gene pool of any species. At the same time, however, concentrated gene pools can sometimes have status—for example, those producing thoroughbred horses or show dogs.

Why, then, does folk wisdom advise that cross-breeds ("mutts") are healthier animals?

Royal families can trace their ancestries through many hundreds of generations of intermarriage. Certain disorders have thus been transmitted repeatedly. The best known is hemophilia. Why, then, do you think, has intermarriage continued almost until the present?

Can you see any advantages to maintaining a particular pool of genes, either in the animal world or among humans?

Are there certain genetic combinations that you think would be advantageous to a species?

In the animal world?

For humans?

Activity 3.5

Objective: To consider the political/ethical implications of genetic engineering.

Genetic screening and genetic engineering have rather threatening implications. For example, Darwin's theory of evolution was, during the latter part of the nineteenth century, corrupted to social Darwinism. This newer theory claimed that poor people were condemned to live in squalor because of inherited incompetence. Thus a society would be best served by allowing such populations to die out or even by sterilizing their adults. This philosophy extended to the mentally retarded and, finally, in Nazi Germany, to those ethnic groups (Jews, Gypsies, and so on) considered politically undesirable. Only a few years ago in the United States, there was a proposal to screen male children in order to detect chromosomal abnormalities associated with learning disabilities and even criminal tendencies. Such a program might indeed be cost-effective, if it worked.

What is your position on genetic screening?

What would your arguments be if you took the opposite position?

Activity 3.6

Objective: To observe children affected by genetic abnormalities and to interview parents of such children.

If possible, visit a program for handicapped children, such as an infant stimulation program that serves children with abnormalities, and then record your impressions after talking with personnel at the program and a parent of one of the children if possible. *Note:* Many parents report that raising a Down syndrome child was a special joy in comparison with raising "normal children" because the Down syndrome child was especially affectionate and appreciative of the parents.

Comments

Activity 3.7

Objective: To gain an appreciation of the tremendous strides made in molecular biology in conjunction with and since the elucidation of the DNA molecule by Nobel Prize winners Watson and Crick in 1953.

Ask a reference librarian at your college or university library to help you locate some resource material on molecular biology. Better yet, briefly interview a biology professor, asking questions about the complexity of the DNA molecule and about recent discoveries in molecular biology. Record your findings and conclusions below.

Answer Key

Overview and Key Concepts

1. deoxyribonucleic acid; DNA (p. 76)

2. gametes; mitosis (pp. 76-78)

3. meiosis; chromosomes; 23 (p. 78)

4. genotype; phenotype (p. 79)

5. Dominant genes; recessive genes (p. 80)

6. alleles; homozygous; heterozygous (pp. 81–82)

7. X; Y; XY; XX (p. 83)

8. Down; Turner's; Klinefelter's (pp. 85–86)

9. abnormal genes; Rh; sickle-cell; Huntington's (pp. 86–88)

10. Genetic counselors (p. 90)

11. amniocentesis; chorionic villus sampling (pp. 90–91)

12. behavioral genetics; genotype; phenotype (p. 94)

13. Identical twins; twin design; adoption design (p. 97)

14. close relatives; relatives' tendencies; strong concordance (pp. 98–102)

15. temperament; personality (pp. 98–100)

Multiple-Choice Self-Test

1. Choice (b) is correct; the gamete (or sex) cell has half of the number of chromosomes found in humans. (p. 76)
   Each chromosome contains thousands of genes; thus (a) and (d) are incorrect. Body cells contain forty-six chromosomes; thus (b) is incorrect.

2. Choice (b) is correct. Genes are made up of DNA molecules. (p. 76)
   Chromosomes, choice (a), are made up of genes. Gametes, choice (c), are a type of cell.

Nucleic acids, choice (d), are part of the term "deoxyribonucleic acid" (DNA) but do not appropriately stand alone in this context.

3. Choice (c) is correct; mitosis is the normal process of cell division for all body cells. (p. 78) Choice (b) is the process by which gamete cells divide; (d) is the movement of substances through cell walls or other semipermeable membranes; and (a) is a made-up term, although the root "amnio" refers to the closed sac around the embryo.

4. Choice (a) is correct. In order for Pam to have blue eyes (phenotype), she would need two recessive blue-eyed genes (genotype); thus, her phenotype and genotype are the same. (pp. 79–81) Choice (b) is incorrect based on what is stated above. Phenotype, choice (c), is neither heterozygous nor homozygous—the term simply refers to the outward appearance of a characteristic. Pam's genotype, choice (d), is homozygous—she has two recessive blue-eyed genes.

5. By definition, when a number of gene pairs determines a specific trait, the trait is termed polygenic, choice (c). (p 83) Choice (a) refers to the situation where one gene is dominant and the other recessive, in which case the dominant gene is the expressed characteristic. Choice (d) refers to the situation where the two genes are identical and thus express the same characteristic. Choice (b) is not a term used in genetics.

6. Choice (a) is correct. The ovum is always an X-chromosome; sperm cells can have either an X-chromosome or a Y-chromosome. Females have an XX configuration, males XY. Thus if an X-bearing sperm cell fertilizes the X-bearing ovum, a female will result. (p. 83) To produce a male, choice (b), a Y-bearing sperm cell would have to fertilize the ovum. The sperm cell, not the ovum, determines the sex of the child; thus, (c) and (d) are incorrect.

7. Choice (a) is correct. Sex-linked recessive traits occur when a recessive gene appearing on the X-chromosome has no corresponding gene on the Y-chromosome. Males, by virtue of having the Y-chromosome, are more likely to fall into this situation. (p. 84) Females, choice (b), rarely have sex-linked recessive traits since two recessive genes (as opposed to one in males) would be required for the trait to appear. Although choice (c) may contain a bit of truth (sex-linked recessive traits versus recessive traits), clearly (a) is a better answer since the number of recessive traits is not necessarily related to the number of sex-linked recessive traits. Choice (d) is clearly incorrect: in the heterozygous case, the dominant, not the recessive, trait is expressed.

8. Choice (a) is correct. Under most circumstances, the fetus is unable to fully develop if there are either too many or too few chromosomes; thus death occurs prior to birth. (p. 85) If the child were to survive, severe abnormalities such as Down syndrome would occur; thus, (b) and (d) are incorrect. However, survival is unlikely in most cases, and therefore (c) is incorrect; Down syndrome and other abnormalities are considered exceptions rather than typical results of too many or too few chromosomes.

9. Choice (a) is correct. The nondisjunctive form of Down syndrome, the most common form, results from an extra chromosome. (p. 85)
Down syndrome is the result of neither a missing chromosome, choice (b), nor a sex-linked recessive trait, choice (d). A misplaced chromosome, choice (c), accounts for about 4 percent of Down syndrome cases.

10. Choice (b) is correct. An individual with Klinefelter's syndrome has at least one extra sex chromosome, most often an extra X. (p. 86)
Down syndrome, choice (a), results from an extra chromosome, but not a sex chromosome. Sickle-cell anemia, choice (c), is caused by a recessive allele of a gene. Turner's syndrome, choice (d), results from a single X chromosome.

11. Choice (c) is correct. Ultrasound uses sound waves to create a television image of the unborn child. (p. 91)
EEGs, choice (a), and EKGs, choice (b), can be done, but neither involves the use of sound waves. Listening to the fetal heartbeat, choice (d), is a means of assessing health but is not ultrasound.

12. By definition, canalization, choice (c), is the concept involving the strength of genetic predispositions. (p. 94)
Choice (a) is a related concept indicating that the genotype can set limits on the phenotype; (c) refers to a person's genetic make-up; and (d) is an index of the influence of heredity on various traits.

13. Choice (b) is correct. Studies have been able to raise maze-bright and maze-dull rats. (p. 96)
Choices (a), (c), and (d) are inaccurate because selective breeding studies have been able to influence intellectual traits in rats.

14. Choice (b) is correct. Identical twins have the same genetics, so any differences found would be attributed primarily to environmental influences. (p. 97)
Choice (a) is the opposite of the correct answer. Choice (c) refers to outward traits; differences in these traits are attributed to the environment. Choice (d), equal weight, is not correct, although even in identical twins, there may be some differences in genetics since heredity and environment interact with one another.

15. Choice (a) is correct. Research suggests that at birth there are temperamental differences. Given how early they occur (before the environment has had time to play a strong role), one would conclude a strong genetic component. (pp. 98–99)
Choice (b): There is no evidence to suggest that these influences increase. Choice (c): There is only moderate evidence of temperamental stability in some traits through childhood and no evidence beyond that time. Choice (d): Evidence suggests a major rather than a minor role for genetics in early temperament.

CHAPTER 4
Prenatal Development and Birth

Learning Objectives

1. Describe the process of conception and the factors that affect it.

2. Identify and describe the three stages of prenatal development. Discuss the characteristics and major events during each stage.

3. Identify and describe the major biological risk factors during the prenatal period.

4. Discuss the effects of various illnesses (such as rubella and syphilis) on prenatal development. Identify critical periods in development.

5. Identify and describe the effect that various teratogens have on prenatal development.

6. Discuss the effects of pregnancy on the parents and others, with special attention to the hormonal changes in the expectant mother.

7. Describe the birth process and identify the characteristics of the three stages of labor. Identify and describe the various birthing techniques.

8. Discuss the problems that can occur during birth and their solutions.

Chapter Outline

I. PRENATAL STAGES OF DEVELOPMENT
Following *conception*, the major stages in prenatal development are the *germinal stage*, the *embryonic stage*, and the *fetal stage*.

A. Conception

1. A *zygote* is created at the moment of conception, when one of the male reproductive cells (*spermatozoa* produced in the testes) fertilizes one of the egg cells (an *ovum* produced in the ovaries) from the woman.

2. For a couple to conceive successfully, every one of a number of conditions must be met.

3. Timing is critical since the ovum normally lives only about twenty-four hours and the sperm only about forty-eight hours.

B. The Germinal Stage (the first two weeks)

1. Successive cell divisions in the zygote produce the *blastocyst*—a tiny sphere of cells.

2. Further cell division produces three layers of cells—*ectoderm, mesoderm,* and *endoderm*—as the blastocyst moves down the fallopian tube.

3. About one week after conception, the process of *implantation* begins and the blastocyst attaches to the uterine wall, becoming the *embryo* once implantation is complete.

C. The Embryonic Stage (third through eighth weeks)

1. Growth now occurs in two patterns: a *cephalocaudal* (head to tail) pattern and a *proximodistal* (near to far, from body's center outward) pattern.

2. The heart is already beating, and the embryo has a small digestive system and a nervous system.

3. While these developments are taking place, a *placenta* forms between the mother and embryo for exchange of oxygen and nutrients.

4. The embryo is connected to the placenta by the *umbilical cord*.

5. By the end of the eighth week, the *amniotic sac* has developed.

D. The Fetal Stage (ninth week to birth)

1. The development of bone cells at about the eighth week marks the end of differentiation of major structures.

2. The embryo is now the *fetus* and begins the long process of developing relatively small features.

3. Most physical features become more adult-looking and more truly human in proportion at this stage.

4. By the third month, the fetus can spontaneously move its head, legs, and feet.

5. The fetal heartbeat can now be heard through the wall of the uterus, and by the fourth or fifth month, the mother may feel *quickening*, or movement of the fetus in her womb.

6. By the seventh month, the fetus is about sixteen inches long and weighs three to five pounds. It can cry, breathe, swallow, digest, excrete, move about, and suck its thumb.

II. PRENATAL INFLUENCES ON THE CHILD

Though human beings are unique, they develop with a complex regularity called *canalization*; however, certain *risk factors* can interfere with the highly canalized processes of prenatal development. Timing of the sequence is particularly important in reference to *critical periods*, or genetically determined "one-time-only" periods, during which a specific change can occur.

A. Biological Risks

1. Women over thirty-five and those in their early teens are at greatest risk for birth complications.

2. Certain physical characteristics of the mother lead to increased chances of spontaneous abortion or miscarriage.

B. Illnesses

1. Until recently, rubella (German measles) was the most common disease creating problems during pregnancy.

   a. Exposure during the first two months of pregnancy has extremely serious consequences.

   b. Numerous other viruses can also cross the placenta and infect the embryo or fetus.

2. Syphilis and gonorrhea have varying influence depending on the progression of the infection in the mother.

3. Genital herpes is commonly transmitted to the baby at birth, but transmission can be prevented by Caesarean delivery.

4. The Task Force on Pediatric AIDS predicted a tremendous increase in pediatric cases of AIDS between 1986 and 1991. Seventy-eight percent of AIDS cases in children involve perinatal (at the time of birth) transmission from an infected mother.

5. The mother's infection with toxoplasmosis can lead to fetal brain damage, blindness, or death.

6. Hypertension is frequently associated with *eclampsia* and may lead to premature delivery.

C. Teratogens
During the early weeks of its life, the embryo is especially vulnerable to unusual or unnatural substances, called *teratogens*.

1. Drugs such as thalidomide and DES, intended to prevent morning sickness and miscarriage, can cause deformity in the embryo and disease later in life.

2. Infants born to users of heavy narcotics such as heroin experience withdrawal symptoms at birth.

3. Cocaine is also a powerful teratogen.

4. Babies born to mothers who consume too much alcohol have *fetal alcohol syndrome* (FAS); even moderate drinking can be dangerous.

5. Smoking of cigarettes by the mother interferes with the fetal oxygen supply.

D. Diet and Nutrition

1. Studies of animals show that undernourishment during pregnancy hurts the offspring in various ways.

2. Deprivation early in gestation leads to physical deformities, and later deprivation leads to overall low birth weight.

3. Indicators reveal that the mother's current diet, not her fat reserves, is the source of the fetus's nutrition.

4. Underweight mothers experience more birth complications than other women, and it is recommended that pregnant women eat more than usual.

E. Stress
Women who experience severe anxiety before and during pregnancy are more likely to have medical complications and to give birth to infants with abnormalities than are women who do not.

F. Environmental Hazards
A broad range of environmental hazards can be destructive to prenatal development: exposure to radiation from nuclear explosions, nuclear plant accidents, industrial materials, and medical X-rays.

III. PARENTAL REACTIONS TO PREGNANCY
Expectant parents create, even if unconsciously, a set of images of what parenthood will be like.

A. Reasons for Having a Child
Prospective parents report a number of different reasons for wanting to have a child—for example, validation of adult status, expansion of self, achievement of moral values, and enhancing of power and influence.

B. Effects of Pregnancy on the Mother

1. Implantation initiates changes in about thirty different bodily chemicals, or *hormones*, that regulate pregnancy and may produce morning sickness.

2. Effects of hormonal changes are varied, and many changes occur in the mother's body.

3. Despite discomfort in later pregnancy, many women take great pleasure in their changing bodies because they have a sense of participating in the creation of a new life.

C. Effects of Pregnancy on the Father and Other Family Members

1. Although fathers do not experience physical changes, they share many of the problems and joys of anticipating a child.

2. An extended network of family members can share the experience of pregnancy.

3. Brothers and sisters are keenly interested in the "new arrival" but may have mixed feelings.

IV. BIRTH
At thirty-eight weeks the infant is considered "full term" and weighs perhaps seven and one-half pounds. During the last weeks in the womb, it becomes positioned for birth, most commonly and most desirable medically in a *cephalic presentation* (head downward). Two other presentations, *breech presentation* (feet and rump first) or *transverse presentation* (shoulders first), may also occur.

A. Stages of Labor

1. The *first stage of labor* begins with contractions producing dilation of the cervix and may last from eight to twenty-four hours before a period of *transition* begins.

2. The *second stage of labor* is from complete dilation of the cervix to birth, lasting between one and one and a half hours.

3. During the *third stage of labor*, which lasts only a few minutes, the afterbirth (consisting of placenta and umbilical cord) is expelled.

B. Managing Discomfort in Childbirth
Women vary widely in their experience of pain as well as in their tolerance for pain.

1. Nonmedicinal Methods

a. Various methods of *prepared childbirth* have been devised to help parents rehearse the actual sensations of labor. Methods such as Lamaze emphasize educational, physical, and emotional preparation for birth.

b. "Gentle birth" emphasizes the infant's experience in the birth process.

2. Medicinal Methods

a. Many mothers endure discomfort without the need for medication but in some instances may need pain-reducing drugs such as narcotics or other sedatives.

b. In the final stages of delivery, a sedative may be injected into the base of the spine to allow the woman to remain awake and alert.

c. A more drastic approach is to administer a general anesthetic and remove the baby surgically, a procedure called *Caesarean section*.

C. Problems During Labor and Delivery

1. *Faulty power* refers to failure of the uterus to contract strongly enough, in which case the doctor may administer the hormone oxytocin to initiate *induced labor*.

2. *Faulty passageway* occurs when the placenta develops too close to the cervix and blocks the baby from moving down the birth canal.

3. *Faulty passenger* refers to problems with the baby's position or size.

4. *Fetal monitoring* is used to record uterine contractions and the fetal heart rate in high-risk and emergency situations.

D. Premature Birth

1. Approximately 10 to 15 percent of live births in the United States occur before full term is reached. *Premature* (or *preterm*) infants have a prenatal age of less than thirty-seven weeks.

2. *Respiratory distress syndrome* (RDS) is a leading cause of death among preterm infants. RDS involves breathing problems in preterm infants.

3. Preterm babies experience a higher incidence of abnormalities than full-term babies, require procedures that may interfere with bonding, and account for 23 to 40 percent of all battered children.

Overview and Key Concepts

Stages of prenatal development are traced from fertilization and conception through phases of the germinal stage, the embryonic stage, and the fetal stage. Prenatal influences such as biological risks, illnesses, teratogens, maternal nutrition, stress, and environmental hazards are discussed. Parental reactions to pregnancy are presented along with reasons for having a baby and the effects of pregnancy on the mother and her family. The chapter concludes with stages of labor and aspects of the birth process.

Directions: Identify the following key concepts introduced in Chapter 4.

1. _____ and _____ unite at _____ to create the _____ (a fertilized egg cell).

2. The zygote divides and redivides, forming a tiny sphere called the _____ , which eventually differentiates into three layers of tissue: the _____ , the _____ , and the _____ .

3. The blastocyst buries itself in the wall of the uterus in the process of _____ , which marks the end of the _____ stage (the first two weeks) and the beginning of the _____ stage (third through eighth weeks).

4. Growth during the embryonic stage (and later) occurs in two patterns: a _____ (head to tail) pattern and a _____ (near to far) pattern.

5. Structures supporting the embryo are the _____ , which forms between the mother and embryo and through which the mother can supply oxygen and nutrients to the child, the _____ , by which the embryo is connected to the placenta,

and the _____ , which by the eighth week completely surrounds the embryo.

6. At about eight weeks, major structures are differentiated and bone cells begin to develop. At this point, the embryo acquires a new name, _____ . The _____ lasts from the ninth week to birth.

7. By the third month the fetus is able to move its head, legs, and feet; and by the fourth or fifth month, the mother may feel _____ of the fetus, or movement in her womb.

8. The biological regularity of prenatal development is called _____ . As the prenatal sequence proceeds, time is crucial because there is a "one-time-only" _____ during which each change can occur. Conditions interfering with canalized events are sometimes called _____ .

9. The nine months of pregnancy are generally divided into three _____ . Development is most vulnerable during the first of these. Harm may result from unnatural substances, sometimes called _____ .

10. At thirty-eight weeks, the fetus is considered _____ and will have become positioned in the womb, most commonly in the _____ presentation, with the head pointing downward, but sometimes in the _____ presentation (feet and rump first) or the _____ presentation (shoulders first).

11. The _____ usually begins with mild and irregular contractions. The cervix dilates for the baby's head to fit through, and a period of _____ begins.

12. The _____ is from complete dilation of the cervix to birth (about one to one and a half hours). During the _____ , which lasts a few minutes, the afterbirth is expelled.

13. To counteract the possibilities of anxiety and pain, various methods of _____ have been devised to help parents rehearse the actual sensations of labor. One well-known program, the _____ , strongly advocates participation of both _____ and _____ .

14. Despite good psychological preparation, medicinal methods may be needed to decrease pain. A rather drastic approach is to give the mother a general anesthetic and remove the baby surgically in a procedure called _____ .

15. Problems can develop during labor and delivery in three ways: through _____ , through _____ (the birth canal), or through a _____ (the baby itself). An infant is considered _____ , or _____ , if he has a prenatal age of less than thirty-seven weeks.

Key Terms

Directions: Provide a definition for each of the following key terms. Check your answers against the Glossary or the text page number that follows each term.

Amniotic sac (p. 113) _____

_____

_____

Artificial insemination (p. 116) _____

_____

_____

Blastocyst (p. 110) _____

_____

_____

Breech presentation (p. 130) _____

_____

_____

Caesarean section (p. 135) _____

_____

_____

Canalization (p. 115) _____

_____

_____

Cephalic presentation (p. 130) _____

_____

_____

Cephalocaudal development (p. 111) _____

_____

_____

Conception (p. 109) _____

_____

_____

Critical period (p. 115) _____

_____

_____

Eclampsia (p. 120) _____

_____

_____

Ectoderm (p. 111) _____

_____

_____

Embryo (p. 111) _____

_____

_____

Embryonic disk (p. 111) _____

_____

_____

Embryonic stage (p. 108) _____

_____

_____

Endoderm (p. 111) _____

_____

_____

Fetal alcohol syndrome (p. 121) _____

_____

_____

Fetal stage (p. 108) _____

_____

_____

Fetus (p. 113) _____

_____

_____

First stage of labor (p. 131) _____

_____

_____

Forceps (p. 137) _____

_____

_____

Germinal stage (p. 108) _____

_____

_____

Hormone (p. 125) _____

_____

_____

Implantation (p. 111) _____

_____

_____

Induced labor (p. 136) _____

_____

_____

In vitro fertilization (p. 116) _____

_____

_____

Mesoderm (p. 111) _____

_____

_____

Osmosis (p. 112) _____

_____

_____

Ovum (p. 108) _____

_____

_____

Placenta (p. 112) _____

_____

_____

Premature (p. 138) _____

_____

_____

Prepared childbirth (p. 133) _____

_____

_____

Preterm (p. 138) _____

_____

_____

Proximodistal development (p. 111) _____

_____

_____

Quickening (p. 114) _____

_____

_____

Respiratory distress syndrome (RDS) (p. 138) _____

_____

_____

Risk factor (p. 115) _____

_____

_____

Second stage of labor (p. 132) _____

_____

_____

Spermatozoa (p. 109) _____

_____

_____

Surrogate mothering (p. 117) _____

_____

_____

Teratogen (p. 120) _____

_____

_____

Third stage of labor (p. 132) _____

_____

_____

Transition (p. 132) _____

_____

_____

Transverse presentation (p. 130) _____

_____

_____

Trimester (p. 116) _____

_____

_____

Umbilical cord (p. 112) _____

_____

_____

Zygote (p. 109) _____

_____

_____

Study Questions

1. What are seven conditions that must be met in order for a couple to conceive successfully? (p. 109)

_____

_____

_____

_____

2. During the germinal stage, what changes take place in the fertilized ovum? (pp. 110–111)

_____

_____

_____

_____

3. What two patterns of growth prevail and what major changes occur in the embryonic stage? (pp. 111–112)

_____

_____

_____

_____

4. What are three major structures supporting the developing embryo and how do they form? (pp. 112–113)

_____

_____

_____

_____

5. What major changes occur during the fetal stage? (pp. 113–115)

_____

_____

_____

_____

6. How is the concept of canalization related to critical periods in development? (pp. 115–116)

_____

_____

_____

_____

7. What are the alternatives to normal conception? (pp. 116–117)

_____

_____

_____

_____

8. What is the relationship between the age of the mother and biological risks associated with child-bearing? (pp. 116–118)

_____

_____

_____

_____

9. What illnesses may threaten the developing child? (pp. 118–120)

_____

_____

_____

_____

10. What are the effects of several well-known teratogens? (pp. 120–122)

_____

_____

_____

_____

11. What is the impact of the mother's current diet on her pregnancy? (pp. 122–123)

_____

_____

_____

_____

12. What is the impact of stress and environmental hazards on pregnancy? (pp. 123–124)

_____

_____

_____

_____

13. What are nine major reasons parents typically give for having a child? (pp. 124–125)

_____

_____

_____

_____

14. What are the major effects of hormonal changes and psychological changes on the mother? (pp. 125–127)

_____

_____

_____

_____

15. What are some of the effects of pregnancy on the father and other family members beside the mother? (pp. 127–128)

_____

_____

_____

_____

16. What three presentations may the baby assume during the last weeks of pregnancy? (p. 130)

_____

_____

_____

_____

17. What happens during each of the stages of labor? (pp. 131–132)

_____

_____

_____

_____

18. What are two well-known methods of prepared childbirth? Describe each briefly. (pp. 133–134)

_____

_____

_____

_____

19. In what three ways can problems that interfere with labor and delivery develop? (pp. 135–137)

_____

_____

_____

_____

20. What are the risks to a premature (or preterm) baby? (pp. 138–139)

_____

_____

_____

_____

Multiple-Choice Self-Test

1. In order for conception to take place, the sperm and the ovum must meet in the
   a. ovary.
   b. vagina.
   c. fallopian tubes.
   d. uterus.

2. A sperm cell typically survives for about _____ once it is released in the female.
   a. six hours
   b. twenty-four hours
   c. forty-eight hours
   d. seventy-two hours

3. The blastocyst differentiates into three different layers of cells during the
   a. embryonic stage.
   b. fetal stage.
   c. germinal stage.
   d. latency stage.

4. The beginning of the embryonic stage is signified by the
   a. appearance of bone cells.
   b. beginning of the heartbeat.
   c. completion of implantation.
   d. formation of the amniotic sac.

5. Exchanges of oxygen and nutrients between the mother and embryo are made in the placenta through the process of
   a. amniosis.
   b. filtration.
   c. meiosis.
   d. osmosis.

6. The fetal stage begins with _____ and ends with _____ .
   a. appearance of bone cells; birth
   b. conception; structural differentiation
   c. conception; birth
   d. implantation; birth

7. Which of the following is *not* considered a risk factor during pregnancy?
   a. being very small in stature
   b. being under twenty years old
   c. being a little overweight
   d. having your fifth or sixth pregnancy

8. Compared with problems that occur in the first trimester, problems in the second and third trimesters typically result in
   a. less severe deficits in development.
   b. loss of the fetus through miscarriage.
   c. more physical than cognitive deficits.
   d. problems in basic structures such as the heart and the central nervous system.

9. If contracted during the first two months of pregnancy, which of the following typically can result in blindness, deafness, and heart defects?
   a. gonorrhea
   b. rubella
   c. genital herpes
   d. AIDS

10. Thalidomide and DES are best classified as
    a. collagens.
    b. prenatal diseases.
    c. prenatal vitamins.
    d. teratogens.

11. Alcohol during pregnancy tends to
    a. depress brain functioning in the fetus.
    b. depress breathing and heart rate in the fetus.
    c. slow motor development in the fetus.
    d. all of the above.

12. The hormonal changes in the mother that regulate pregnancy begin to have their effect
    a. immediately after conception.
    b. right after the first cell division.
    c. as soon as implantation occurs.
    d. at the beginning of the fetal stage.

13. The first stage of labor is characterized by
    a. Braxton-Hicks contractions.
    b. birth.
    c. dilation of the cervix.
    d. expulsion of the placenta.

14. _____ is the hormone used to artificially induce labor if progression of normal labor is insufficient.
    a. Epidural
    b. Oxytocin
    c. Dystocia
    d. Thalidomide

15. Which of the following conditions might necessitate a Caesarean section?
    a. cephalopelvic disproportion
    b. placenta previa
    c. ruptured uterus
    d. all of the above

Activities

Activity 4.1

> **Objective:** To emphasize that life begins at conception.

The Chinese count a person's age from conception rather than from the birthday. The arguments in favor of this Chinese custom could be helpful to prospective parents. Under the following headings, present evidence to support this other way of defining age.

The Germinal Stage

The Embryonic Stage

The Fetal Stage

Diet and Nutrition During Pregnancy

Activity 4.2

Objective: To review the issues involved in a teenage pregnancy.

You are preparing a course outline for a class of pregnant teenagers. Although almost all of the students will be expectant mothers, a few fathers may be present as well.

1. On what basis would you establish a relationship of trust and credibility?

   Seem knowledgable in the field, be sure to appear concerned and caring. don't talk down to them, relate occurances in your own pregnancy to them

2. Assuming that the young parents-to-be have a low income, what information would you provide on nutrition (e.g., essential nutrients, sources of food supplements, food stamps)?

   -Slender or underweight mothers experience birth complications more often than other women do, including more premature births and babies who are small

3. How would you discuss teratogens?

4. Since the young women are probably well into the first trimester, what would you have to say about exposure to illnesses such as rubella?

5. About labor?

Activity 4.3

> **Objective:** To examine the arguments for and against a home delivery.

Although many hospitals provide alternative birthing centers, a substantial number of couples still elect to have their baby at home. Prepare arguments for a debate on the topic "Home Is the Best Place for a Normal Birth."

On the pro side, consider the following advantages:

- Being with people who know and love the parents.

- Those in attendance to assist with the delivery are also known to the parents.

- When decisions must be made, there is less outside pressure on one's own territory.

- The mother in labor has more autonomy at home.

- The atmosphere is less threatening.

- One can always get to the hospital in an emergency.

On the con side, consider:

- Who can absolutely predict a normal delivery?

- It is reassuring to know that personnel and equipment are already there.

- Hospitals today are far more sensitive to the feelings of families than they have been in the past.

- The burden of guilt, if something went wrong, would be overwhelming.

An alternative to a debate might be a panel discussion that includes people who deliver babies at home and at hospitals, as well as parents who have been through each experience.

Activity 4.4

Objective: To become aware of differences in pregnancy and childbirth customs between generations.

Recall comments made by your parents' generation and by new parents today. Comment on differences or similarities about the following.

Recommended weight gain

Teratogens

Feelings about the change the new baby will make in living patterns

Preparation for the birth

Where the birth will take place

Obstetricians versus midwives

Prenatal influences on the baby

Fathers' participation during the birth

Inviting family and friends to the birth

Nutrition

Plans for breast- or bottle-feeding

Anesthesia during delivery

Other

Activity 4.5

> **Objective:** To recognize that profound grief may accompany a miscarriage or spontaneous abortion.

A member of your family or a friend has just had a miscarriage.

What can do you, without being intrusive, to help both parents with their loss?

What practical household assistance can you give?

If other children are present, how could you help?

What might you want to say?

What would you not say, just yet?

How long might you expect the parents to be stunned?

Might there be a difference between the father's and the mother's responses?

How would you know when and whether to encourage the parents to try for another pregnancy?

Other

Activity 4.6

Objective: To focus on human dimensions of the birth process and to collect naturalistic data about pregnancy and the birth process.

To build on scientific and biological information about the birth process, interview a new mother about her personal experiences during pregnancy and the birth process. Record your findings below.

Activity 4.7

Objective: To further analyze the steps in prenatal development.

Break the stages of prenatal development down into a month-by-month sequence through the nine months of gestation—recording major changes that occur in each month of pregnancy.

First Month

Second Month

Third Month

Fourth Month

Fifth Month

Sixth Month

Seventh Month

Eighth Month

Ninth Month

Activity 4.8

Objective: To consider different perspectives on the controversial issue of abortion.

In light of the material in Chapter 4 on conception and human genetics, formulate when you personally think the developing human organism fully becomes a person, and contemplate whether your own position on legalized abortion (as upheld in *Roe* v. *Wade*) is predicated on moral grounds or on pragmatic grounds. The following questions may be helpful.

1. When do you think the developing organism becomes a person entitled to the rights of a human being?

2. What impact do you think that moral arguments—for example, that the unborn child has a right to life—should have on the abortion issue?

3. Do you think that pragmatic concerns such as the population explosion should have a strong impact on this issue?

Activity 4.9

> **Objective:** To reassess the relative contributions of heredity and environment.

Now that you have studied some of the major mechanisms of human genetics in Chapter 4, would you change your earlier calculations about the relative importance of heredity and environment in development?

There is hardly a more widely discussed issue than heredity versus environment in all the literature of developmental psychology and child development. Why do you think this issue commands so much attention?

Why do you think the discovery of the structure of the DNA molecule is considered to be one of the greatest scientific advances of the twentieth century?

Answer Key

Overview and Key Concepts

1. ovum; sperm; conception; zygote (p. 109)

2. blastocyst; ectoderm; mesoderm; endoderm (pp. 110–111)

3. implantation; germinal; embryonic (pp. 110–111)

4. cephalocaudal; proximodistal (p. 111)

5. placenta; umbilical cord; amniotic sac (pp. 112–113)

6. fetus; fetal stage (p. 113)

7. quickening (p. 114)

8. canalization; critical period; risk factors (p. 115)

9. trimesters; teratogens (pp. 116–120)

10. full-term; cephalic; breech; transverse (p. 130)

11. first stage of labor; transition (pp. 131–132)

12. second stage of labor; third stage of labor (p. 132)

13. prepared childbirth; Lamaze method; mother; father (p. 133)

14. Caesarean section (p. 135)

15. faulty power in the uterus; faulty passageway; faulty passenger; premature; preterm (pp. 135–138)

Multiple-Choice Self-Test

1. Choice (c) is correct. The ovum needs to descend most of the way down the fallopian tube, and the sperm cells must migrate through the vagina to the fallopian tubes. (p. 108)
    The ovary, choice (a), releases the ovum. The sperm travel through the vagina, choice (b), to get to the fallopian tubes to meet the ovum. The fertilized ovum develops in the uterus, choice (d).

2. Sperm cells live about forty-eight hours, choice (c), after they are released. (p. 109)
    Six hours, choice (a), is too little time. After twenty-four hours, choice (b), the number of sperm cells is reduced; but there are still more than enough sperm cells for conception to occur. The life span of a released ovum is about twenty-four hours. Seventy-two hours, choice (d), is the length of the crucial period in which conception can occur.

3. Differentiation of the ectoderm, mesoderm, and endoderm occurs in the germinal stage, choice (c), prior to implantation. (p. 111)
    Differentiation has already occurred during (a) and (b), the other two prenatal stages. Choice (d) is one of Freud's psychosexual stages.

4. The embryonic stage begins about two weeks after conception, once implantation, choice (c), is complete. (p. 111)
    Bone cells, choice (a), mark the end of the embryonic stage and beginning of the fetal stage. The heartbeat, choice (b), begins during the embryonic stage. The amniotic sac, choice (d), does not form until about eight weeks after conception.

5. Blood vessels of the mother and infant intermingle in the placenta, where the primary means of transmission is osmosis, choice (d), the passage of substances through the cell membrane. (p. 112)
    Choice (a) is not a term used in prenatal development. Although not everything passes through the placental barrier and thus some filtration, choice (b), occurs, osmosis involves not only size but also concentration and thus is more involved than simple filtration. Meiosis, choice (c), is a form of cell division.

6. Choice (a) is correct. The fetal stage begins about eight weeks after conception, when bone cells, the last structure to be differentiated, first appear. The fetal stage is the last stage of prenatal development and ends at birth (pp. 113–115).
    Choice (b) is roughly the germinal stage; (c) is the entire prenatal period; and (d) is the embryonic and fetal stage.

7. Choice (c) is correct. There is risk for women who are more than 25 percent overweight or underweight; however, being a little over or under does not add any additional risk. (p. 118)
    Choices (a) and (d) have been associated with a greater chance of miscarriage; (b) has been associated with greater chance of low birth-weight infants, stillborn infants, and problem deliveries.

8. Choice (a) is correct. The most critical periods for development occur in the first trimester; problems in the second and third trimesters are generally less severe. (pp. 125–126)
    The first trimester has a greater risk from miscarriage, choice (b); major physical defects, choice (c); and basic structural problems, choice (d).

9. Choice (b) is correct. The critical period for rubella, or German measles, is approximately the first two months of pregnancy. Rubella can result in blindness, deafness, heart defects, and central nervous system defects. (p. 118)
   Fetuses can contract gonorrhea, choice (a), while passing through the birth canal; it may result in blindness. Genital herpes, choice (c), is also contracted at birth; it may result in blindness, brain damage, and other neurological disorders. AIDS, choice (d), may also be contracted at birth when the contaminated blood of the mother mixes with the infant's blood.

10. Choice (d) is correct. A teratogen, an unnatural substance taken by the mother, permanently damages the embryo's growth. Both thalidomide, a mild sedative, and DES, a drug to prevent miscarriage, may be classified as teratogens because harmful effects are associated with them. (p. 120)
    Choice (a) is a fibrous protein. Neither thalidomide nor DES is a disease, choice (b), or a vitamin, choice (c). Both are drugs.

11. Choice (d) is correct. Alcohol has been found to depress fetal brain functioning, choice (a); breathing and heart rate, choice (b); and motor development, choice (c). (pp. 121–122)

12. Implantation, choice (c), allows the first exchanges between mother and infant and initiates changes in about thirty different hormones that regulate pregnancy. (p. 125)
    At conception, choice (a), the ovum is still free floating; therefore, there is no effect on the mother. The first cell division, choice (b), also occurs prior to implantation. By the time the infant reaches the fetal stage, choice (d), hormones have already exercised and are continuing to exercise considerable influence.

13. Choice (c) is correct. The first stage begins with mild and irregular contractions and continues until the cervix is completely dilated. (p. 131)
    Choice (a), also known as false labor, often occurs prior to true labor. Choice (b) occurs at the end of the second stage of labor, and (d) occurs during the third, and last, stage of labor.

14. Choice (b) is correct. Oxytocin is a hormone that can either induce or strengthen contractions. (p. 136)
    An epidural, choice (a), is an injection used to eliminate pain during labor. Dystocia, choice (c), is the term used for failure to progress in labor. Thalidomide, choice (d), is a mild sedative that has been found to cause severe birth defects.

15. Choice (d) is correct. Choice (a) is a condition in which the head is too large for the pelvis; (b) is a condition in which the placenta blocks the birth canal; and (c) is a condition in which the uterus breaks and may cause the mother to bleed to death. (p. 137)

CHAPTER 5
The First Two Years: Physical Development

Learning Objectives

1. Describe the physical characteristics of an infant at birth and the first few hours of an infant's life.

2. Describe methods for assessing the newborn and know what different assessment scores mean.

3. Describe the development of the nervous system both structurally and functionally.

4. Describe infant sleep patterns in terms of type and duration. Contrast infant sleep with adult sleep.

5. Discuss the infant's sensory abilities.

6. Identify and describe the newborn's reflexes.

7. Describe the development of such motor skills as reaching and walking during the first year. Discuss the roles of learning and maturation in motor development.

8. Discuss the common causes of low birth-weight infants, the consequences of that condition, and the methods used to help these infants.

9. Describe gender, cultural, and racial differences in growth and motor development and be able to provide possible explanations for these differences.

10. Characterize the nutritional needs of the infant.

Chapter Outline

I. APPEARANCE OF THE YOUNG INFANT

A. The First Few Hours

1. When first delivered, *neonates* do not resemble stereotypes of beautiful babies.

2. They may be covered by a white waxy substance called *vernix*, and their bodies may be covered with fine, downy hair called *lanugo*.

3. *Fontanelles*, or gaps in the skull bones, exist so the head can be compressed into an elongated shape to move through the birth canal.

4. Newborns react vigorously to their surroundings during the first fifteen or thirty minutes of life before falling asleep; thus these first minutes are a prime time for early parent-infant bonding.

B. Is the Baby All Right?

1. The Apgar scale

a. The Apgar consists of simple 0 to 2 ratings of the heart function, breathing, muscle tone, skin color, and reflex irritability.

b. Babies are rated at one and five minutes. Most earn nine or ten points by five minutes after delivery.

c. A score of less than four shows the baby is at serious medical risk.

2. The Brazelton Neonatal Behavioral Assessment Scale

a. The Brazelton is a neurological and behavioral test given on the third day of life and repeated several days later.

b. The Brazelton is intended to determine how well infants can regulate their responses to various stimuli.

c. Altogether, the examiner notes twenty neurological reflexes and responses to twenty-six different stimuli.

C. Newborn Weight

1. At birth a typical baby weighs about seven and a half pounds, or 3,400 grams.

2. Neonates have a large surface area compared to their weight; thus they lose heat more easily than adults.

3. Also, they need to gain weight, typically doubling their birth weight by four months.

4. In order to gain weight and keep warm, they must consume calories and need to drink about one quart of breast milk or formula every twenty-four hours.

D. Size and Bodily Proportions

   1. The length of a newborn matches adult proportions more than the weight does.

   2. Babies' heads take up about one-fourth of their length, and babies appear chubby and overweight.

   3. Babies' general appearance may have psychological consequences by fostering attachments or bonds.

   4. The cuteness of infants' faces is particularly notable. The pattern of babyish features occurs widely among animals and may be genetically based (Lorenz, 1970).

II. DEVELOPMENT OF THE NERVOUS SYSTEM
The *central nervous system* consists of the brain and nerve cells of the spinal cord. Together, they coordinate the perception of stimuli as well as motor responses. Brain growth is rapid from just before birth until beyond the second birthday. Brain size increases not so much because of the increasing numbers of *neurons* but because neurons put out many new fibers that connect them with each other and because brain cells called *glial cells* put out fatty sheathing, or *myelin*, that gradually encases neurons and their fibers.

A. Growth of the Brain

   1. Early neural activity is dominated by "lower" areas of the brain called the *brain stem* and the *midbrain*.

   2. As babies approach their first birthday, the "higher" part of the brain, the *cerebral cortex*, becomes more active.

   3. By the end of infancy, overall anatomical features of the brain are complete, but various parts continue to develop specialized functions. For example, the left hemisphere specializes in language.

   4. Despite specialization within brain areas, the *cerebrum* can supply alternate areas for such functions as language (in case of brain damage).

5. To a large extent, brain specialization appears to be driven by sensory experiences.

B. States of Sleep and Wakefulness

1. One important function of the brain is to control infants' states of sleep and wakefulness.

2. Very young infants vary from deep sleep to wakefulness. Newborns sleep about sixteen hours a day.

3. Newborns divide sleeping time about equally between active (*REM sleep*) and quiet periods of sleep.

4. Adults also alternate between cycles of REM and non-REM sleep.

5. Although sleep dominates in infancy, *states of arousal* offer opportunities for the baby to form impressions of her surroundings.

6. There is evidence that babies carry on some form of mental processing of stimulation even while asleep.

III. SENSORY DEVELOPMENT
Observations and experiments with neonates show that all the human senses operate at birth.

A. Visual Acuity

1. Infants can see at birth but lack the clarity of focus or acuity (keenness) of adult vision.

2. Infant vision is nearsighted. Acuity improves during infancy and reaches adult levels at the end of the preschool years.

B. Auditory Acuity

1. Infants can hear at birth and respond to sudden loud sounds with a dramatic startle reaction (the Moro reflex).

2. Pure tones produce little response; complex noises usually produce more of a response.

3. Electrodes attached to the infant's head register small electrical responses to ordinary sounds.

C. Taste and Smell

1. Even at birth infants prefer sweet tastes and suck sugar water faster than plain water. Other preferences are more difficult to establish.

2. Newborns react to a variety of smells, both good and bad.

3. Breast-feeding newborns can recognize the odor of their mothers' breasts.

D. Touch

1. Newborn infants have many reflexes that show sensitivity to touch.

2. Touch may aid development and tactual behaviors, such as holding and carrying, and relax both baby and care-giver.

3. Certain innate responses to touch can also facilitate visual development (Bushnell, 1981).

4. Sensitivity to pain increases with age.

IV. MOTOR DEVELOPMENT
The infant's first movements appear to be inborn and are called *reflexes*. Reflexes disappear or are incorporated into purposeful movements called *skills*. Both reflexes and skills are called *motor abilities*.

A. Early Reflexes

1. There are more than two dozen inborn reflexes, some of which, like sucking, enhance adaptation to the postuterine environment.

2. Stroking the baby's cheek causes a turning to the side being stroked. This *rooting* behavior helps the baby locate his mother's breast.

3. When the baby locates the nipple, he begins *sucking* powerfully and rhythmically without being taught.

4. A newborn will startle dramatically in response to sudden loss of support, even if not threatened. Such a startle is called the *Moro reflex*.

5. Like the *stepping* reflex, the early *grasping* reflex may facilitate later, more intentional grasping behaviors needed for exploration.

6. *Survival reflexes*, such as breathing, serve obvious functions. Other reflexes, such as the tonic neck reflex, are *primitive reflexes*.

B. The First Motor Skills

1. *Motor skills* are voluntary movements of the body.

2. *Gross motor skills* involve large muscles of the arms, legs, and torso.

3. *Fine motor skills* involve the small muscles located throughout the body.

4. The sequence in which motor skills develop follows both the *cephalocaudal principle* (head to tail) and *proximodistal principle* (near to far).

5. Large motor development in the first year permits the baby to engage increasingly in voluntary movements including *locomotion*.

6. Early *reaching and grasping* are fused in a single act; however, older babies reach first and then grasp the object.

7. In most children a predictable series of events culminates in true *walking* at twelve to thirteen months.

8. Acquisition of skills involved in walking illustrates the important issue of relative contributions of genetic endowment (nature) and of experience (nurture).

9. Confusion between nature and nurture seems inevitable and leads to the related issue of *maturation versus learning*.

V. VARIATIONS IN GROWTH AND MOTOR DEVELOPMENT

A. Low Birth-Weight Infants

1. *Low birth-weight* infants, either *preterm* or *small for date*, can result from malnourishment of mother or harmful practices such as smoking.

2. Physically immature infants look different from normal, full-term babies.

3. Preterm infants exhibit reflexes that are weak and poorly organized.

4. Neurological limitations persist in some preterm infants for the first two or three years, causing them to develop specific motor skills a bit later than full-term infants.

5. Ways have been devised to help low birth-weight infants by capitalizing on the benefits of rocking babies and providing extra handling.

6. Low birth-weight babies tend to respond to their parents less than normal babies do.

B. Gender Differences

1. During the first two years, the genders do not differ in competence and differ only sometimes in performance.

2. Boys show much more activity than girls and engage in more gross motor activity than girls do.

3. Gender differences may stem partly from different encouragement by parents and may also be genetically based.

4. Girls excel more often than boys at fine motor skills.

C. Cultural and Racial Differences

1. Physical growth and motor development vary among racial and cultural groups around the world.

2. In general, infants in a number of African societies develop motor skills sooner than North American infants, even when the families live in similar economic circumstances.

VI. NUTRITION DURING THE FIRST TWO YEARS

A. Special Nutritional Needs of Infants

1. Compared with other children, infants eat less in overall or absolute amount.

2. In proportion to their body weight, however, infants need to consume much more than others.

B. The Breast Versus the Bottle

1. Breast-feeding is recommended when possible because it builds immunity and closely matches the infant's nutritional needs.

2. Breast-feeding also satisfies the infant's sucking needs and fosters attachment.

C. Nutrition in Later Infancy

1. After about six months infants can be introduced gradually to solid foods.

2. Often North American diets fail to provide enough specific nutrients.

3. In calorie-rich societies such as ours, eating too much can cause overweight or *obesity*.

4. Weight in infancy correlates very little with weight in childhood and adulthood.

5. Extremely overweight infants develop enlarged fat cells as well as extra fat cells that do not disappear.

6. An infant or preschool child who fails to grow at normal rates for no apparent medical reason is suffering from a condition called *failure to thrive*.

7. Failure to thrive seems to have many sources.

8. The *infant mortality rate* is the proportion of babies who die during the first year of life. The number has declined steadily during this century.

9. Infant mortality in the United States and Canada is two or three times lower than in many Third World countries. Mortality in the United States, however, is higher than in nineteen other developed nations.

Overview and Key Concepts

Chapter 5 deals with the condition and appearance of the neonate as well as with newborn weight, size, and bodily proportions. Development of the nervous system, sensory development, and motor development are considered along with variations in growth and motor development. Gender differences and cultural-racial differences are considered. A concluding discussion presents nutritional needs and problems related to nutrition, such as malnutrition, obesity, failure to thrive, and infant mortality.

Directions: Identify the following key concepts introduced in Chapter 5.

1. When first delivered, the newborn baby, or _____ , definitely does not resemble most people's stereotype of a baby.

2. Many babies, especially if born a bit early, have a white waxy substance called _____ on their skin, and their bodies may be covered with fine, downy hair called _____ .

3. A quick, easily learned assessment of the infant's condition at birth is the _____ scale. A more thorough assessment, which may be given on the third day of life, is the _____ .

4. The _____ consists of the brain and nerve cells of the spinal cord. Most of the postnatal increase in brain size results not from increasing numbers of nerve cells, or _____ , but because brain cells called _____ put out fatty sheathing, or _____ , that gradually encases the neurons and their fibers.

5. At about six months, neural activity is dominated by the relatively primitive or "lower" areas of the brain called the _____ and the _____ , which regulate relatively automatic functions such as breathing.

6. As babies approach their first birthday, the "higher" part of the brain, called the _____ , becomes more active.

7. Newborns divide their sleeping time about equally between relatively active and quiet periods of sleep. The more active kind is named _____ , after the rapid eye movements that accompany it. In the quieter kind of sleep, called _____ , infants breathe regularly and more slowly.

8. Infants can see at birth but lack the _____ or _____ (keenness) characteristic of adults with good vision.

9. The infant's very first movements appear to be inborn and automatic; they are called _____ . During the first months of life, most reflexes disappear or become incorporated into purposeful movements that are called _____ . Both reflexes and skills are also called _____ .

10. Some reflexes, such as breathing, serve obvious physical needs and are called _____ . Others, such as the tonic neck reflex, serve no obvious physical purpose and are called _____ .

11. _____ are voluntary movements of the body or of parts of the body. _____ involve the large muscles of the arms, legs, and torso. _____ involve the small muscles located throughout the body.

12. On the whole, the sequence in which skills develop follows two trends that guide development. The _____ refers to the fact that upper parts of the body become usable and skillful before lower parts do. The _____ refers to the fact that central parts of the body become skillful before peripheral or outlying parts do.

13. After a few months, _____ become more common than the reflexes with which babies are born. By the age of seven months, on the average, babies become able to _____ , or move around on their own.

14. Questions about the acquisition of motor skills illustrate an important issue that pervades developmental psychology: the relative contributions of genetic endowment (_____) and of experience (_____) to children's

overall growth. Most developmental trends obviously depend on both
_____ and _____ , but the way in which each factor contributes is often unclear.

15. For medical purposes, newborns are considered _____ infants if they weigh less than 2,500 grams, which is about five and one-half pounds. Such low weight can happen for either of two reasons. First, some babies do not develop as quickly as normal, even though they are carried for about the usual term of forty weeks. They are called _____ infants. Second, some babies develop normally, but their gestation ends earlier than usual; they are called _____ .

Key Terms

Directions: Provide a definition for each of the following key terms. Check your answers against the Glossary or the text page number that follows each term.

Apgar scale (p. 152) _____

_____

_____

Attachment (p. 156) _____

_____

_____

Brain stem (p. 157) _____

_____

_____

Brazelton Neonatal Behavioral Assessment Scale (p. 153) _____

_____

_____

Central nervous system (p. 156) _____

_____

_____

Cephalocaudal principle (p. 165) _____

_____

_____

Cerebral cortex (p. 157) _____

_____

_____

Cerebrum (p. 157) _____

_____

_____

Failure to thrive (p. 182) _____

_____

_____

Fine motor skill (p. 165) _____

_____

_____

Fontanelle (p. 151) _____

_____

_____

Glial cell (p. 156) _____

_____

_____

Gross motor skill (p. 165) _____

_____

_____

Infant mortality rate (p. 182) _____

_____

_____

Kinesthetics (p. 175) _____

_____

_____

Kwashiorkor (p. 180) _____

_____

_____

Lanugo (p. 151) _____

_____

_____

Low birth weight (p. 171) _____

_____

_____

Marasmus (p. 180) _____

_____

_____

Midbrain (p. 157) _____

_____

_____

Moro reflex (p. 164) _____

_____

_____

Motor ability (p. 163) _____

_____

_____

Motor skill (p. 165) _____

_____

_____

Mouthing reflex (p. 164) _____

_____

_____

Myelin (p. 156) _____

_____

_____

Neonate (p. 151) _____

_____

Neuron (p. 156) _____

_____

Preterm (p. 171) _____

_____

Primitive reflex (p. 164) _____

_____

Proximodistal principle (p. 165) _____

_____

Reflex (p. 163) _____

_____

REM sleep (p. 158) _____

_____

Rooting reflex (p. 163) _____

_____

_____

Secretory IgA (p. 177) _____

_____

_____

Skill (p. 163) _____

_____

_____

Sleep apnea (p. 160) _____

_____

_____

Small for date (p. 171) _____

_____

_____

Sucking reflex (p. 164) _____

_____

_____

Sudden infant death syndrome (SIDS) (p. 160) _____

_____

_____

Survival reflex (p. 164) _____

_____

_____

Vernix (p. 151) _____

_____

_____

Study Questions

1. How does the appearance of an infant immediately after birth differ from the pictures we see on greeting cards? (p. 151)

   _____

   _____

   _____

   _____

2. What is the purpose of the Apgar scale, and, briefly, how does it work? (pp. 152–153)

   _____

   _____

   _____

   _____

3. What infant behaviors are assessed by the Brazelton Neonatal Behavioral Assessment Scale? (pp. 153–154)

_____

_____

_____

_____

4. How does the baby's general physical appearance have psychological consequences for fostering attachments, or bonds, between the baby and the people who care for him? (pp. 155–156)

_____

_____

_____

_____

5. What occurs in the process of myelinization within the central nervous system? (pp. 156–157)

_____

_____

_____

_____

6. What are three or four basic areas of the brain and their function in infancy? (pp. 157–158)

_____

_____

_____

_____

7. What are common patterns of sleep and wakefulness in infants? (pp. 158–160)

_____

_____

_____

_____

8. At birth, what can the infant see? (pp. 160–161)

_____

_____

_____

_____

9. What are a few of the ways in which a newborn baby responds to sound? (pp. 161–162)

_____

_____

_____

_____

10. What preferences for particular tastes and smells do babies show at birth? (p. 162)

_____

_____

_____

_____

11. In what ways does touch seem to enhance development in infancy? (pp. 162–163)

_____

_____

_____

_____

12. What is the difference between survival reflexes and primitive reflexes? (p. 164)

_____

_____

_____

_____

13. What are two principles of motor skill development? (p. 165)

_____

_____

_____

_____

14. What is the general sequence of events in the development of locomotion? (pp. 166–167)

_____

_____

_____

_____

15. How do early and later reaching and grasping differ from each other? (pp. 167–168)

_____

_____

_____

_____

16. What steps are involved in the fairly predictable series of events that leads up to true walking in most children? (pp. 168–169)

_____

_____

_____

_____

17. How do questions about the development of walking illustrate the important issue of nature and nurture in skill development? (pp. 169–170)

_____

_____

_____

_____

18. What are three possible causes of low birth weight? (p. 171)

_____

_____

_____

_____

19. What are three examples of differences in physical and motor development in infants and toddlers that could be explained by gender and cultural/racial variations? (pp. 173–176)

_____

_____

_____

_____

20. What are three advantages of breast-feeding over formula feeding? What are three disadvantages? (pp. 176–178)

_____

_____

_____

_____

Multiple-Choice Self-Test

1. At birth, the infant is often covered with a white waxy substance called
   a. myelin.
   b. vernix.
   c. fontanelles.
   d. lanugo.

2. An infant's Apgar score indicates the infant's
   a. gestational age.
   b. level of intelligence.
   c. relative health at birth.
   d. size and weight relative to what is normal.

3. Frank and Ronda have just been told that their newborn's Apgar score is five; this means that their baby
   a. is probably in good health.
   b. will probably have above-average intelligence.
   c. is in immediate need of special medical attention.
   d. is not likely to survive.

4. The area of the brain that regulates such activities as breathing and digestion and is responsible for early infant functioning is the
   a. brain stem and midbrain.
   b. cerebral cortex.
   c. cerebrum.
   d. spinal cord.

5. Infants with abnormal breathing patterns and a high incidence of sleep apnea are thought to be at risk for
   a. prematurity.
   b. kwashiorkor.
   c. REM.
   d. SIDS.

6. If given a choice between sugar water and salt water, a newborn is likely to
   a. prefer sugar water.
   b. prefer salt water.
   c. dislike both.
   d. prefer both equally.

7. A sudden loud noise is likely to elicit the _____ reflex in a newborn.
   a. Moro
   b. rooting
   c. stepping
   d. sucking

8. The fact that an infant's head and upper body develop before the lower body illustrates the
   a. cephalocaudal principle.
   b. integrational principle.
   c. maturational principle.
   d. proximodistal principle.

9. Very early reaching and grasping behavior seems to be guided primarily by
   a. reflexes.
   b. touch.
   c. vision.
   d. both touch and vision.

10. After forty weeks' gestation, Brad weighed five pounds at birth. Brad would be considered
    a. hypergestational.
    b. normal.
    c. preterm.
    d. small for date.

11. Use of waterbeds with low birth-weight infants has
    a. not been successful in reversing the effects of low birth weight.
    b. been associated with improved health and physical development in some low birth-weight infants.
    c. been clearly shown to increase intelligence in low birth-weight infants.
    d. not been studied.

12. Which of the following is true of gender differences?
    a. Boys tend to excel in fine motor skills.
    b. Girls tend to be more active than boys.
    c. Girls tend to excel at tasks requiring balance and rhythm.
    d. Girls tend to excel at tasks requiring speed and strength.

13. Currently in North America, the percentage of mothers who choose to breast-feed their infants is about
    a. 10 percent.
    b. 30 percent.
    c. 50 percent.
    d. 70 percent.

Activities

Activity 5.1

> **Objective:** To observe a real infant in various states of arousal.

Arrange to observe an infant, roughly six months to one year old, during the baby's naptime. If you are fortunate enough to already be baby-sitting such as infant, so much the better. Or you might ask a parent's permission to observe and take notes. With advance notice, most infant day-care centers welcome students who come to observe.

Allow about two hours for this activity. You may use the table on the following page for your notes. It is based on Table 5-2 of the text.

During your observation, remember that these states of arousal vary from baby to baby. A few families are in the happy circumstance of having a baby who does not show signs of distress on awakening. The baby just looks around quietly and smiles if someone happens to be in view.

In class, you will find it helpful to compare your observations with those of other students. There may or may not be differences based on the babies' ages, genders, or ethnic/racial groups. You may find what appear to be differences in temperament or even personality. As you discuss your findings, you will become increasingly aware of similarity and variation from one infant to another. You may find that most of the babies do have various states of arousal but the way in which they are expressed is unique to each one.

States of Arousal

Infant's age _____ months   Gender _____

Cultural/ethnic/racial heritage _____

Other factors that may be relevant. (Is the baby teething? Does it have a cold? Do the adults describe this baby as a "good" sleeper?)

State	Infant's Behavior	For How Long?
non-REM	Complete rest; muscles relaxed; eyes shut, lids quiet; breathing even and rather slow	
REM sleep	A few twitches, jerks, facial grimaces; irregular and intermittent eye movements; breathing irregular and relatively rapid	
Drowsiness	Occasional movement, but less than in REM sleep; eyes open and close; glazed look; breathing regular, but faster than in non-REM sleep	
Alert inactivity	Eyes open and scanning; body rather still; breathing rate similar to drowsiness, but more irregular	
Alert activity	Eyes open, but not attending or scanning; frequent diffuse body movements; vocalizations; irregular breathing; skin flushed	
Distress	Whimpering or crying; vigorous or agitated movements; facial grimaces pronounced; skin very flushed	*Do not time this!* If you are in charge, take care of the distress. If not, call the person who takes care of the baby.

Activity 5.2

> **Objective:** To examine the distinction that hospital personnel make between preterm and small-for-date infants.

Telephone for an appointment with a doctor or nurse who works in the obstetrics unit of a hospital in your community. If possible, visit the neonate nursery. You may be restricted to looking through the nursery window.

The purpose of the appointment and visit is to discuss the criteria for distinguishing between a preterm infant and a low birth-weight baby.

It would be appropriate to ask about differences in the care of these two categories of infants.

Other questions you may wish to ask are:

What determines whether the baby will be cared for in the regular nursery or in the intensive care unit?

What instructions do you give the parents of preterm and low birth-weight babies?

How long do the low birth-weight babies who remain in the regular nursery usually stay?

If there is only one hospital in your community, this activity would be more feasible for a small committee of students (fewer than six) than for the entire class. Other students might wish to interview parents of preterm or low birth-weight babies. Finding such parents may be done quite informally, by asking in class, asking friends, or asking your family. Or were *you* a low birth-weight or preterm baby? Examples of questions you could ask parents are:

What were you told about your baby's health?

Were you worried?

What special care did you need to give your baby—care that differed from care given to other babies?

How old was the baby when you were no longer concerned about weight or gestational age?

If you were a low birth-weight or preterm baby:

What did your parents say about you during that period?

To the degree that you can remember, do you think that there was a carry-over of parental concern during your preschool and primary-grade years?

We might assume that your parents' concern is long past, but are there still vestiges of concern over your nourishment, sleep, and so on?

Activity 5.3

> **Objective:** To note the resources for health and development available to parents of newborn infants in your community.

With the help of social service and health agencies, identify three services that parents may use to ask questions and get help with their new baby's feeding and general physical condition.

Name, address, telephone	Would you feel OK as a client?	Is it easy to find in the phone book?
1.		
2.		
3.		

Activity 5.4

Objective: To observe the degree of consistency between the popular press and Chapter 5 of the text.

There are many magazines available specifically for parents. Look through one or two issues of a magazine like *Parents*. Do the comments on nutrition, sleep, growth, and so on complement or contradict what is said in Chapter 5?

For each magazine, use the following form.

Title of the magazine _____

Publication date of issue you examined _____

Topic	Comments in Magazine	Text's Comments	Consistent/ Contradictory
1.			
2.			
3.			
4.			
Would you recommend this magazine to a parent? Why or why not?			

Activity 5.5

Objective: To recognize several developmental characteristics during three periods of infancy and toddlerhood.

Imagine that you are a teacher in a remote community, isolated from the health services we usually take for granted. Perhaps you teach in a one-room school in an Eskimo village in Alaska. Supplies and services are flown in. The nearest hospital and health center is six hundred miles away; patients are flown to and from the facility. Babies are usually born at home with the help of a respected midwife.

You have lived and worked in the community long enough to earn the trust of the families there, particularly the parents of the children you have taught. Folks have formed the habit of coming to you for advice about their children. Like parents everywhere, they want healthy, functioning children and often turn to you, rather than to health-care personnel, for reassurance. You do your best, recognizing your limitations.

You have been using the text as a reference book, and in this case, you have been asked the universal question, "Is my baby all right?" There are three babies under discussion, and you have decided to do the best you can, recognizing obvious limitations. One of the babies, a girl, was born last week; another is a four-month-old girl; and there's an old-timer of thirteen months, a boy. They all seem fine, but you want to be more specific. You have gone to the text and settled on Table 5-3, "Major Reflexes in Newborn Infants," as most useful for the newborn and Table 5-4, "Milestones of Motor Development," for the other two little ones. The items in Table 5-4 are based on the Denver Developmental Screening Test and have been validated for many years. You are on firm ground.

What characteristics, transcending all cultural boundaries, would you check for?

The Newborn

Survival Reflexes

1.
2.
3.

Primitive Reflexes

1.
2.
3.

Head Support

The Four-Month-Old

Reflexes

1.
2.

Motor Skills

1.
2.
3.
4.
5.
6.

The Thirteen-Month-Old

Motor Skills
1.
2.
3.
4.
5.
6.
7.
8.
9.
10.
11.
12.
13.
14.

Answer Key

Overview and Key Concepts

1. neonate (p. 151)

2. vernix; lanugo (p. 151)

3. Apgar; Brazelton Neonatal Behavioral Assessment Scale (p. 153)

4. central nervous system; neurons; glial cells; myelin (p. 156)

5. brain stem; midbrain (p. 157)

6. cerebral cortex (p. 157)

7. REM sleep; non-REM sleep (p. 158)

8. clarity of focus; acuity (p. 160)

9. reflexes; skills; motor abilities (p. 163)

10. survival reflexes; primitive reflexes (p. 164)

11. motor skills; gross motor skills; fine motor skills (p. 165)

12. cephalocaudal principle; proximodistal principle (p. 165)

13. voluntary movements; locomote (p. 166)

14. nature; nurture; genetics; experience (p. 169)

15. low birth-weight; small for date; preterm (p. 171)

Multiple-Choice Self-Test

1. Choice (b) is correct. Vernix is a white waxy substance that covers the skin at birth, especially if the infant is born a bit early. (p. 151)
   Myelin, choice (a), is a fatty sheath that develops on neurons. Fontanelles, choice (c), refers to the "soft spot" on the baby's head. Lanugo, choice (d), refers to the fine downy hair present at birth.

2. Choice (c) is correct. The Apgar is a measure of infant health made at one and five minutes after birth. It includes heart rate, breathing, muscle tone, skin color, and reflexes. (p. 152) The Apgar does not assess gestational age, choice (a); intelligence, choice (b); or size and weight, choice (d).

3. Choice (c) is correct. A score of five indicates that something is wrong and that the newborn is in need of immediate medical attention. (p. 153) Infants with scores of eight and above are probably in good health, choice (a). Infants with scores of three and below need immediate intensive care and may not survive, choice (d). The Apgar sheds no light on later intelligence, choice (b).

4. Choice (a) is correct. The lower areas of the brain, the brain stem and midbrain, regulate breathing, digestion, and alertness. (p. 157) Choices (b) and (c) are higher areas of the brain that tend to be involved in more voluntary functioning, particularly as the infant gets older. Choice (d) is involved in transmitting information to and from the brain and in some reflex activity.

5. Choice (d) is correct. Abnormal breathing patterns and sleep apnea are associated with a higher risk for sudden infant death syndrome (SIDS). (pp. 160–161) The symptoms described are postnatal, not prenatal, symptoms; thus (a) is incorrect. Choice (b) is a protein deficiency associated with malnutrition; and (c), rapid eye movement, is a stage of sleep associated with dreaming.

6. Choice (a) is correct. Studies indicate that infants clearly prefer sugar water over salt water and will suck faster for sugar water than for plain water. Thus, (b), (c), and (d) are incorrect. (pp. 297–298)

7. The Moro reflex, choice (a), a startle response, is produced in response to a loud noise. (p. 161) The rooting reflex, choice (b), is initiated by stimulation to the cheek. The stepping reflex, choice (c), occurs when an infant is held upright—it lifts its legs as if to step. The sucking reflex, choice (d), occurs when something is placed in the infant's mouth.

8. Choice (a) is correct. The cephalocaudal principle refers to the fact that upper parts of the body become usable and skillful before lower parts. (p. 165) Choices (b) and (c) are not general principles of development. Choice (d) refers to the fact that the central parts of the body develop before the peripheral or outer parts.

9. Early reaching is guided primarily by vision, choice (c). Studies show that infants will use vision to guide them to an optical illusion but will not close their hands on that illusion once they apparently "touch it." (p. 167) Reaching and grasping are primarily voluntary behaviors; therefore, (a) is incorrect. Touch, choice (b), and touch and vision together, choice (d), seem to play a role in later reaching and grasping.

10. Choice (d) is correct. Forty weeks is the average gestational age. Weight under five and one-half pounds is considered low birth weight. An infant who is full term but has low birth weight is termed small for date. (p. 171)
Choice (a) is a term not generally used. The infant has low birth weight and therefore is not normal, choice (b). Preterm, choice (c), refers to infants whose gestational age is less than thirty-seven weeks.

11. Choice (b) is correct. Interventions such as waterbeds, rocking, and extra stimulation have improved health and physical development in low birth-weight infants. (pp. 172–173) Although waterbeds have been associated with positive outcomes, changes in intelligence, choice (c), have not been reliably found. Choices (a) and (d) are inaccurate statements.

12. Choice (c) is correct. During the first two years, girls tend to excel in coordination-based tasks and boys tend to excel in strength-based tasks. (p. 174)
Girls tend to do better on fine motor tasks, choice (a). Boys are more active, choice (b), and better at tasks requiring speed and strength, choice (d).

13. Choice (c) is correct. Current surveys indicate that one in every two mothers, or fifty percent, breast-feeds her infants. (p. 178)

CHAPTER 6
The First Two Years: Cognitive Development

Learning Objectives

1. Define perception and cognition and describe ways of studying these processes.

2. Characterize infant visual perception, including object constancy and depth perception.

3. Describe the infant's ability to localize sounds, indicating how this ability differs from that of older children and adults.

4. List the major characteristics of and achievements in each of Jean Piaget's six stages of sensorimotor development.

5. Provide an overall evaluation of Piaget's theory, including a discussion of the five areas of concern covered in the text.

6. Identify the three kinds of behavioral learning in infancy, and describe the circumstances under which each can occur.

7. Discuss and evaluate the basic features of learning theory and the nativist theory with respect to language acquisition.

8. Describe what is meant by phonology, semantics, and syntax in terms of infant language acquisition.

9. Describe the individual differences in choice of first words and indicate how parents influence early language.

Chapter Outline

I. WAYS OF STUDYING PERCEPTION AND COGNITION IN INFANTS
Infants gather information about the environment through the psychological processes of perception and cognition. *Perception* refers to the brain's immediate organization of sensations. *Cognition* is a more general term for all processes by which humans acquire knowledge. It includes perception, reasoning, and language skills.

A. Arousal and Infants' Heart Rates

1. Infant psychologists have developed several interrelated techniques for inferring the perceptions and "thoughts" of babies.

2. One way to understand an infant's cognition is to measure his heart rate (HR) with a small electronic stethoscope attached to his chest.

3. Changes in HR signify variations in the baby's arousal, alertness, and general contentment.

4. Infant psychologists believe this to be true because HR varies reliably with attention and arousal in adult subjects.

5. Typically HR slows when adults notice something interesting but not overly exciting.

6. If adults attend to something very stimulating, their HRs speed up, or accelerate.

7. Precautions must be taken when using HR to study infants because of unique qualities of infants' attention. Infants should be observed when they are truly alert.

8. Many stimuli that seem harmless to adults apparently overstimulate very young infants.

B. Recognition, Memory, and Infant Habituation

1. Babies' responses to the familiar and the unfamiliar provide infant psychologists with a second way of understanding infant perception and cognition.

2. Psychologists study infants' tendency to get used to and therefore to ignore stimuli as they experience them repeatedly; this tendency is called *habituation*.

3. This method has shown that babies recognize quite a lot of past experiences.

4. Sometimes, recognition persists for very long periods.

5. Overall, monitoring infants' HR has given psychologists a useful method for learning something about what infants attend to and perceive in their environment.

II. INFANT PERCEPTION
Children acquire a number of perceptual skills during infancy, each corresponding to one of the five human senses: vision, hearing, touch, taste, and smell.

A. Visual Perception

1. Newborns are particularly attracted to contours, or the edges of areas of light and dark.

2. When infants get to the age of two or three months their perceptual interest shifts to complexity and curvature.

3. *Object constancy* refers to the perception that an object remains the same in some way in spite of constant changes in the sensations that it sends to the eye.

    a. A baby's toy duck never casts exactly the same image on her retina from one second to the next. Somehow the baby must learn that this kaleidoscope of images refers to only one constant duck.

    b. *Size constancy* refers to the perception that an object stays the same size even when viewed at different distances.

    c. *Shape constancy* refers to viewing the same object at different angles and having the ability to recognize apparent but unreal changes of shape.

    d. Young infants at about three months show constancy only for simple shapes. Older infants can recognize complex forms, but it is hard to say when exactly babies acquire either shape or size constancy.

    e. Whatever the timing of their appearance, shape and size constancies enable the infant to distinguish familiar objects and to begin seeing the world as predictable and secure.

4. Depth and Space Perception

    a. *Depth perception* refers to a sense of how far away objects are or appear to be. This type of perception emerges at around two or three months of age, as demonstrated in the classic *visual cliff* experiment.

    b. Infants also show depth perception in their responses to looming motions.

  c. Research shows a variety of degrees of sensitivity to spatial orientation in infants.

 B. Auditory Perception
  Infants respond to sounds even as newborns, but what sense they make of sounds will be a crucial factor in their acquisition of language.

  1. Research confirms that under certain conditions infants can indeed hear as well as perceive what they hear.

  2. For example, infants just two days old can locate sounds, as shown by the way they orient their heads toward the noise of a rattle.

III. INFANT COGNITION
 At first infant cognition has little to do with the symbolic forms that develop later; instead, it emphasizes active experimentation with and manipulation of materials.

 A. Piaget's Theory of Sensorimotor Intelligence
  Piaget described six stages in *sensorimotor intelligence,* dealing with how infants think by way of sensory perceptions and motor actions.

  1. Piaget believed infants follow three trends as they grow older.

   a. Their thinking becomes less *egocentric.*

   b. They show a trend toward abstract or symbolic thinking.

   c. As their motor skills become more complex, they form structures that Piaget called *schemes.*

  2. Piaget typically referred to later cognitive structures and patterns as *operations* or *systems.*

  3. Piaget argued that sensorimotor intelligence develops by means of two complementary processes, *assimilation* and *accommodation.*

   a. Stage 1—early reflexes: using what you're born with (birth to one month): Piaget believed that cognitive development begins with reflexes and modifications of reflexes.

   b. Stage 2—primary circular reactions: modifying what you're born with (one to four months): Soon after the baby begins modifying his early reflexes, he begins building and differentiating action schemes rapidly. Babies produce repeated actions (*circular reactions*) involving the body and engage in commonly occurring schemes.

c. Stage 3—secondary circular reactions: making interesting sights last (four to eight months): As they practice their first schemes, babies move their attention beyond their own bodily actions to include objects and events immediately around them. Circular reactions now orient to external objects, and the baby has a hazy notion of *object permanence*.

d. Stage 4—combined secondary circular reactions: deliberate combinations of means and ends (eight to twelve months): At this stage, instead of just happening on connections among schemes, the infant purposely uses her knowledge gained in the prior stage. Heavy reliance on motor action causes babies to make the *AnotB error;* however, a developing intentional quality allows him to anticipate events in the near future.

e. Stage 5—tertiary circular reactions: active experimentation with objects (twelve to eighteen months): At Stage 5, the infant deliberately varies the schemes for producing interesting results or ends and engages in systematic application of schemes.

f. Stage 6—the first symbols: representing objects and actions (eighteen to twenty-four months): At this stage, motor schemes begin to occur symbolically. For the first time, the baby can begin to imagine or envision actions and their results without having to try them out beforehand. True object permanence is achieved, and *deferred imitation* is made possible by mental representation.

B. Baby Jill's Intelligence: An Example
Relationships among the six stages of sensorimotor intelligence become clearer if we look at how Baby Jill handled a ball at each stage of her development.

C. Assessment of Piaget's Theory of Infant Cognition

1. Piaget's theory has stimulated considerable study of infant cognition. Some research has confirmed the main features of the theory; other research has pointed out aspects of infancy that at least complicate Piaget's theory.

2. For example, evidence for connections among early schemes complicates Piaget's assertion that schemes primarily begin as separate entities.

3. Some infant psychologists question Piaget's six stages because they feel that the stages confuse the child's motor abilities with his cognitive abilities (Bower, 1981).

4. Whereas effects of memory may explain much of infant performance (e.g., the AnotB error), Piaget explained most infant thinking in terms of motor schemes.

5. Piaget may have taken the role of motivation for granted and in emphasizing the nature of competence may have neglected the immediate causes of performance.

IV. BEHAVIORAL LEARNING IN INFANCY

Behaviorism, or learning theory has supplied a framework for studying specific performance in infants. Learning theorists focus on changes in specific behaviors or responses and on observable causes (stimuli and reinforcements) of behavior.

A. Classical Conditioning

1. Classical conditioning depends on transferring control of a reflex response by pairing two stimuli (the UCS and the CS).

2. Classical conditioning occurs reliably from about the age of six months onward. Prior to that age, mixed results have been obtained with infants.

3. Young infants may be genetically predisposed to learn some connections or associations and genetically restrained from learning others.

B. Operant Conditioning

1. In operant learning, infants get a reward or reinforcement if they perform some simple action.

2. The large majority of studies of infant learning involve operant conditioning.

3. Babies tend to repeat actions that are reinforced, and many studies have found infants quite capable of learning through operant conditioning.

4. Operant learning is easily confused with reflex responses since it typically involves behaviors that young babies can already do.

C. Imitation

1. Infants can engage in different types of imitation at different points during infancy.

2. Only children nearing their second birthday could engage in deferred imitation.

V. LANGUAGE ACQUISITION

To become competent in language, infants must learn sounds (*phonology*), they must begin learning language's meanings (*semantics*), and they must piece together its organization (*syntax*).

A. Theories of Language Acquisition

1. Learning theories of language must confront the limits of reinforcement in language acquisition.

2. More likely learning processes are mutual imitation and accommodation.

3. For some linguists, even imitation and accommodation do not go far enough in explaining the ease and speed with which infants acquire language. They propose a nativist theory and argue that humans are genetically predisposed to acquire language through the *language acquisition device* (LAD) (Chomsky, 1976).

B. Phonology

1. Every language uses a finite number of sounds, or *phonemes*, which combine to make words.

2. In acquiring language, infants must learn to notice phonemes and to ignore meaningless sounds.

3. Infants seem to be genetically and physiologically disposed toward noticing phonemic differences as well as predisposed toward the categorical perception of sounds.

4. Babies begin babbling in very complex ways between four and eight months and seem to be intrinsically motivated to produce sounds far beyond those uttered by their parents. Even deaf children babble in normal ways.

5. Babbling can be reinforced, but it is not susceptible to teaching.

6. Late in infancy, some babbling may sound rather like true language because it becomes complex and acquires normal *intonation* or "melody."

C. Semantics and First Words

1. The semantics (or meanings) of a language are never mastered fully, even by adults.

2. Around their first birthday, infants begin to use their first words, and they may use as many as fifty words by their second birthday.

3. *Expressive language* refers to words children actually use in conversation. It is complemented by *receptive language*, which is the ability to comprehend language used by others.

4. The first words are sometimes called *holophrases* because the child often uses one word to express a complete thought.

5. First words tend to refer to objects that stand out in the child's environment.

6. Children may bias their selection of first words in favor of words that they already find easy to pronounce.

7. Children vary in their emphasis on words that refer to objects and objective events and those that refer to feelings and relationships.

8. There are numerous parental influences on language acquisition.

Overview and Key Concepts

From the moment of birth, infants begin interacting with the environment around them, and they begin the lifelong process of figuring out the world. Chapter 6 assesses perceptual and cognitive processes in the first two years of life from both the Piagetian and the behavioristic standpoint. It discusses evidence for the baby's cognitive development even before the baby is able to communicate verbally. The chapter surveys numerous studies from infant psychology and introduces the topic of language acquisition.

Directions: Identify the following key concepts introduced in Chapter 6.

1. _____ refers to the brain's immediate or direct organization and interpretation of sensations. _____ is a more general term for all the processes by which humans acquire knowledge. It includes perception, reasoning, and language skills.

2. Infants' tendency to ignore stimulation that they are thoroughly used to is called _____ .

3. Infants tend to pay attention to _____ stimuli, and they tend to _____ to the familiar. Evidence for this may be found in changes in the _____ .

4. Infants seem to favor looking at facial patterns and other patterns marked by interesting _____ , _____ , and _____ .

5. _____ refers to the perception that an object remains the same in some way in spite of constant changes in the sensations that it sends to the eye.

6. The well-known experiment used to test a baby's depth perception uses the _____ .

7. Piaget refers to intelligence in infancy as _____ .

8. Piaget's six stages of infant cognitive development show three trends: _____ , _____ , and _____ .

9. According to Piaget, cognitive development begins with _____ . In fact, Stage 1 is called _____ .

10. In _____ , the baby seems to be stimulated by the outcome of his own behavior, so he responds for the sheer joy of feeling himself act.

11. In Piaget's third stage, _____ _____ _____ emerge.

12. A belief (gained in Stage 3) that objects have existence separate from one's own actions and continue to exist even when they cannot be seen is called _____ .

13. In Piaget's fourth and fifth stages, the baby's actions become more intentional and more varied. Sensorimotor intelligence culminates in the sixth stage with schemes beginning to occur _____ .

14. A framework that studies the specific performance of infants has come from _____ , or what psychologists sometimes also call _____ . Typically, learning theorists identify three kinds of behavioral learning: _____ , _____ , and _____ .

15. Learning theories of language suggest several processes that may affect language acquisition. Three of these are _____ , _____ , and _____ . Nativist theories argue that human beings are genetically predisposed to acquire language and sometimes call these inborn linguistic skills the _____ .

Key Terms

Directions: Provide a definition for each of the following key terms. Check your answers against the Glossary or the text page number that follows each term.

Accommodation (p. 199) _____

_____

_____

AnotB error (p. 202) _____

_____

_____

Assimilation (p. 198) _____

_____

_____

Behaviorism (p. 210) _____

_____

_____

Circular reaction (p. 200) _____

_____

_____

Cognition (p. 188) _____

_____

_____

Deferred imitation (p. 204) _____

_____

_____

Depth perception (p. 194) _____

_____

_____

Egocentric (p. 198) _____

_____

_____

Expressive language (p. 217) _____

_____

_____

Habituation (p. 190) _____

_____

_____

Holophrase (p. 218) _____

_____

_____

Intonation (p. 216) _____

_____

_____

Language acquisition device (LAD) (p. 215) _____

_____

_____

Learning theory (p. 210) _____

_____

_____

Motherese (p. 219) _____

_____

_____

Object constancy (p. 192) _____

_____

_____

Object permanence (p. 201) _____

_____

_____

Perception (p. 188) _____

_____

_____

Phoneme (p. 215) _____

_____

_____

Phonology (p. 214) _____

_____

_____

Primary circular reaction (p. 200) _____

_____

_____

Receptive language (p. 217) _____

_____

_____

Scheme (p. 198) _____

_____

_____

Secondary circular reaction (p. 200) _____

_____

_____

Semantics (p. 214) _____

_____

_____

Sensorimotor intelligence (p. 198) _____

_____

_____

Shape constancy (p. 193) _____

_____

_____

Size constancy (p. 192) _____

_____

_____

Syntax (p. 214) _____

_____

_____

Tertiary circular reaction (p. 202) _____

_____

_____

Visual cliff (p. 194) _____

_____

_____

Study Questions

1. How are heart rate and habituation used to study cognitive response in infants? (pp. 189–190)

_____

_____

_____

_____

2. What is meant by *object constancy, size constancy,* and *shape constancy*? (pp. 192–193)

_____

_____

_____

_____

3. What are the major implications of Gibson and Walk's famous visual cliff experiment? (pp. 194–195)

_____

_____

_____

_____

4. There is no doubt that babies are born able to hear. During the first eighteen months, what sequence is involved in learning to perceive the meaning and the location of sounds? (pp. 196–197)

_____

_____

_____

_____

5. It has been said that Piaget's theory of cognitive development describes a journey away from the self. Explain the meaning of this statement. (p. 198)

_____

_____

_____

_____

6. How do assimilation and accommodation work together as complementary processes in the emergence of sensorimotor intelligence? (pp. 198–199)

_____

_____

_____

_____

7. How did Piaget explain the origin of sensorimotor intelligence from simple reflexes in Stage 1 of his sensorimotor period in cognitive development? (pp. 199–200)

_____

_____

_____

_____

8. What are circular reactions and how do primary circular reactions differ from secondary circular reactions? (pp. 200–201)

_____

_____

_____

_____

9. What early signs of object permanence appear in Stage 3 of Piaget's sensorimotor period? (p. 201)

_____

_____

_____

_____

10. How are "deliberate combinations of means and ends" manifested in the baby's behavior between eight and twelve months? (pp. 201–202)

_____

_____

_____

_____

11. What is the AnotB error? (p. 202)

_____

_____

_____

_____

12. What is an example of a behavioral episode that fits the pattern of a tertiary circular reaction? (pp. 202–203)

_____

_____

_____

_____

13. What are the major achievements of Stage 6? (pp. 203–204)

_____

_____

_____

_____

14. Once a theory in psychology becomes widely known and accepted, thoughtful colleagues begin to refine it by noting exceptions and developing alternative explanations. So it is with Piaget's theory of cognitive development. What questions that may modify Piaget's theory have been raised about the integration of schemes, motor limitations versus cognitive limitations, the effects of motivation, and performance versus competence? (pp. 205–210)

_____

_____

_____

_____

15. How does behaviorism provide a framework different from Piaget's for viewing cognitive development in infants? (pp. 210–213)

_____

_____

_____

_____

16. What are some examples of classical conditioning and operant conditioning in infants? (pp. 210–212)

_____

_____

_____

_____

17. What are two competing theories of language acquisition? (pp. 214–215)

_____

_____

_____

_____

18. What is the evidence that humans are genetically and physiologically predisposed to noticing phonemic differences? (p. 216)

_____

_____

_____

_____

19. Few babies say real words before their first birthday, but they are surely developing their ability to speak a language. How can adults tell that this is happening? (pp. 216–218)

_____

_____

_____

_____

20. What are some ways in which parents facilitate language acquisition? (pp. 219–222)

_____

_____

_____

_____

Multiple-Choice Self-Test

1. Perception refers to the process by which
   a. external stimuli trigger neurons.
   b. our brain organizes and interprets sensations.
   c. we acquire all knowledge.
   d. we form symbolic representations.

2. The tendency for an infant to look less and less at a stimulus that is repeatedly presented is called
   a. classical conditioning.
   b. habituation.
   c. operant conditioning.
   d. stimulus generalization.

3. Newborns tend to prefer looking at objects that
   a. are high in contour.
   b. have simple shapes.
   c. they have seen before.
   d. are innately preprogrammed.

4. Object constancy refers to
   a. the fact that infants show consistent preferences for certain kinds of objects.
   b. the notion that objects exist even when they are out of sight.
   c. the perception that an object stays the same despite changes in sensation.
   d. none of the above.

5. The visual cliff has been used to study
   a. depth perception.
   b. infant crawling and walking.
   c. reaching and grasping.
   d. all of the above.

6. Which of the following is true of a newborn's ability to localize sounds?
   a. Newborns are incapable of sound localization.
   b. Newborns can locate high-pitched sounds better than low-pitched sounds.
   c. Newborns can locate high- and low-pitched sounds equally well.
   d. Newborns cannot locate low-pitched sounds.

7. Assimilation refers to the process of
   a. becoming more organized with the addition of new experiences.
   b. interpreting new experiences on the basis of already existing schemes.
   c. modifying existing schemes to incorporate new experiences.
   d. reducing attention to a repeatedly presented stimulus.

8. Which of Piaget's sensorimotor stages is characterized by the development of secondary circular reactions?
   a. first
   b. second
   c. third
   d. sixth

9. According to Piaget, the first signs of object permanence appear at
   a. birth.
   b. about one month of age.
   c. about four months of age.
   d. about twelve months of age.

10. Which of the following statements best summarizes our knowledge about the newborn's capacity to learn?
    a. Research has clearly demonstrated that newborns can learn through classical conditioning, operant conditioning, and imitation.
    b. Research suggests that newborns learn primarily through classical conditioning.
    c. Research suggests that newborns can be operantly conditioned but that there are mixed results for the other forms of learning.
    d. Newborns do not learn; their behavior is dominated by innate reflexes.

11. Semantics refers to
    a. the organization of a language.
    b. the sound patterns within a language.
    c. the meaning of a language.
    d. all of the above.

12. In general, expressive language
    a. appears at about three months of age.
    b. follows receptive language.
    c. is part of babbling.
    d. precedes receptive language.

13. If a child utters the word "drink" to indicate "I want a drink," we refer to this utterance as
    a. a holophrase.
    b. a phoneme.
    c. receptive language.
    d. motherese.

Activities

Activity 6.1

Objective: To observe infant behavior firsthand.

In order to appreciate the research, ideas, and theories presented in Chapter 6, capitalize on opportunities to observe and analyze infant behavior for yourself. Try to visit an infant stimulation or infant day-care program on your campus or in your community. Record some episodes of infant behavior and some of your impressions below.

Activity 6.2

Objective: To understand the arguments used by two theories of cognitive learning.

Some proponents of psychological theory tend to believe that their theory is the "best" and that other theories are too flawed to be particularly useful. Other psychologists can put the various theories into perspective and recognize the contribution of each.

Prepare the arguments and rebuttal *for* and *against* (1) operant conditioning and (2) Piaget's theory of cognitive development.

Operant Conditioning	
For	**Against**

Piaget's Theory of Cognitive Development	
For	**Against**

Activity 6.3

Objective: To develop facility in understanding and using Piagetian terms.

The terms that Jean Piaget attached to the concepts in his theory of cognitive development are daunting. Some people have postponed looking into this approach because the terms seem so mysterious. But good teachers know that one of the best ways of learning something is to teach it!

A group of well-educated parents has asked you to explain what the fuss over Piaget and infant cognition is all about. You have decided to give clear explanations of a few key terms, with examples. After that, you will discuss the six stages of sensorimotor intelligence, also with examples. Prepare your notes for the key terms, as indicated below.

Sensorimotor intelligence

Egocentric thinking

Schemes

Assimilation

Accommodation

Symbolic thinking

Stage 1: Early reflexes

Stage 2: Primary circular reactions

Object permanence

Stage 3: Secondary circular reactions

Stage 4: Combining secondary circular reactions

AnotB error

Stage 5: Tertiary circular reactions

Stage 6: First symbols

Activity 6.4

Objective: To determine whether a baby has object permanence.

Visit a baby who is three to five months old.* When you have made friends with the baby, offer an attractive object for the baby to examine (some people use keys on a key ring). After the baby becomes interested, gently take the keys back. With the baby watching, hide the keys under a scarf or a cushion. Note whether the baby searches for the keys.

Visit a baby who is six or seven months old. Use the same procedure as above. Does the baby search?

Now repeat the procedure with a baby nine to twelve months old. This time you have two scarves or cushions. *With the baby watching,* hide the keys under one scarf; then move the keys so that they are hidden under the second scarf. Note the baby's procedure for finding the keys.

With respect to object permanence, at what stage is

Baby 1 (three to five months)?

Baby 2 (six or seven months)?

Baby 3 (nine to twelve months)?

*The question of how to find a baby justifiably concerns many students. Only a few are fortunate enough to be a parent, and those students may feel free to observe their own children. For those who are not parents, there may be a campus children's center that serves infants and toddlers. If there is an early childhood education progam on campus, get in touch with the faculty who teach the courses. They probably can tell you the names and locations of infant day-care centers in the community.

Another good source of infants and toddlers comes from your own class. Ask your professor to set aside a few minutes for inquiring about infants and willing parents.

When you observe in a home, be sure to tell the parents what you have learned. They sometimes worry about what you have found out about their children. Let them see your notes and be sure you say something reassuring about their baby. Every mom and dad wants an A in parenting.

In this activity, it may be expedient for the class to be divided into thirds. Each third can then choose one of the age ranges.

What might the connection between object permanence and memory be?

How might it have altered the baby's scheme of objects and people in the environment?

Activity 6.5

Objective: To identify symptoms of hearing loss among infants and toddlers, with a focus on language development.

Sometimes a hearing loss is not identified until a child reaches preschool or kindergarten. Teachers have learned to look for certain signs. If you suspected that a child's hearing was impaired, what questions would you ask about the following behaviors?

Babbling during infancy

The child's score on a standardized IQ test

The child's verbal ability compared with that of his or her age mates

The child's ability to follow verbal instructions

The child's opportunities, from birth, to vocally interact with adults

The child's use of breath and voice sounds, | s | and | sh |

The child's attention to the mouth of the speaker

Activity 6.6

Objective: To hear a tape recording of the actual sounds and first words in the sequence of language development.

Using Table 6-3 as a guide, locate six infants and toddlers. Ask the parent or care-giver to record the vocalizations as indicated below.

Approximate Age	Vocal Accomplishment
4 weeks	Cries of displeasure (optional)
12 weeks	Contented cooing, squealing, gurgling, occasional vowel sounds
20 weeks	First signs of babbling; most vowel sounds, but only occasional consonants
6 months	Babbling well established; full range of vowel sounds and many consonants
12 months	Babbling includes the melody or intonation of the language; utterances signal emotions; first words are produced; the child understands simple commands
18 months	Expressive vocabulary between three and fifty words; intricate babbling interspersed with real words; occasional two- and three-word sentences
24 months	Expressive vocabulary between fifty and three hundred words, though not all used accurately; babbling gone; many two-word sentences or even longer; nonadult grammar; the child understands most simple language intended for him/her

Source: DeVilliers & DeVilliers, 1978.

Play the tapes in class in order of chronological age, and ask for class consensus.

Do the recordings correspond with the chart in ages and sounds?

If not, how can you account for the discrepancy?

Was there any correlation between the use of the first words and walking?

For the recordings with words: Are they understandable? If not, do you have a translation?

Other comments

Activity 6.7

Objective: To note individual variations in the age at which language develops.

Interview a parent of an infant or toddler twelve to twenty-four months of age. Ask the parent the following questions.

1. Is your child using words yet?

2A. If so, at what age did you recognize the first word?

Have you noticed any sentences, even of one word?

Can you recall any of the sentences?

How clearly does your youngster speak?

Does he/she still need to learn to pronounce certain consonants (e.g., "I yove you")? (Tell the parent that it usually takes a long time for a child to learn to pronounce all of the sounds correctly.)

2B. If the child is *not* speaking in words:

How does your baby tell you what he/she wants?

Can you understand any of the sounds the baby makes?

Are the baby's inflections something like talking?

Do you get the feeling that talking is about to happen? (Unless you're truly concerned, reassure the parent by commenting on the wide variation in age of language acquisition.)

3. What does your child (try to) say the most often?

4. Can you understand everything your child wants to say?

5. Does your child understand almost everything you say to him/her?

In class, compare notes with other students.

Activity 6.8

Objective: To apply major concepts of behaviorism and learning theory to real-life situations involving infants.

Try to recall episodes from your own infant behavior that have been related to you by your family over the years (or refer to your baby book or album) or episodes of infant behavior involving family members or neighbors and friends, or even hypothesize at least one behavioral vignette that fits each category listed below.

Classical Conditioning

Operant Conditioning

Imitation

Activity 6.9

Objective: To apply Piagetian concepts of infant cognitive development to real-life episodes of infant behavior.

Piaget's original writings are richly sprinkled with examples of his own children's behavior, and nothing is really appropriately illustrative of Piaget's ideas except real vignettes of child behavior. Because Piaget's theory figures so heavily in the study of child development, it would be good for you to keep a small notebook across the term of this course in which you can jot down interesting episodes of child behavior that you observe. For this exercise you will need some observations of children, birth to age two, from which you can match behavioral episodes with the following Piagetian concepts.

Reflexes

Modified Reflexes

Circular Reactions

Object Permanence

Deferred Imitation

Answer Key

Overview and Key Concepts

1. perception; cognition (p. 188)

2. habituation (p. 190)

3. novel; habituate; heart rate (p. 190)

4. contours; complexity; curvature (p. 192)

5. object constancy (p. 192)

6. visual cliff (p. 194)

7. sensorimotor intelligence (p. 198)

8. less egocentrism; more symbolic thinking; development of schemes (p. 198)

9. reflexes; early reflexes: using what you're born with (p. 199)

10. circular reactions (p. 200)

11. secondary circular reactions (p. 200)

12. object permanence (p. 201)

13. symbolically (p. 203)

14. behaviorism; learning theory; classical conditioning; operant conditioning; imitation (p. 210)

15. reinforcement; imitation; accommodation; language acquisition device (pp. 214–215)

Multiple-Choice Self-Test

1. Choice (b) is correct. Perception refers to the brain's immediate or direct organization and interpretation of sensations. (p. 188)
   Choice (a) refers to sensation; (c) refers to cognition; and (d) is a process involving mental operations or thinking.

2. Habituation, choice (b), is the process by which we tend to look less at a stimulus that has been repeated, presumably because we remember that we have seen the stimulus

before (p. 190)
Classical conditioning, choice (a), involves the association of a stimulus with a response.
Operant conditioning, choice (c), is the association of a response with a stimulus. Stimulus
generalization, choice (d), is the process by which we expand responses to similar stimuli.

3. Choice (a) is correct. Studies have found that newborn infants tend to look at and prefer
   stimuli with a high degree of contour, such as the human face. (p. 192)
   Infants tend to prefer the most complex stimulus they are capable of perceiving, choice (b).
   Items they have seen before seem to be preferred later, choice (c). There does not seem to
   be strong evidence for innately preprogrammed stimuli, choice (d).

4. Choice (c) is correct. Object constancy, which includes size and shape constancies, is the notion that although something may look different from different distances or angles, we perceive it as the same object. (p. 192)
   Choice (a) refers to object preferences; (b) refers to object permanence.

5. Choice (a) is correct. The visual cliff consists of a table covered with a strong transparent
   surface, and underneath the table there is a checkered surface. In one case the checkered
   surface appears to be close; in another, far. The illusion of depth is used to study depth perception in infants. (p. 194)
   Infants can crawl or walk, choice (b), on the surface; or they can attempt to reach and grasp,
   choice (c). But its primary purpose is to look at avoidance of one side or the other.

6. Choice (b) is correct. Studies indicate that although newborns can locate both high- and
   low-pitched sounds, they are much better at locating high-pitched sounds. (p. 197)
   Newborns are capable of sound localization, choice (a); but they differ in their ability, depending on the pitch, choices (c) and (d).

7. Choice (b) is correct. Assimilation is the process of taking in new information and acting on
   that information in light of already present behaviors, ideas, or schemes. (p. 198)
   Choice (a) refers to the process of organization; (c) to accommodation; and (d) to
   habituation.

8. Choice (c) is correct. Piaget's third stage is the stage of secondary circular reaction, in which
   the infant focuses on repeated actions of objects. (p. 200)
   Piaget's first stage is the stage of early reflexes, choice (a). The second stage is the stage of
   primary circular reactions, choice (b). The sixth stage involves the first symbols, choice (d).

9. Choice (c) is correct. According to Piaget, the first signs of object permanence involve
   briefly looking for an object that is partially visible or within easy reach. This occurs during
   the third stage, which begins at about four months of age. (p. 201)
   At birth, choice (a), and at one month, choice (b), out of sight is out of mind; there is no
   sense of object permanence. By twelve months of age, choice (d), infants have a fairly well-
   developed (but not complete) sense of object permanence.

10. Choice (c) is correct. Of the three forms of learning, clear demonstrations of operant conditioning have been found in the newborn infant. Classical conditioning and imitation are not as clear. (pp. 210–212)
Choices (a), (b), and (d) do not accurately reflect current information.

11. Choice (c) is correct. The study of the purposes and meaning within a language is known as semantics. (p. 214)
Choice (a) defines syntax; (b) defines phonology.

12. Choice (b) is correct. Expressive language is the ability to use words appropriately in conversation. Receptive language is the ability to understand or comprehend language used by others. Receptive language typically occurs before expressive. (p. 217)
Expressive language is typically not seen before one year of age, choice (a). It is more complex than babbling, choice (c), because it involves the use of actual words. It follows receptive language, choice (d).

13. Choice (a) is correct. A holophrase is a single word used to express a complete thought. It is characteristic of children's first speech. (p. 218)
A phoneme, choice (b), is a unit of sound. Receptive language, choice (c), is the ability to comprehend the speech of others. Motherese, choice (d), is a dialect used by mothers to talk with their children. It consists of short sentences and simple vocabulary.

CHAPTER 7
The First Two Years: Psychosocial Development

Learning Objectives

1. Discuss the roles of the father, siblings, peers, and other care-givers in social interactions, and contrast these roles with mother-infant synchrony.

2. Characterize the infant's emotional capacities and indicate how they are expressed and measured.

3. Define what is meant by temperament and describe the three types found in infants.

4. Describe and contrast the three theories of early personality development (Sigmund Freud's, Erik Erikson's, and Margaret Mahler's).

5. Identify and describe the four phases of attachment. Cite the major characteristics of each phase and be able to generate examples.

6. Describe the three common outcomes of attachment, how they are assessed, and what the long-term consequences of each are.

7. Discuss the similarities and differences in mothers' and fathers' roles in attachment.

8. Define what is meant by the development of autonomy and indicate how parents might influence it. Differentiate the four major theoretical positions (identification, operant conditioning, observational learning, and social referencing) concerning the development of autonomy.

9. Describe the development of self-knowledge and self-awareness during the first two years.

10. State the various definitions of child abuse, provide data concerning the incidence of child abuse, identify and describe the causes of child abuse, and evaluate the various treatment and prevention techniques.

Chapter Outline

I. EARLY SOCIAL RELATIONSHIPS

A. Parent-Infant Synchrony

1. Frequently the social interactions between parent and infant involve a pattern of closely coordinated exchanges called *parent-infant synchrony*.

2. Studies using videotapes reveal that a mother and her baby actually have "conversations" that resemble adult dialogues in many ways except for the child's lack of words.

3. Until an infant is several months old, responsibility for coordinating this activity rests with the parent. But after a few months the baby becomes capable of initiating social interchanges and of influencing the content and style of the parent's behavior.

B. Social Interactions with Fathers, Siblings, and Peers

1. Father-infant interactions

a. Fathers are important figures in the child's social network, even though they are not usually the primary care-giver.

b. Play episodes between father and baby tend to have more active interchanges than play episodes between mother and baby.

c. Stylistic differences between mother and father, however, do not indicate that fathers are less competent care-givers than mothers.

2. Interactions with siblings

a. Approximately 80 percent of children in the United States and Europe grow up with siblings.

b. In many cultures children are cared for by siblings.

c. Interactions with siblings are likely to make an important positive contribution to an infant's development.

C. Interactions with Other Care-Givers

1. Infants interact with other nonparent care-givers, including day-care teachers, other relatives, and family friends.

2. Studies indicate that on measures of sociability, social competence, language persistence, achievement, self-confidence, and problem solving, children who had been in day care as infants did as well as or better than children who had not.

3. Living in an extended or three-generation family can contribute to the quality of infant social development. Maternal grandmothers, for example, have been found to buffer infants against negative effects of insensitive parents or siblings.

4. Interactions with peers

   a. Until recently there were few studies of infant-infant interactions.

   b. Recent observations have found that even young babies show considerable interest in other babies.

   c. When given a choice, infants often prefer playing with their peers to playing with their mothers.

   d. Peers support the autonomy of toddlers from mothers and offer toddlers an alternative source of support and comfort.

II. EMOTIONS, TEMPERAMENT, AND PERSONALITY DEVELOPMENT IN INFANCY

A. Emotions in Infancy

   1. Emotions in infancy cover a great range and complexity.

   2. Physiological aspects of emotion (such as HR) are easy to measure, but their relationship to specific emotions is less clear and infants express many variations in basic emotions.

   3. Infants generally show joy and laughter by three to four months, fear by five to eight months, and more complex emotions in the second year of life.

B. Temperament

   1. The classic New York Longitudinal Study identified nine aspects of *temperament* and three main temperamental patterns.

      a. Average or easy children were regular and adaptable.

      b. Slow-to-warm-up children were relatively inactive and slow to adapt.

      c. Difficult children were irregular and moody in their general activities.

2. The type of temperament the baby has can have a strong influence on the parent-infant bond.

C. Personality Development During the First Two Years

1. Temperament and reactions from care-givers may provide the initial basis for a child's *personality*—her unique pattern of physical, emotional, social, and intellectual traits.

2. The Freudian view proposes that the *oral stage* occurs during the first year of infancy and that at about age one infants enter the *anal stage*.

3. Erikson's crises begin in infancy in the oral sensory period, in which the social crisis of *trust versus mistrust* must be resolved. Between ages one and three, children enter the muscular anal period and must resolve the crisis of *autonomy versus shame and doubt* (Erikson, 1963).

4. Mahler's theory of symbiosis and individuation proposes that following early "normal autism," infancy is characterized by a *symbiotic mother-child relationship*. About halfway through the first year and into the second year, the process of *separation-individuation* occurs.

III. ATTACHMENT FORMATION
Attachment refers to the intimate and enduring emotional relationship between infant and care-giver during the first year of life and is inferred from signaling behaviors and approach behaviors.

A. Phases of Attachment Formation
Attachments are thought to develop in a series of phases (Bowlby, 1969).

1. Phase I: indiscriminate sociability (birth through two months): The baby is not very selective in the use of her attachment behaviors.

2. Phase II: attachments in the making (two through seven months): Babies begin forming bonds but still accept attention and care from comparative strangers.

3. Phase III: specific, clear-cut attachments (seven through twenty-four months): The infant's preferences for specific people become stronger.

4. Phase IV: goal-coordinated partnerships (twenty-four months and onward): The baby is able to tolerate delays and interruptions in parental attention and can also tolerate short parental absences.

B. Assessing Attachment: The "Strange Situation"

1. The most widely used method for evaluating attachment is called the "strange situation," consisting of eight brief social episodes with different combinations of the infant, her mother, and a strange adult (Ainsworth, 1978).

2. About 70 percent of babies display a *secure attachment* (Type B) pattern of response in the "strange situation"; about 20 percent display an *anxious-avoidant attachment* pattern (Type A); and 10 percent display an *anxious-resistant attachment* pattern (Type C).

C. Consequences of Different Attachment Patterns

1. Secure attachment (Type B) early in infancy benefits babies in several ways during their second year of life.

2. Less securely attached infants (Types A and C) may not learn as well from their parents.

3. Also Types A and C showed greater dependency and less satisfaction with the attention they received.

D. Influences on Attachment Formation

1. The role of the mother

   a. A major determinant of individual differences in attachment is the quality of the infant-mother relationship during the first year.

   b. A mother's capacity to respond sensitively seems to be more important than the sheer amount of time spent in contact with baby.

   c. An appropriate amount and a moderate degree of maternal stimulation are important.

2. The role of the father

   a. Infants appear to be equally attached to both father and mother, even though the mother is the primary care-giver.

   b. Fathers are more vigorous and physical with infants; mothers quieter and more verbal.

3. The effects of maternal employment

   a. Fifty-three percent of married mothers with children age one and younger are in the labor force. This is double the 1970 rate.

   b. The effects of maternal employment are rarely direct and are influenced by a variety of intervening conditions; thus findings should be cautiously interpreted.

   c. Children of working mothers tend to show better social and emotional adjustment, as reflected in higher self-esteem, than children of nonworking mothers.

4. The effects of day care

   a. The growing number of dual-career and single-parent families is leading to increased interest in nonmaternal child care.

   b. Participation in out-of-home care that is responsive to children's needs does not appear to interfere with attachments between an infant and her parents.

   c. Day-care experiences seem to promote peer-oriented social skills.

IV. THE EMERGENCE OF AUTONOMY
Secure attachment to parents by the second year of life enables the child to shift attention to the physical and social world and to develop a sense of autonomy through greater mobility and communication as well as parental support.

A. Sources of Autonomy

   1. *Identification*, according to psychoanalytic theory, is the process by which children wish to become like their parents.

   2. *Operant conditioning* stresses the importance of reinforcement for desirable behaviors.

   3. *Observational learning* stresses that the key to autonomy and self-control is in the child's ability to imitate parents.

   4. *Social referencing*, the child's sensitive awareness of how his parents and others are feeling and his ability to use these emotional cues as a basis for guiding his own emotional responses and actions, is a common denominator in all the explanations of developing autonomy.

B. Development of Self-Knowledge and Self-Awareness
The sense of self that develops late in infancy shows up in everyday situations. Studies have used mirror recognition and TV recognition to assess babies' sense of self.

1. Aspects of self-awareness are expressed in a variety of ordinary situations and involve knowledge of standards of behavior, comparisons of the child's performance with that of others, smiles of accomplishment, and self-descriptive utterances.

2. The child is also gaining an important sense of others in the family and roles they play.

C. Development of Competence and Self-Esteem

1. From the beginning of infancy through the end of toddlerhood, children achieve a growing sense of trust, autonomy, competence, and self-esteem.

2. *Competence* develops as a result of the child's exploration of the world and sense of satisfaction in mastering the world.

3. *Self-esteem* is the child's feeling that he is an important, competent, and worthwhile person.

V. CHILD ABUSE AND NEGLECT

A. Defining Abuse

1. The definition of any problem influences attempts to solve it. Kempe originally defined abuse exclusively in terms of its physical effects.

2. Currently five types of *maltreatment* are included in legal and professional definitions: physical abuse, sexual abuse, physical neglect, emotional neglect, and psychological abuse.

B. Incidence of Abuse
Incidence is difficult to assess.

C. Causes of Abuse

1. The *ontogenic level*, or background, of the abusing parent plays a key role in child abuse.

2. The *microsystem*, a person's everyday environment, including family interactions, plays a major role in child abuse.

3. The *ecosystem*, broad influences outside the family, indirectly contributes to the quality of life and patterns of abuse.

4. The *macrosystem*, social and economic conditions of the society as well as societal values and beliefs, influences child abuse.

D. Treatment and Prevention
   Treatment and prevention are the two major approaches to solving the problem of child abuse.

Overview and Key Concepts

Chapter 7 covers aspects of early social relationships of the infant and toddler and the crucial process of attachment and bonding to parents and care-givers. Emotional development, types of temperament, and personality development in infancy are discussed with supporting research. Factors influencing attachment and the emerging sense of autonomy are explored, as are aberrations in the child's social system that result in abuse and neglect.

Directions: Identify the following concepts introduced in Chapter 7.

1. Social interactions between parent and infant can involve a closely coordinated interaction called _____ .

2. Until an infant is several months old, responsibility for coordinating this interaction rests with the _____ .

3. Recent observations have found that even young babies show considerable interest in other _____ and in much the same ways that they show interest in their _____ .

4. _____ refers to the infant's typical or characteristic way of feeling and responding.

5. In the now classic _____ , more than 130 infants were studied and rated on nine aspects of temperament.

6. According to _____ psychosexual theory, the _____ of development occurs during the first year of infancy. It corresponds to Erikson's psychosocial crisis of _____ versus _____ .

7. Freud's anal stage of psychosexual development corresponds to Erikson's psychosocial crisis of _____ versus _____ .

8. Margaret Mahler and her colleagues have proposed that following a period of "normal autism," infancy is characterized by a _____ . Beginning halfway through the infant's first year and through the second, the process of _____ occurs.

9. _____ refers to the intimate and enduring emotional relationship between infant and care-giver during the infant's first year of life. Because it cannot be observed directly, it must be inferred from common infant behaviors. Three of these—crying, cooing, and babbling—are _____ behaviors. Others, such as smiling, are _____ behaviors.

10. Attachments are thought to develop in a series of phases. Phase I is _____ .

11. Both _____ , an infant's upset at being separated from her care-giver, and _____ , a wariness and avoidance of strangers, appear near the beginning of Phase III.

12. The most widely used method for evaluating attachment is called the _____ . It was originally developed by Mary Ainsworth.

13. During the first two years, most studies indicate that babies are equally attached to both _____ and _____ .

14. Three explanations of developing autonomy, all of which involve social referencing, are _____ , _____ , and _____ .

15. _____ (skill and capability) develops as a result of the child's natural curiosity and desire to explore the world and the pleasure that she experiences in successfully mastering and controlling that world. _____ refers to a child's feeling that he is an important, competent, powerful, and worthwhile person who is valued and appreciated by those around him.

Key Terms

Directions: Provide a definition for each of the following key terms. Check your answers against the Glossary or the text page number that follows each term.

Anal stage (p. 240) _____

_____

_____

Anxious-avoidant attachment (p. 245) _____

_____

_____

Anxious-resistant attachment (p. 246) _____

_____

_____

Approach behaviors (p. 242) _____

_____

_____

Attachment (p. 242) _____

_____

_____

Autonomy (p. 250) _____

_____

_____

Autonomy versus shame and doubt (p. 240) _____

_____

_____

Causal environment (p. 257) _____

_____

_____

Competence (p. 255) _____

_____

_____

Contact comfort (p. 242) _____

_____

_____

Ecosystem (p. 257) _____

_____

_____

Failure-to-thrive syndrome (p. 256) _____

_____

_____

Identification (p. 251) _____

_____

_____

Macrosystem (p. 258) _____

_____

_____

Microsystem (p. 257) _____

_____

_____

Ontogenic level (p. 257) _____

_____

_____

Oral stage (p. 240) _____

_____

_____

Parent-infant synchrony (p. 229) _____

_____

_____

Personality (p. 240) _____

_____

_____

Role reversal (p. 257) _____

_____

_____

Secure attachment (p. 244) _____

_____

_____

Self-esteem (p. 255) _____

_____

_____

Separation anxiety (p. 244) _____

_____

_____

Separation-individuation (p. 241) _____

_____

_____

Signaling behaviors (p. 242) _____

_____

_____

Social referencing (p. 252) _____

_____

_____

Stranger anxiety (p. 244) _____

_____

_____

"Strange situation" (p. 244) _____

_____

_____

Symbiotic mother-child relationship (p. 241) _____

_____

_____

Temperament (p. 235) _____

_____

_____

Trust versus mistrust (p. 240) _____

_____

_____

Study Questions

1. What is meant by *parent-infant synchrony?* (pp. 229–231)

   _____

   _____

   _____

   _____

2. What is the myth and the reality of the quality of babies' social interaction with their fathers, their siblings, and their peers? (pp. 231–235)

   _____

   _____

   _____

   _____

3. What is the nature of emotions in infancy? (pp. 235–237)

   _____

   _____

_____

_____

4. How is *temperament* defined? How can various temperaments be categorized? How can temperament influence interactions between infants and care-givers? (pp. 237–239)

_____

_____

_____

_____

5. What similarities and differences exist between the Freudian and Eriksonian views of the development of personality in infancy? (pp. 240–241)

_____

_____

_____

_____

6. What is Margaret Mahler's contribution to the concepts of attachment and autonomy? (pp. 241–242)

_____

_____

_____

_____

7. How do Harlow's studies of monkeys correlate with notions of attachment in humans? (p. 242)

_____

_____

_____

_____

8. What major milestones in psychosocial development are described in Bowlby's four phases of attachment formation? (pp. 243–244)

_____

_____

_____

_____

9. What types of attachment have been determined on the basis of Mary Ainsworth's "strange situation" research? (pp. 244–245)

_____

_____

_____

_____

10. What are the consequences of different patterns of attachment? Give examples that include other cultures. (pp. 245–247)

_____

_____

_____

_____

11. What are some of the major influences in attachment formation? (pp. 247–249)

_____

_____

_____

_____

12. What are some of the specific findings about the role of maternal employment as well as the effects of day care on the child's social and emotional development? (pp. 247–249)

_____

_____

_____

_____

13. What are three major sources of autonomy? (pp. 250–252)

_____

_____

_____

_____

14. How is social referencing related to the three major explanations of autonomy? (p. 252)

_____

_____

_____

15. What are two ways in which researchers have studied self-recognition as a component of self-knowledge in infants? (pp. 252–253)

_____

_____

_____

_____

16. What are some of the ordinary situations in which young children express a sense of self-awareness? (pp. 253–255)

_____

_____

_____

_____

17. How can parents best promote the development of competence and high self-esteem in their children? (p. 255)

_____

_____

_____

_____

18. What types of ontogenic levels in parents and what types of infants create family interactions that place the family at risk for abuse? (p. 257)

_____

_____

_____

_____

19. What influences in the community, the society, and the culture are conducive to child abuse? (pp. 257–258)

_____

_____

_____

_____

20. What measures would you recommend for the prevention of abuse? (pp. 258–260)

_____

_____

_____

_____

Multiple-Choice Self-Test

1. Psychosocial development during the first two years is characterized by the development of
   a. independence and intimacy.
   b. self-control.
   c. self-identity.
   d. trust and autonomy.

2. Observation of young infant behavior indicates that there is
   a. a synchrony between parent and infant responses.
   b. an inborn tendency to trust the parent.
   c. very little social awareness.
   d. all of the above.

3. As compared with the amount of time mothers spend interacting with their families, fathers tend to spend
   a. more time.
   b. about the same amount of time.
   c. less time.
   d. less total time but more quality time.

4. When three-month-old Shelia took her first bath in the bathtub, she responded by crying through most of it. The following day, she still showed some apprehension but did not cry. By the third day, she started to enjoy her bath. Shelia's temperament would most likely be classified as
   a. difficult.
   b. easy.
   c. impulsive.
   d. slow to warm up.

5. According to Freud, the newborn infant is in the _____ stage of psychosexual development.
   a. anal
   b. autonomy
   c. oral
   d. trust

6. Erikson indicated that if the parent provides care that is consistent and responds to the infant's needs during the first year, the infant will
   a. develop a sense of autonomy.
   b. develop a sense of basic trust.
   c. have successfully resolved the muscular-anal conflict.
   d. probably have a reflective personality in later life.

7. During which phase of attachment does the infant begin to actively seek proximity to her care-giver and develop clear-cut attachment?
   a. Phase I
   b. Phase II
   c. Phase III
   d. Phase IV

8. The "strange situation" is used to assess
   a. creativity.
   b. level of attachment.
   c. perception of novelty.
   d. tolerance level of stimulation.

9. Which of the following best describes the behavior of an anxious-resistant attached toddler?
   a. Adam runs to a stranger when he enters the room but not when his mother enters.
   b. George gets upset when his mother prepares to leave the room and clings to her when she returns.
   c. Judy ignores both a stranger and her mother when they enter a room.
   d. Todd stops playing with his toys when a stranger enters the room.

10. Dependency during the preschool years seems to be a common occurrence in
    a. Type A attached children only.
    b. Type B attached children only.
    c. Type A and Type B attached children.
    d. Type A and Type C attached children.

11. In general, long-term effects of maternal employment tend to show that children of working mothers
    a. tend to be less sex-stereotyped.
    b. have better family and peer relations.
    c. have a better sense of self-esteem.
    d. all of the above.

12. Which of the following is a consequence of failure to develop a sense of autonomy during the second year of life?
    a. extreme shyness
    b. being overly demanding and self-critical
    c. self-blame and self-doubt
    d. all of the above

13. Which approach describes the development of autonomy as a function of parental reinforcement of a child's grown-up behavior or independent exploration and self-restraint?
    a. classical conditioning
    b. identification
    c. observational learning
    d. operant conditioning

14. A study that evaluated various treatment programs for child abusers found that the most effective method for reducing child abuse was
    a. family counseling.
    b. foster care.
    c. Parents Anonymous groups.
    d. traditional psychotherapy.

Activities

Activity 7.1

> **Objective:** To demonstrate that most parents' descriptions of their babies' tempera-
> ments fall into the categories described in the New York Longitudinal Study.

Compare parents' responses to the questions listed below with the three NYLS categories: average or easy babies, slow-to-warm-up babies, and difficult babies.

Ask several parents of babies the following questions.

1. Tell me about your baby. What is he/she like?

2. What are your baby's general personality traits?

3. What type of temperament does your baby have?

4. How are you and your family adjusting to the baby?

5. Is your baby a happy baby most of the time?

In class, write the three categories on the board and tally each student's report across the
categories.

Do most of the responses fit the categories?

Do any responses require that you add new categories?

Was a preponderant temperament reported by the class?

Activity 7.2

Objective: To be prepared with a courteous, informed response to those who think that today's parents overindulge their children.

The local newspaper recently published the following letter:

Dear Editor:

I've had it with these wimpy parents who let their children walk all over them! My baby is two weeks old and I've already begun to teach her that I'm not going to jump every time she hollers. No eight-and-a-half-pound person is going to rule my life. She'll learn to eat when it's time for her to eat, and she'll only play with the toys I give her. None of this baby-proofing the house for me. Our home belongs to me and my husband, and we have enough self-respect not to let her get away with murder. By the time she weighs thirty pounds, she'll be an obedient child, not like those squalling, obnoxious brats I see around here.

Yours for better children,

Feisty Mom

You are inspired to write an answer to "Feisty Mom." Based on the material you read in Chapter 7, what would the text of your letter be?

Activity 7.3

> **Objective:** To reinforce awareness of the interlocking levels of child abuse in the microsystem, the ecosystem, and the macrosystem.

The legislators in your home state are at an impasse. Incidence of child abuse has reached an alarming rate, and a bill is being prepared to allocate funds for alleviating the problem. The impasse is due to pressure from two well-meaning but opposing factions.

One faction wants the money to go to programs that would identify families at risk and thus remedy the underlying causes, such as unemployment, emotional disturbance, lack of education, and gaps in public policy. This faction wants to prevent abuse from happening.

The other faction says that we must first put out the fire—that is, give immediate help to parents and children already in crisis, the result of living in abusive households. They want funds allocated to treatment programs for parents, therapeutic day-care programs for children, and foster care when necessary.

As a taxpayer in your state, what is your position?

Politicians know the art of negotiation and compromise. What do you recommend to validate the arguments of both factions?

Activity 7.4

> **Objective:** To become aware of the quantity of literature available on the topics discussed in Chapter 7.

Prepare an annotated bibliography to supplement the excellent readings listed on pages 262–263. Include at least two references under each of the following headings:

- Early social accomplishments

- Emotions and temperament in infancy*

- Attachment formation

- Child abuse and neglect

The references may include books and articles written both for professionals and for the lay public.

*Be sure to include the crises of trust versus mistrust and autonomy versus shame and doubt.

Activity 7.5

Objective: To be able to highlight the key concepts in Chapter 7.

You are writing an essay exam on the material in Chapter 7. Your students will have three hours to answer the questions and will be allowed to choose three out of five questions. What five questions would you ask? Under each question, jot down the points you would look for when reading the students' responses.

Answer Key

Overview and Key Concepts

1. parent-infant synchrony (p. 229)

2. parent (p. 230)

3. babies; parent (p. 234)

4. temperament (p. 235)

5. New York Longitudinal Study (NYLS) (p. 237)

6. Freud's; oral stage; trust; mistrust (p. 240)

7. autonomy; shame and doubt (p. 240)

8. symbiotic mother-child relationship; separation-individuation (p. 241)

9. attachment; signaling; approach (p. 242)

10. indiscriminate sociability (p. 243)

11. separation anxiety; stranger anxiety (p. 244)

12. "strange situation" (p. 244)

13. mother; father (p. 247)

14. identification; operant conditioning; observational learning (pp. 251–252)

15. competence; self-esteem (p. 255)

Multiple-Choice Self-Test

1. Choice (d) is correct. The major themes of infancy are trust during the first year and autonomy during the second year. (p. 229)
   Choice (a): Although independence is the task of the second year of life, intimacy is not found until early adulthood. Choice (b): Issues of self-control are likely to be found in later childhood. Choice (c): Issues of identity are found in early adolescence.

2. Choice (a) is correct. Social interactions between parent and infant involve close coordination in which each waits for the other to finish before beginning to respond. (p. 229)

There is no evidence to suggest innate trust, choice (b). Rather, trust seems to develop over the first year. Even young infants show a remarkable ability in the area of social competency and awareness, choice (c).

3. Choice (c) is correct. Studies have shown that fathers spend about two or three hours per day interacting with the infant and mothers spend about nine hours. (p. 231)
   Choices (a) and (b) are not true. Although fathers' interactions are somewhat different from mothers', both tend to be of good quality, choice (d).

4. Choice (d) is correct. Shelia showed some initial reluctance toward the bathtub; however, as time passed, the infant's response became more positive. This is the behavior of a slow-to-warm-up infant. (p. 237)
   The difficult infant, choice (a), is likely to show continued negative reactions (crying) for some time; three days would not be enough time to adjust. The easy infant, choice (b), may show initial apprehension but would adapt quickly during the first bath. Impulsive, choice (c), is not a temperament style; impulsiveness would be characteristic of an infant who would act without much caution.

5. Choice (c) is correct. Freud's first stage of psychosexual development is the oral stage. (p. 240)
   Choice (a) is Freud's second stage, which begins at about one year of age. Choice (b) is Erikson's second stage, which also begins at about one year of age. Choice (d) is Erikson's first stage, which begins at birth.

6. Choice (b) is correct. According to Erikson, the first year involves the establishment of trust. This is accomplished through consistent and sensitive response to the infant's needs. (p. 240)
   Autonomy, choice (a), is the second-year conflict. Choice (c) would be a resolution involved in Freud's second stage. Erikson's theory does not deal with reflective personality, choice (d).

7. Choice (c) is correct. Phase III, which occurs from seven to twenty-four months, is characterized by greater mobility, separation anxiety, and stranger anxiety. (p. 244)
   Choice (a) is the phase of indiscriminate sociability; (b) is attachment in the making; and (d) is goal-coordinated partnership.

8. Choice (b) is correct. The "strange situation" is a series of eight brief social episodes involving an infant, his or her mother, and a stranger; it is used to assess attachment. (p. 438)
   The "strange situation" has nothing to do with choice (a), (c), or (d).

9. Choice (b) is correct. The anxious-resistant attached toddler shows signs of anxiety even before separation, is intensely upset during separation, actively seeks close contact upon reuniting, but resists attempts to be comforted. (p. 245)
   Choices (a) and (c) are similar to patterns found in anxious-avoidant attachment. Choice (d) is similar to what might be found in a securely attached child.

10. Choice (d) is correct. In preschool, both Type A (anxious-avoidant) and Type C (anxious-resistant) have difficulties that center on dependency. (p. 245)
Type B (secure attachment) does not show problems with dependency in preschool; thus choices (b) and (c) are inaccurate. Choice (a) is inaccurate because Type C preschoolers have difficulty with dependence.

11. Choice (d) is correct. Although these results need to be interpreted with some caution, long-range effects of maternal employment include children who show fewer sex-stereotyped attitudes, choice (a); better family and peer relationships, choice (b); and better self-esteem, choice (c). (p. 248)

12. Choice (d) is correct. Studies have found that failure to develop a sense of autonomy results in extreme shyness, choice (a); children who are overly demanding and self-critical, choice (b); and children who tend to be self-blaming and have self-doubt, choice (c). (p. 250)

13. Choice (d) is correct. The use of reinforcement by parents to shape desirable behavior is characteristic of an operant conditioning approach. (p. 251)
Choice (a), classical conditioning, would involve pairing a stimulus with an already established reflex-like response. Choice (b), from the psychoanalytic perspective, involves autonomy based on the adoption of the behaviors and values of the same-sex parent. Choice (c) involves imitation of parental and other adult autonomous behavior.

14. Choice (c) is correct. The use of parental support groups, such as Parents Anonymous, in conjunction with a caseworker saw a 53 percent reduction in abuse and neglect (although there was a great likelihood of recurrence). (pp. 258–260)
Family counseling, choice (a), led to some reduction in abuse and neglect. Foster care, choice (b), has been viewed as a temporary measure, not a permanent solution. Traditional psychotherapy, choice (d), has been found to be the least effective.

CHAPTER 8
The Preschool Years: Physical Development

Learning Objectives

1. Describe normal physical development in the preschool years, including the various characteristics and patterns of growth.

2. Identify and discuss the various irregularities that can occur in physical development.

3. Discuss the changes that occur in brain development during the preschool years. Identify the areas of growth and brain specialization.

4. Describe the role that illness plays in physical development during the preschool years.

5. Identify and describe the changes that occur in motor skills, indicate how they come about, and discuss the effects of training. Differentiate between fundamental and specialized motor skills.

6. Identify and describe the changes that occur in fine motor skills, including cross-cultural differences.

7. Discuss the gender differences in physical development during the preschool years, including information on real and perceived changes.

8. Discuss the effects of children's physical growth on themselves and on adults.

Chapter Outline

I. NORMAL PHYSICAL DEVELOPMENT

A. Rate of Growth in the Preschool Years

1. The *velocity* of growth is the rate or speed by which children change size over a period of time.

2. These velocities and their relationships to each other lead to steady changes in bodily proportions and cause preschool children to look less and less like babies.

3. Velocities of growth vary among children and among the major parts of children's bodies and help to accentuate the unique appearance of each child.

B. Influences on Growth

1. For any preschool child who is reasonably healthy and happy, physical growth is remarkably smooth and predictable, especially compared with many cognitive and social developments.

2. Genetic background: Most dimensions of growth are influenced substantially by heredity.

3. Races and ethnic groups around the world differ in growth patterns (Eveleth, 1979).

4. Nutrition and the secular trend: During the last one hundred years or so, children in industrialized countries have been getting larger and heavier. This developmental pattern is often called the *secular trend*.

   a. Of greater significance than the secular trend is the fact that present-day children reach maturity more rapidly.

   b. Some of the secular trend may result from *hybrid vigor:* the tendency of genetically dissimilar individuals to produce comparatively larger and more vigorous offspring.

   c. The secular trend may be coming to an end because diet and medicine have reached their natural limits.

5. Disease: To hold back growth, an illness must be fairly major.

   a. Certain diseases do retard growth by reducing the normal absorption of nutrients over time.

b. A deficiency in the *endocrine glands* can also retard growth.

c. Once causes are diagnosed and treated, children can often experience the process of *catch-up growth*.

d. Degree of *ossification* (hardening of bones) can be an important index of normal growth.

6. Emotional factors: Sometimes too much stress in a family can keep children from growing normally, a condition called *deprivation dwarfism*, or *failure to thrive*.

a. Because of the attendant social impairment, deprivation dwarfism has lately been called *reactive attachment disorder* (RAD).

b. RAD apparently results from situations that interfere with normal positive relationships between parent and child.

c. Recent research suggests that RAD results from a lack of synchrony or "mesh" between parents' expectations and children's inherent styles of responding (Drotar, 1985).

d. If RAD has not persisted too long, it can usually be reversed through nutritional and medical intervention.

C. Understanding Physical Growth
Because physical growth can be measured simply and objectively, studying large populations has proved relatively easy. However, trends among populations can be misleading for three major reasons.

1. Group trends hide important individual differences.

2. Population differences in growth can create the impression that heredity and environment affect all aspects of growth to the same extent, when they do not.

3. A third caution has to do with the complex relationship between size and health.

II. BRAIN DEVELOPMENT

A. Organization of the Brain

1. The brain does not work like a telephone switchboard; rather, a stimulus tends to lead to generalized brain activity over large areas or even over the entire brain.

2. In spite of responding widely to most stimuli, the brain shows relationships between the kind of stimulation it receives and the area that responds the most strongly. For example, visual stimuli produce activity in the *visual cortex*.

B. Hemispheric Lateralization
During the preschool years, children begin showing definite *hemispheric lateralization*, which is the tendency for the left and right halves of the brain to perform separate functions.

1. Generally, the left hemisphere deals with information on an item-by-item or linear basis.

2. The right hemisphere identifies relationships or patterns among the items.

C. Lateralized Behaviors

1. In contrast to hemispheric lateralization, lateralized behaviors are quite evident in everyday life, even among preschool-age children.

2. *Lateralized behaviors* are actions that individuals prefer to perform with one side of their body more than with the other—for example, handedness.

III. OTHER BODILY CHANGES

A. Preschool Sensory Development

1. *Visual acuity* improves during the preschool years.

2. Vision for moving objects remains difficult for much longer.

3. *Auditory acuity* is more fully developed by the preschool years than is visual acuity.

B. Childhood Diseases

1. Colds and other minor viruses

a. During the preschool years, children catch numerous viral illnesses, but the number declines as they get older.

b. Illnesses cause inconvenience, but they do teach young children about the nature of disease.

2. Serious illnesses during early childhood

a. Serious illnesses are ones that incapacitate children for many days or weeks.

b. There has been a decrease in the incidence of serious disease; however, AIDS has recently appeared and, for a variety of reasons, there is considerable variation in the incidence of fatalities from serious disease in the preschool years.

C. Bladder and Bowel Control

1. Sometime during the preschool years, most children acquire control of their bladder and bowels.

2. Most commonly, daytime control comes before nighttime control, some time before the third birthday.

IV. MOTOR SKILL DEVELOPMENT

A. Fundamental Motor Skills

1. Walking and its variations

a. After about a year's experience, children can typically walk without looking at their feet.

b. Running appears early in the preschool years, shortly after walking begins to smooth out.

2. Jumping and its variations

a. Early jumping embraces several behaviors.

b. A complex variation of jumping is hopping.

3. Climbing

a. A child may climb stairs even before she learns to walk.

b. Going down stairs, or descending, is more difficult.

4. Throwing and catching

a. Early throwing is characterized by stereotyped methods.

b. Catching proceeds through similar phases to throwing.

B. Can Fundamental Motor Skills Be Taught?
Among physically normal children, fundamental motor skills (such as jumping and throwing, which every child seems to learn just by living in human society) are not as

teachable as specialized motor skills (such as swimming and ballet dancing). Children seem to learn fundamental motor skills from naturally occurring experiences.

C. Fine Motor Coordination: The Case of Drawing Skills
Motor activities that require the coordination of small movements are said to require *fine motor coordination*. One very common fine motor skill is drawing, which shows non-representational and representational stages of development.

1. Prerepresentational drawing

   a. Around the end of infancy, children begin to scribble.

   b. A child's interest in the results of her drawing shows up in the patterns she imposes on even her earliest scribbles.

2. Representational drawing

   a. While preschool children improve their scribbling, they develop an interest in representing people, objects, and events.

   b. During the preschool years, the child's visual representations are limited by his comparatively rudimentary fine motor skills.

3. Cross-cultural differences in picture perception

   a. What children draw is somewhat culturally conditioned and depends on what they see around them.

   b. However, not all aspects of children's drawings show variation among cultures. One example is perception of depth.

   c. Neither do fine motor skills for drawing show much cultural variation.

V. GENDER DIFFERENCES IN PHYSICAL DEVELOPMENT
In spite of wide individual differences, preschool boys and girls develop at almost exactly the same average rates. Whereas gender differences are small, individual differences are large.

VI. EFFECTS OF CHILDREN'S PHYSICAL GROWTH

A. Effects on Adults

1. As the child's physical competence increases, parents are required to spend significant time making sure the child comes to no physical grief in his motor explorations.

2. By the end of the preschool period, minute-to-minute surveillance decreases.

3. During the preschool period, many parents discover a special need for patience in their dealings with their children.

4. Physical development makes possible new forms of recreation. New skills add teachable elements and create a new sort of contact between the child and parents.

B. Effects on the Child

1. Physical growth gives preschool children many opportunities for increased self-esteem.

2. By age five, children are firm believers in the value of physical growth.

Overview and Key Concepts

Chapter 8 focuses on aspects of normal physical development in preschoolers, including size and rate of growth. Brain development is discussed along with organization of brain functions and their relationship to motor skills. Health concerns of preschoolers, bodily changes accompanying growth, and motor skill development are presented. The chapter concludes with a consideration of gender differences and the effect that children's growth has on adults and the children themselves.

Directions: Identify the following concepts introduced in Chapter 8.

1. The _____ of growth is the rate or speed by which children change size over a period of time.

2. The _____ is the tendency over the last one hundred years or so for children in the industrialized countries to become larger and heavier. This may partially result from _____ , or the tendency of genetically dissimilar individuals to produce comparatively larger and more vigorous offspring.

3. Diseases often influence growth by affecting nutrition; however, about one child in ten thousand develops a deficiency in her _____ , which produce growth hormones.

4. Once causes of slow growth are diagnosed and treated, children can often recover by a process called _____ .

5. Bone hardening is called _____ . It is a normal growth process that continues until adolescence. By comparing a child's skeletal growth with X-rays of normally developing children, experts can estimate _____ for a particular child.

6. Although most variations in growth stem from genetic health or physical causes, differences can occasionally also result from emotional factors. Sometimes too much stress can produce a condition called _____ , or _____ . Partly because of social impairment, psychologists have lately used the term _____ .

7. By age two, the normal child's brain weight is about _____ percent that of an adult. By age five, its weight is about _____ percent that of an adult.

8. Brain growth during early childhood happens in two ways. First, a lot of growth comes from the development of _____ , the insulating covers that surround mature nerve fibers. In addition to _____ , some nerve cells continue to extend fibers between and among themselves.

9. The brain responds widely to most stimuli; however, it also shows relationships between the kind of stimulation it receives and the area that responds most strongly. A visual image produces strongest activity in an area called the _____ . The sounds of speech produce their primary response in the _____ and specifically in a place called _____ . Simple voluntary movements produce their largest neural activity in the _____ , and the child's own speech usually produces its primary activity in a place called _____ .

10. During the preschool years, children begin showing definite _____ , which is the tendency for the left and right halves of the brain to perform separate functions.

11. _____ are actions that individuals prefer to perform with one side of their body more than with the other (for example, handedness).

12. _____ are those that nearly every child learns eventually simply by participating in human society. _____ are ones that not everyone learns and that require special training, such as ballet dancing.

13. Many motor activities require the coordination of small movements but not strength. Tying shoelaces calls for this _____ .

14. One especially widespread fine motor skill among young children is drawing, which shows two overlapping phases: _____ and _____ drawings.

15. In spite of wide _____ , preschool boys and girls develop at almost exactly the same average rates. By the time children begin kindergarten at age five, slight _____ in physical development and motor skills appear. Boys tend to be slightly bigger, stronger, and faster; yet these differences are noticeable only as averages.

Key Terms

Directions: Provide a definition for each of the following key terms. Check your answers against the Glossary or the text page number that follows each term.

Auditory cortex (p. 280) _____

_____

_____

Broca's area (p. 280) _____

_____

_____

Catch-up growth (p. 277) _____

_____

_____

Deprivation dwarfism (p. 278) _____

_____

_____

Dichotic listening (p. 280) _____

_____

_____

Endocrine gland (p. 277) _____

_____

_____

Failure to thrive (p. 278) _____

_____

_____

Fine motor coordination (p. 294) _____

_____

_____

Hemispheric lateralization (p. 280) _____

_____

_____

Hybrid vigor (p. 275) _____

_____

_____

Lateralized behavior (p. 282) _____

_____

_____

Motor cortex (p. 280) _____

_____

_____

Ossification (p. 277) _____

_____

_____

Reactive attachment disorder (RAD) (p. 278) _____

_____

_____

Secular trend (p. 275) _____

_____

_____

Velocity (p. 273) _____

_____

_____

Visual cortex (p. 280) _____

_____

_____

Wernicke's area (p. 280) _____

_____

_____

Study Questions

1. What are the basic effects of genetic background, nutrition, and the secular trend on the growth of young children? (pp. 274–276)

_____

_____

_____

_____

2. What are the effects of disease and hormone deficiency on physical development? (pp. 276–277)

_____

_____

_____

_____

3. How can X-rays be used to determine bone age? (pp. 277–278)

_____

_____

_____

_____

4. What growth syndromes are associated with emotional rather than with genetic or physical factors? (p. 278)

_____

_____

_____

_____

5. What are three reasons that trends in growth among populations can be misleading? (p. 279)

_____

_____

_____

_____

6. In what two ways does brain growth happen during early childhood? (pp. 279–280)

_____

_____

_____

_____

7. How is hemispheric lateralization related to dichotic listening? (pp. 280–281)

_____

_____

_____

_____

8. What is the general status of sensory development in the preschool years? (p. 284)

_____

_____

_____

_____

9. What contrast can be made between minor viral illnesses and more serious illnesses during early childhood? (pp. 284–287)

_____

_____

_____

_____

10. What is the sequence of bladder and bowel control? (pp. 287–289)

_____

_____

_____

_____

11. Name and describe the emergence of some of the fundamental motor skills. (pp. 290–293)

_____

_____

_____

_____

12. Can fundamental motor skills be taught? (p. 293)

_____

_____

_____

_____

13. In what sequence do drawing skills develop in the preschool years? (pp. 294–296)

_____

_____

_____

_____

14. What variations and similarities exist cross-culturally in children's drawings? (p. 296)

_____

_____

_____

_____

15. How would you describe the magnitude of gender differences in the physical development of preschoolers? (pp. 298–299)

_____

_____

_____

_____

16. What type of differences account much more for variation between children than gender differences do? (pp. 298–299)

_____

_____

_____

_____

17. How does the ongoing physical development of a preschooler modify the way in which adults relate to the child? (pp. 300–302)

_____

_____

_____

_____

18. How does ongoing physical development in the preschool years affect the child himself? (p. 302)

_____

_____

_____

_____

Multiple-Choice Self-Test

1. During the preschool years
   a. head circumference remains unchanged.
   b. height more than triples.
   c. overall weight tends to decrease.
   d. the proportion of body fat tends to decrease.

2. Physical growth during the preschool years
   a. is affected by the seasons of the year.
   b. is rather smooth and predictable.
   c. may be suppressed by stress.
   d. includes all of the above.

3. In general, the growth pattern of a child tends to resemble that of
   a. the same-sex parent.
   b. the opposite-sex parent.
   c. both parents equally.
   d. neither parent.

4. Hybrid vigor is promoted by
   a. careful matching of particular genetic features.
   b. cloning.
   c. genetically dissimilar individuals.
   d. genetically similar individuals.

5. The present secular trends in growth will most likely slow down or cease in the near future primarily because
   a. new forms of cancer are evolving that will shorten life.
   b. of hybrid vigor.
   c. of environmental pollution.
   d. the positive effects of medicine and diet have reached their limits.

6. By age five, the brain has about _____ percent of its final adult weight.
   a. 30
   b. 50
   c. 75
   d. 90

7. Hemispheric lateralization
   a. begins to appear during the preschool years.
   b. essentially turns off the right hemisphere of the brain.
   c. is complete by about two years of age.
   d. refers to the continuation of brain cell division during the preschool years.

8. Who is most likely to die from an infectious disease?
   a. a poor rural boy
   b. a poor urban boy
   c. a poor urban girl
   d. a rich urban boy

9. Changes in a preschooler's gross motor skills indicate that
   a. considerable vacillation.
   b. deterioration and regression in development.
   c. general improvement.
   d. little or no improvement.

10. Which of the following is a specialized motor skill?
    a. swimming
    b. reaching
    c. running
    d. walking

11. Mark is three years old. He is most likely able to
    a. balance on one foot.
    b. catch a large ball.
    c. make simple representational drawings.
    d. run in a straight line.

12. Scribbling by preschoolers is a characteristic of
    a. abstract drawing.
    b. nonrepresentational drawing.
    c. associative drawing.
    d. primitive drawing.

13. Gender differences in gross and fine motor skills during the preschool years
    a. exist.
    b. exist for fine motor skills but not for gross motor skills.
    c. exist for gross motor skills but not for fine motor skills.
    d. are perceived as existing but actually do not.

Activities

Activity 8.1

> **Objective:** To plan an outdoor environment that would support a preschooler's motor development.

Your preschool has just been awarded a grant of $10,000 to improve a yard that until now has been a square plot of fenced-in dirt. There are twenty-five children in the school, but as a rule, no more than fifteen children use the yard at the same time. It is customary to allow at least 100 square feet of outdoor space per child enrolled.

Design, to scale, an outdoor area for preschoolers two to five years of age. Tricycle riding and swings are fine, but in addition, you want to enhance other opportunities for large motor development.

Activity	Area in Yard	Special Equipment
Walking		
Running		
Hopping		
Climbing		
Throwing/Catching		

When the weather is too cold or rainy, what indoor activities can the teachers plan to support these skills?

Activity 8.2

Objective: To observe developmental differences in children's drawings.

Make an appointment to visit a preschool or child-care center in your area. Ask the director whether you may photograph examples of children's drawings. If possible, get at least one sample of a freehand drawing, done without adult direction, from the following ages: two, two and one-half, three, three and one-half, four, four and one-half, five, and five and one-half.

Check out a camera from your AV department. A Polaroid is easiest, but 35mm cameras usually have enough automatic features for the most inexperienced novice. If you use the latter, use a fast (400 or faster) film for slides.

If the use of a camera is not feasible, you may be able to trace some of the drawings. *Do not attempt to copy the drawings.* It is very difficult for an adult to reproduce children's art with authenticity.

Note: If the child's name is on the drawing, cover it with a blank scrap of paper. Do not copy names without parents' permission.

Activity 8.3

Objective: To identify nutritious snacks that look inviting to children and would be enjoyed by them.

Young children enjoy a cup of something nourishing to drink and like to have it accompanied by a food to munch, crunch, or nibble on. Sodas or fruit drinks have too much sugar. Even apple juice is too sweet, but all right once in a while.

List at least four foods in each category (no popcorn or peanuts). Assume that substitutes are available to accommodate children with allergies and that Lactaid is added to milk products for children who cannot tolerate lactose.

Drinks Fruit or vegetable juice	1. 2.	3. 4.
Snacks Grains: wheat, rice, or sesame seed crackers	1. 2.	3. 4.
Fruits: in season, cut to bite size	1. 2.	3. 4.
Raw vegetables, bite size: green pepper, peas, turnips, carrots	1. 2.	3. 4.
Combinations: apple stuffed with peanut butter, celery stuffed with cream cheese	1. 2.	3. 4.
Dips: guacamole, yogurt with onion soup	1. 2.	3. 4.

Activity 8.4

Objective: To identify safety measures for young children.

You are writing accident prevention procedures to be used by a nursery school staff. Emergency numbers will be posted next to the phone.

Fill in the phone numbers for your community, as follows:

Poison Control Center
Ambulance
Fire Department
Police Department

Does your community have a 911 service?

And, of course, you will have a file of emergency phone numbers for each child.

What measures would you require of the staff to prevent the following:

Ingestion of toxic substances?

Serious falls that could lead to fractures and head injuries?

Choking on small objects or pieces of food?

Profuse bleeding from cuts?

Burns?

Severe bruises?

Running out of the school yard?

Other?

Find out where, in your community, you can arrange for first-aid training for your staff—for example, Red Cross, school health department, volunteer pediatrician, fire department.

Source of service:
Telephone:

Activity 8.5

Objective: To observe evidence of the secular trend in size.

Visit a museum that has clothing and furniture from 1860 or earlier.

You will be looking at garments worn by adults and furnishings used by adults. Often, ball gowns and formal dress for men are displayed. The furnishings and clothing are usually those of the affluent upper classes. We assume that, during childhood, the wearers and owners had access to more and better food than much of the population. The sizes therefore may be attributed more to genetic constitutional factors than to nutrition. Food choices and eating habits, of course, reflected custom and accessibility rather than knowledge of nutrition.

Compare the following to what we see among the middle classes in the United States today:

Height

Size of hands

Size of feet

Height of seats on chairs and sofas

Height of tables and buffets

Did you see noticeable differences?

If so, could there have been reasons for the differences other than those already mentioned?

Answer Key

Overview and Key Concepts

1. velocity (p. 273)

2. secular trend; hybrid vigor (p. 275)

3. endocrine glands (p. 277)

4. catch-up growth (p. 277)

5. ossification; bone age (p. 277)

6. deprivation dwarfism; failure to thrive; reactive attachment disorder (p. 278)

7. 75; 90 (p. 279)

8. myelin sheaths; myelinization (pp. 279–280)

9. visual cortex; auditory cortex; Wernicke's area; motor cortex; Broca's area (p. 280)

10. hemispheric lateralization (p. 280)

11. lateralized behaviors (p. 282)

12. fundamental motor skills; specialized motor skills (p. 293)

13. fine motor coordination (p. 294)

14. nonrepresentation; representational (p. 294)

15. individual differences; gender differences (p. 298)

Multiple-Choice Self-Test

1. Choice (d) is correct. Body fat decreases as a proportion of total bodily tissue during the preschool years. (p. 273)
Head circumference, choice (a), increases by about an inch. Height, choice (b), increases by about one-third. Weight, choice (c), increases by about 65 percent.

2. Choice (d) is correct. Physical growth is three times faster in the spring than in the fall, choice (a); is rather smooth and predictable during preschool, choice (b); and can be retarded by stress, choice (c). (pp. 274–278)

3. Choice (c) is correct. Most dimensions of growth are influenced by heredity. For example, if one parent is tall and the other is short, the child has an equal chance of being tall or short. (p. 274)
The result is independent of sex; thus choices (a) and (b) are incorrect. The result is influenced by heredity; thus choice (d) is incorrect.

4. Choice (c) is correct. Hybrid vigor is the tendency for genetically dissimilar individuals to produce comparatively larger and more vigorous offspring. (p. 275)
Choice (a), matching (especially if matching similar qualities); choice (b), cloning; and choice (d), genetic similarity, work against hybrid vigor.

5. Choice (d) is correct. Recent studies have begun to show a slowdown in secular growth trends. Much of this has been attributed to reaching the natural limits of the effects of medicine and diet. (p. 276)
New forms of cancer and other diseases, choice (a), will probably cause the current trends to stay balanced; their impact is not that significant. Hybrid vigor, choice (b), will probably continue at the present rate. It is hard to say what effects pollution, choice (c), might have on secular growth trends.

6. Choice (d) is correct. At age two, the brain has reached about 75 percent of its adult weight, and that percentage increases to 90 by age five. (p. 279)

7. Choice (a) is correct. During the preschool years, children begin showing a definite tendency for the left and right halves of the brain to perform separate functions. (p. 280)
Both hemispheres are functional throughout the life span, choice (b). Lateralization begins, rather than ends, at about two years of age, choice (c). Brain cell division, for the most part, has ended by about six months of age, choice (d).

8. Choice (a) is correct. Three factors contribute to death rates from infectious diseases. Low-income, rural, male children are most likely to die of infectious disease. (pp. 286–287)
Choices (b), (c), and (d) have a somewhat lower probability of death than choice (a).

9. Choice (c) is correct. Children become more skilled in basic physical actions across the preschool period. (p. 289)
Gross motor skills show improvements, choice (d), that are steady, choice (a), with no evidence of deterioration or regression, choice (b).

10. Choice (a) is correct. Specialized motor skills are skills that not everyone learns and that require special training. Swimming, which requires some training, is considered a specialized motor skill. (p. 293)
Reaching, choice (b); running, choice (c); and walking, choice (d), are all considered fundamental motor skills because all children eventually learn them.

11. Choice (d) is correct. Running appears rather early in the preschool years. The other activities listed may take more time to develop. (pp. 290–292)

Balancing on one foot, choice (a), typically appears at about age five. Catching a large ball, choice (b), and making a representational drawing, choice (c), appear at about age four.

12. Choice (b) is correct. By definition, scribbling and the drawing of simple shapes are nonrepresentational drawing. (p. 294)
Choices (a), (c), and (d) are not terms typically used in this context.

13. Choice (d) is correct. Although there are rather wide individual differences, gender differences in both gross and fine motor behaviors are nonexistent. (p. 298)
Choices (a), (b), and (c) hypothesize the existence of gender differences. In actuality, average rates of development are the same for both males and females during preschool.

CHAPTER 9
The Preschool Years: Cognitive Development

Learning Objectives

1. Describe Jean Piaget's stage of preoperational thinking and identify the major developments and limitations found during this stage.

2. Discuss what Piaget meant by egocentrism and indicate how it affects other developments during the preoperational stage.

3. Describe the classic Piagetian tasks concerning class inclusion. Indicate how extensions of these studies differ from Piaget's original work.

4. Describe the major features of perceptual development during the preschool period, including visual, auditory, and tactile modes.

5. Describe the basic features of language acquisition during the preschool years, with particular focus on the development of syntax.

6. Discuss the two major theories of language development and review the basic assumptions and concepts of each. Evaluate the two theories.

7. Compare and contrast the two views concerning the relationship between thought and language.

Chapter Outline

I. THINKING IN PRESCHOOLERS

   A. Piaget's Preoperational Stage

      1. At about age two, according to Piaget, children enter the preoperational stage, which extends to age seven and during which children become increasingly proficient at using symbols.

      2. Limitations of the preoperational stage are related to the fact that children often confuse their own points of view with those of other people.

   B. Symbolic Thought

      1. Symbols are words, objects, or behaviors that stand for something else.

      2. Probably the most significant cognitive achievement of the preoperational stage is the emergence of symbolic thought.

      3. Symbolic thinking helps preschoolers in three ways.

         a. It gives them convenient ways of remembering objects and experiences.

         b. Symbols help children to think and solve problems about their experiences.

         c. Symbols help children communicate what they know.

   C. Egocentrism in Young Children

      1. *Egocentrism* refers to the inability of a person to distinguish between his own point of view and that of another person. It is literally a centering on the self in thinking.

      2. Young children think egocentrically sometimes but not always. In his famous three-mountains experiment, Piaget basically found that children were not able to take the perspective of a doll across the table from them.

      3. However, with some modifications in the three-mountains situation children were able to relate to the perspective of another person.

      4. Preschoolers' ability to communicate with others is also marked by egocentrism.

D. Animism and Artificialism

1. In the preschool years, a child often expresses *animism*, a belief that nonliving objects are in fact alive and human.

2. *Artificialism* refers to a belief that all objects, whether living or not, are made in the same way, usually by human beings.

3. To a certain extent, animism and artificialism are both special forms of egocentrism.

E. Classification Skills

1. *Classification* refers to the placement of objects in groups or categories according to some sort of standard or criteria.

2. Young children can reliably classify objects that differ in just one dimension or feature.

3. Preschoolers can sometimes also manage more complex classification tasks, such as a class inclusion task: the ability to compare a subset with a larger set.

4. Piaget believed that the preschooler cannot decenter her thinking—that is, she cannot broaden her focus to take account of more than one dimension at the same time.

5. Recent studies have shown that Piaget underestimated the ability of children to solve surprisingly complex problems, including class inclusion problems; however, this does not mean that preschoolers are the cognitive equals of older children.

F. Reversibility and Conservation

1. Many problems require *reversibility* in thinking—the ability to undo a problem mentally and go back to its beginning.

2. Often preschool children cannot or do not use reversible thinking.

3. Conservation of liquid problems may prove difficult, whereas many identity problems are not too difficult for the older preschooler.

4. Problems requiring reversibility are affected a great deal by how they are presented. Certain procedures have been found to increase correct responses, as have other modifications in the way Piaget presented his tasks to children.

G. How Cognitive Development Occurs

1. Inconsistencies in cognitive performance may occur because preschool children depend on social context or circumstances to develop new skills.

2. Children are often assisted by older models: siblings, teachers, parents.

3. The gap in difficulty between independent thinking and socially supported thinking is called the *zone of proximal development* (ZPD). It is the area in which problems are too difficult to solve alone but are not too hard to solve with support from others.

4. The concept of the ZPD originated with Soviet psychologist Lev Vygotsky and has proved a useful model in developmental psychology and education.

H. How Skillful Is Preschool Symbolic Thinking?

1. Symbolic thinking is marked by variability in the preschool years and has a "now you see it, now you don't" quality. Such variations make sense in children who are just learning to represent experiences symbolically.

2. Research on early cognition suggests that children often combine their social motivations and intuitions with their cognitive ones.

II. PERCEPTUAL DEVELOPMENT IN PRESCHOOL CHILDREN

A. Visual Perception

1. During the preschool years, vision becomes increasingly important as a source of information, yet preschoolers are usually farsighted.

2. *Visual discrimination* refers to the ability to distinguish differences in what is seen.

   a. Preschoolers can usually make visual discriminations that involve relatively simple or obvious distinctions.

   b. However, when visual discriminations require noticing underlying dimensions or require abstract grouping, preschool children do not perform as well.

   c. The difficulty of visual discrimination depends a great deal on the particular dimension or distraction in question.

3. *Visual integration* refers to the ability to coordinate particular sights with each other as well as with appropriate physical actions. For example, throwing and catching a ball requires visual integration.

a. A number of such coordination and integration skills improve in the preschool years.

b. Yet there are limits to improvement because preschool children have particular trouble in coordinating actions and sights in the presence of distracting stimuli.

c. Coordinating visual perception with physical actions can also prove challenging. When very young children track a moving object, they have trouble separating their eye movements from their head movements.

4. *Visual memory* refers to the ability to recall or recognize simple sights such as a familiar face.

a. During the preschool years, children become better at this sort of task, at least when they have to remember for only fairly short periods of time (H. Williams, 1983).

b. Younger children lack the cognitive skills that older children and adults have, and they lack, to a large extent, the language that older persons are able to use as an aid to visual memory.

B. Auditory Perception

1. By the age of two or three, most children have very good auditory acuity.

2. However, producing sounds they can hear correctly is difficult, and many common errors occur in producing various phonemes.

III. LANGUAGE ACQUISITION IN THE PRESCHOOL YEARS
For most children, language expands rapidly after infancy. Dramatic developments occur in syntax and in semantics and in communicative competence.

A. The Nature of Syntax

1. The *syntax* of a language is a group of rules for ordering and relating the language's elements. Linguists call the smallest meaningful units of language *morphemes*.

2. Syntactic rules operate on morphemes in several ways; sometimes they mark important relationships between large classes or groups of words.

3. Syntactic rules vary in how regular or general they are. Some apply to large, open-ended groupings or classes of words and are thus *generative*, or capable of generating original sentences.

4. Some syntactic rules are more narrow, and some are completely irregular. Thus, in acquiring syntax, the child confronts a mixed system of rules.

B. Beyond First Words: Duos and Telegraphic Speech

1. Before the age of two, the child begins linking two words together; these utterances are sometimes called *duos* (meaning "twos").

2. By nature, early speech leaves out most small connecting words such as articles and prepositions.

3. Individual differences and undergeneralizations also appear in children's speech.

   a. Children differ significantly in the particular relationships they express and in the rate at which relationships emerge. The child's grammar may not coincide with the linguist's grammar.

   b. Some syntactic relationships apparently have a narrower meaning for some children than for adults. A wide range of such *undergeneralizations* occurs in early sentences (Nelson, 1981).

4. Regularities and overgeneralizations also occur in children's early speech.

   a. After highly individual beginnings, certain aspects of syntax do develop in universal and predictable patterns.

   b. To a certain extent children's language seems to compromise between the new forms that children hear and the old forms that they can already produce easily.

   c. Sometimes, in fact, early syntax becomes too regular, and children make *overgeneralizations* such as "I runned to the store."

5. The predisposition to infer grammar is reflected in children's actual speech, which abounds in original but grammatical utterances.

6. The limits of learning rules are also demonstrated in children's speech. Although children eventually do rely on rule-governed syntax, they probably still learn a lot of language by rote. Many expressions in a language are *idiomatic*, which means they bear no logical relationship to normal meanings or syntax. Children must learn idiomatic expressions one at a time.

C. Mechanisms of Language Acquisition
Current evidence suggests that language seems to grow by the interaction of an active, thinking child with certain key people and linguistic experiences.

1. One common-sense view, which was formerly held, is that children learn to speak through reinforcement; analysis of conversations between parents and children, however, shows that the expected types of reinforcement do not occur.

2. Imitation and practice also play a role; however, the role of imitation is subtle and indirect and often involves playful practice with new expressions.

D. Innate Predisposition to Acquire Language: LAD

1. The ease and speed with which children acquire language suggests that there is an innate predisposition to acquire language (Chomsky, 1976; Slobin, 1973).

2. This tendency is sometimes called the *language acquisition device*, or LAD, which functions as a kind of inborn road map to language.

3. The universality of language acquisition, common features of syntax, critical periods for language acquisition, and early grammars are all supportive of the notion of the LAD.

4. The limits of LAD, however, become apparent when the role of experience is carefully considered.

E. Parent-Child Interactions

1. Certain kinds of verbal interactions help children acquire language, and parents are helpful when they speak in relatively short sentences to their preschool children.

2. One of the most helpful kinds of verbal interactions is *recasting* a child's utterances.

3. Such techniques for stimulating language development provide the preschooler with a framework for trying and learning unfamiliar language forms. This framework is sometimes called *scaffolding* (Bruner, 1983).

F. Language Variations
Not surprisingly, parents vary in how they talk to their children, and certain larger patterns can be identified in at least two respects.

1. Gender differences in language can be identified within any one community.

2. Socioeconomic differences in language can be identified in conjunction with socioeconomic levels.

IV. RELATIONSHIPS BETWEEN LANGUAGE AND THOUGHT
The relationship between language and thought has been explored and is the subject of extensive speculation in the field of psychology and beyond.

A. Piaget: Action as the Basis for Both Language and Thought

1. Piaget argued that action or activity promotes initial language development and that children need to manipulate objects and to have a rich variety of concrete experiences.

2. Piaget believed that sensorimotor experiences precede language and that language development reflects cognitive performance.

B. Vygotsky: The Gradual Integration of Language and Thought

1. As plausible as Piaget's ideas are, they ignore important evidence that language can also guide other cognitive developments, including both early sensorimotor development and later symbolic thinking.

2. Lev Vygotsky concluded that language and thought develop independently at first but gradually become integrated with each other sometime during childhood.

3. Whatever their actual relationship, language and thought remain only partly coordinated during the preschool years.

Overview and Key Concepts

Preoperational thinking develops during the preschool years with the emergence of symbolic thought, allowing the child to more effectively represent the world mentally. Preschoolers, however, are limited in that they tend to focus on the most obvious aspects of situations and have difficulty taking another person's perspective. They often imbue objects and natural events with a living consciousness and are generally egocentric in their world view. Because language emerges very rapidly and almost automatically in the preschool years, Chomsky and others have postulated a language acquisition device, or LAD. Whether language reflects thought or develops independently is open to question. In any case, preschoolers' language capability progresses from one-word utterances to duos and more elaborate statements that are increasingly marked by adultlike syntax.

Directions: Identify the following concepts introduced in Chapter 9.

1. A young preschool child can reenact experiences in new and creative ways through _____ , a form of pretend play in which he simulates people, objects, animals, and activities in his efforts to understand them.

2. At about age two, according to Piaget, children enter a new stage of cognitive development, _____ , in which they become increasingly proficient at using

_____ , which are words or actions that stand for something else. During this stage they also extend their belief in object permanence to include _____ , or constancies.

3. Preoperational children also sense many _____ , or variations in their environments that normally occur together. Probably the most significant cognitive achievement of the preoperational period is the emergence of _____ .

4. _____ refers to the inability of a person to distinguish between his own point of view and that of another person. It is literally a centering on the self in thinking and stems from _____ or _____ , which is the tendency to focus on only one aspect of an object or situation and to ignore other aspects.

5. In the preschool years, a child often expresses _____ , a belief that nonliving objects are in fact alive and human. _____ refers to a belief that all objects, whether alive or not, are made in the same way, usually by human beings.

6. To realize that a puppy is a *poodle*, belongs to the larger class *dogs*, and at the same time belongs to the still larger class *animals* is to understand the concept of _____ . This is not an ability that preoperational children typically have.

7. Many problems require _____ in thinking, which is the ability to undo a problem mentally and to go back to its beginning. Reversibility, it turns out, contributes to a major cognitive achievement of middle childhood called _____ , the ability to perceive that certain properties of an object remain the same or constant in spite of changes in the object's appearance.

8. The gap between independent thinking and socially supported thinking is called the _____ , the area in which problems are too difficult to solve alone but are not too hard to solve with support from adults or from more competent peers. The concept originated with Soviet psychologist _____ .

9. Not only does visual acuity improve during early childhood, but visual perception also improves in several ways. First, children learn to _____ , or notice visual differences among objects, and they _____ what they see increasingly well. Also, they improve their _____ , or ability to recognize and recall specific visual stimuli.

10. In some ways, hearing develops more quickly than vision. By the age of two or three, most children have very good _____ , meaning that they can notice small or soft sounds as well as young adults can. They can also discriminate speech sounds, or _____ , quite well.

11. For most children, language expands rapidly after infancy. Dramatic development occurs in _____ , or the way the child organizes utterances. But significant changes

also occur in _____ , or what the child means by his utterances, and in _____ , or how the child adjusts his utterances to the needs and expectations of different situations.

12. The _____ of a language is a group of rules for ordering and relating its elements. Linguists call the elements of language _____ . Before age two, the child begins linking two words together when she speaks; these utterances are sometimes called _____ .

13. Some syntactic relationships apparently have a narrower meaning for some children than for adults. A wide range of such _____ occurs in early sentences. Also, early syntax sometimes becomes too regular and children make _____ , as in a statement like "I runned to the store."

14. One common-sense view formerly held by some psychologists is that children learn to speak through _____ . _____ may help children acquire language by initiating playful practice with new expressions. Also, the ease and speed with which children acquire language has caused some psychologists and linguists to conclude that children have an innate predisposition to learn language, or a _____ .

15. Parents often help children acquire language through special strategies in their verbal interaction with them. One of the most helpful kinds of verbal interactions is _____ a child's utterances: repeating or reflecting back what the child says but in altered form. The techniques for stimulating language development have in common that they provide young preschoolers with a framework of language, or _____ .

Key Terms

Directions: Provide a definition for each of the following key terms. Check your answers against the Glossary or the text page number that follows each term.

American Sign Language (ASL) (p. 332) _____

_____

_____

Animism (p. 313) _____

_____

_____

Artificialism (p. 314) _____

_____

_____

Auditory acuity (p. 323) _____

_____

_____

Centration (p. 311) _____

_____

_____

Classification (p. 314) _____

_____

_____

Class inclusion (p. 314) _____

_____

_____

Communicative competence (p. 323) _____

_____

_____

Conservation (p. 316) _____

_____

_____

Decenter (p. 315) _____

_____

_____

Duo (p. 325) _____

_____

_____

Egocentrism (p. 311) _____

_____

_____

Functional relationship (p. 309) _____

_____

_____

Generative (p. 324) _____

_____

_____

Identity (p. 309) _____

_____

_____

Idiomatic (p. 328) _____

_____

_____

Inner speech (p. 337) _____

_____

_____

Lexicon (p. 328) _____

_____

_____

Make-believe (p. 308) _____

_____

_____

Morpheme (p. 324) _____

_____

_____

Overgeneralization (p. 326) _____

_____

_____

Perceptual dominance (p. 311) _____

_____

_____

Recasting (p. 333) _____

_____

_____

Reversibility (p. 316) _____

_____

_____

Scaffolding (p. 334) _____

_____

_____

Symbol (p. 309) _____

_____

_____

Symbolic thought (p. 309) _____

_____

_____

Telegraphic speech (p. 325) _____

_____

_____

Undergeneralization (p. 325) _____

_____

_____

Visual discrimination (p. 321) _____

_____

_____

Visual integration (p. 321) _____

_____

_____

Visual memory (p. 322) _____

_____

_____

Zone of proximal development (p. 318) _____

_____

_____

Study Questions

1. What are some of the major milestones of the preoperational stage? (p. 309)

   _____

   _____

   _____

   _____

2. In preoperational children, what is the special meaning of the term *egocentrism*? Give two examples of egocentric and nonegocentric thinking. (pp. 311–313)

   _____

   _____

_____

_____

3. How do young children show their tendency to think animistically and artificially? (pp. 313–314)

_____

_____

_____

_____

4. What are the limitations of a preschooler's ability to classify? (pp. 314–316)

_____

_____

_____

_____

5. Give a Piagetian example of a preschooler's difficulty in conservation and reversibility. Then give an example in which the procedures that were used enhanced the preschooler's ability to conserve and demonstrate reversibility. (pp. 316–317)

_____

_____

_____

_____

6. What is meant by the *zone of proximal development*, or ZPD? (pp. 317–318)

_____

_____

_____

_____

7. Describe gains made by preschoolers in visual discrimination, visual integration, and visual memory. (pp. 319–323)

_____

_____

_____

_____

8. Describe some of the major aspects of language presented in the text: syntax, semantics, phonemes, morphemes, and communicative competence. (pp. 323–325)

_____

_____

_____

_____

9. When young children are learning syntax, they sometimes overgeneralize; at other times, they undergeneralize. What is meant by *overgeneralization* and *undergeneralization*? Give two examples of each error. (pp. 325–326)

_____

_____

_____

_____

10. Describe at least four mechanisms of language acquisition that have been proposed by psychologists. (pp. 328–331)

_____

_____

_____

_____

11. Compare the limits of the LAD with the role of experience in language acquisition. (pp. 331–332)

_____

_____

_____

_____

12. Compare a hearing-impaired child's learning American Sign Language with a hearing child's language acquisition. (p. 332)

_____

_____

_____

_____

13. In terms of parent-child interactions, what are the benefits of recasting? (pp. 333–334)

_____

_____

_____

_____

14. How is Bruner's idea of scaffolding related to Vygotsky's notion of the zone of proximal development? (p. 334)

_____

_____

_____

_____

15. What are some of the gender differences in language cited by the text and what evidence is given for hypothesizing gender differences in language usage? (p. 334)

_____

_____

_____

_____

16. What are some of the socioeconomic differences in language cited in Chapter 9? (pp. 334–335)

_____

_____

_____

_____

17. How did Jean Piaget conceptualize the relationship between thought and language in cognitive development? (pp. 335–336)

_____

_____

_____

_____

18. How does Lev Vygotsky's view of the relationship between language and thought differ from Piaget's? (p. 337)

_____

_____

_____

_____

19. What is the role of inner speech in toddlers' thinking? (p. 337)

_____

_____

_____

_____

20. Describe some of the effects of cognition on social development. (pp. 337–338)

_____

_____

_____

_____

Multiple-Choice Self-Test

1. Piaget's second stage of development, which extends across the preschool years, is called the
   a. concrete operational stage.
   b. prelogic stage.
   c. preoperational stage.
   d. symbolic stage.

2. Which of the following develops during the preoperational stage?
   a. functional relationships
   b. object permanence
   c. reversibility
   d. sensory integration

3. According to Piaget, the most significant cognitive achievement during the preoperational stage is the
   a. emergence of identity permanence.
   b. ability to use reversibility in thinking.
   c. emergence of symbolic thought.
   d. ability to use egocentric logic.

4. Brad believes that everybody sees the world as he sees it. Brad's thinking is characterized by
   a. animism.
   b. centration.
   c. egocentrism.
   d. functional relations.

5. Animism refers to the
   a. attribution of human characteristics, such as feelings, to nonliving objects.
   b. belief that all objects were made simply for the benefit of the child.
   c. ability to formulate a causal relationship between two seemingly unrelated events.
   d. inability to realize that changes in an object do not necessarily change the identity of the object.

6. Given a group of six red cars and four blue cars, Grace says that there are more red cars than cars. Her response indicates a lack of
   a. class inclusion.
   b. conservation.
   c. decentration.
   d. reversibility.

7. In tasks requiring visual integration, preschoolers normally tend to do
   a. quite poorly.
   b. well even on tasks that have a large number of different stimuli.
   c. well even if they are involved in other tasks at the same time.
   d. well unless they are distracted.

8. Rusty is beginning to learn the rules of language, including basic grammar. One would say that he is acquiring
   a. communication.
   b. semantics.
   c. syntax.
   d. telegraphic speech.

9. Kristy says, "Go house," when she means "Go into the house." Kristy is using
   a. egocentric speech.
   b. idiomatic speech.
   c. overgeneralization.
   d. telegraphic speech.

10. Emilio says, "Where are the childs," instead of "Where are the children." Emilio is using
    a. imitation.
    b. overgeneralization.
    c. telegraphic speech.
    d. undergeneralization.

11. The reinforcement view of language predicts that parents will
    a. ignore immature utterances.
    b. reinforce correct grammatical form.
    c. reinforce noises that approximate words.
    d. all of the above.

12. The innate predisposition view of language hypothesizes
    a. a language acquisition device.
    b. that syntactic rules are the same for all languages.
    c. that parents will reinforce correct grammar.
    d. that the primary mechanism of language acquisition is the imitation of speech sounds.

13. Who is most likely to agree with the statement that children's language is limited by their level of cognitive development?
    a. B. F. Skinner
    b. Jean Piaget
    c. Jerome Bruner
    d. Lev Vygotsky

Activities

Activity 9.1

> **Objective:** To be prepared to demonstrate the young child's preoperational thinking about the physical world.

Prepare a kit of materials and instructions that you could use on a moment's notice to observe or demonstrate at least three characteristics of preoperational thinking. Use objects that could be found in any nursery school or home environment. Include the following tasks for three- and four-year-olds.

Conservation of Liquid

Materials (*Hint:* Sand or fine gravel may be used instead of liquids.)

Procedure (*Hint:* Make sure that the child understands the vocabulary and the nature of the task.)

Ask for a justification by asking questions such as "How come?" or "The other day a boy (or girl) told me . . . What do you think about that?"

Perspective from Another Point of View

Materials (*Hint:* Piaget's three mountains problem, on text pages 311–312, works well.)

Procedure

How might you change this task so that a preschooler *could* see another's perspective? (*Hint:* As you reread the situation of the policeman chasing the child on text pages 311–312, consider the possibility of the task that makes human sense.)

Classification

Materials (*Hint:* Simple sorting tasks work well, such as sorting crayons from felt-tip pens and chalk.)

Procedure

Class Inclusion

Materials (*Hint:* Try red and white flowers, as described on text pages 314–315.)

Procedure

Artificialism

No materials needed.

Procedure (*Hint:* See text page 314. What food sources could you ask about?)

Animism

No materials needed.

Procedure (*Hint:* Try a conversation about nonliving objects or natural phenomena, as in the clouds example on text page 314).

From these demonstrations, what generalizations can you make for parents and teachers about the preschooler's

Conservation

Reversibility in thinking

Egocentric thinking

Classification

Class inclusion

Artificialism

Animism

Activity 9.2

Objective: To recognize several different approaches in early childhood education.

A panel of early childhood educators could be easily assembled from preschool programs on your campus and in your neighboring community to discuss varying approaches to preschool education. Comment below on several different types of programs and philosophies of early education.

A Piagetian program

A Montessorian (American Montessori) approach

A Montessorian (Italian-international) approach

A program with strong academic-cognitive emphasis

A program with strong sociopersonal emphasis

Activity 9.3

Objective: To become aware of part of the linguistic process by which some children grow up bilingual.

A baby will soon be born into a family in which two languages are spoken.One parent is Norwegian, and the other is American. Each of the parents has agreed to speak to their offspring only in his or her native tongue. They anticipate that the youngster will become proficient in both languages. A close friend strongly disagrees.

"Oh no! The baby will get all mixed up and speak a garbled version of English and Norwegian. You've got to choose one language or the other."

The three adults turn to you, as a student of child development, to help resolve the dispute. What information would you offer about growing up bilingual?

Activity 9.4

Objective: To identify effective and ineffective strategies for facilitating language development.

A mother and father, both quite articulate, are delighted that their toddler is really talking, although not very well. She is a bright, observant child, and her parents have been conscientiously trying to teach her correct syntax. For example, when she says, "I taked my teddy bear outside," they gently explain that the correct word is *took*. But she doesn't seem to remember, no matter how many times they correct her. She continues to make many mistakes of this sort. The parents turn to you for insight about their daughter's learning to speak correctly. What would you say to them about:

The timing and process of a young child's competence in using correct grammar

Overgeneralizations and undergeneralizations

The advisability of correcting the child's speech

Ways that will help this child acquire language

What else might you add?

Activity 9.5

Objective: To become aware of perceptual skills that are prerequisites of academic skills and learning.

You are the director of a middle-class preschool that has a developmental focus. Direct teaching of reading or computational skills is not part of the curriculum. You are more interested in language interactions and the enjoyment and appreciation of stories and songs. Rather than teach arithmetic, you want the children to have firsthand sensory experiences with all kinds of materials and objects (pouring, measuring, and so on)—somewhat of a Piagetian point of view. To the parents your program looks as though the children are mostly encouraged to play, listen to stories, and sing. They want to know why you are not teaching their children to read and add. In your opinion, perceptual skills are an essential foundation for later academic learning, and that is your focus.

Assuming that the children's visual perception is normal for their ages, what activities and experiences would you provide to enhance:

Visual discrimination

Visual integration

How would you protect their focus and concentration?

What activities would you provide to facilitate:

Visual memory

Tactile perception

In the course of the day's activities, how could you notice the children's auditory perception?

You are accountable to the parents, who still want their children to read. How would you explain to them the connection between perceptual skills and academics?

Activity 9.6

Objective: To become aware of the ongoing controversy between those who advocate early academics in the preschool and those who favor naturalistic approaches with abundant amounts of play and self-selected activities for the children.

At the library or in a local bookstore locate a copy of David Elkind's *The Hurried Child* or another book or article that is critical of early formal instruction in preschool. After reading the book or article, formulate your own position on the issue of how formal or informal learning environments for young children should be. Record your opinion on each school of thought below.

Arguments Supporting Early Academic/Formal Instruction

Arguments for Informal, Social-Interaction Models of Education

Answer Key

Overview and Key Concepts

1. make-believe (p. 308)

2. preoperational stage; symbols; identities (p. 309)

3. functional relationships; symbolic thought (p. 309)

4. egocentrism; perceptual dominance; centration (p. 311)

5. animism; artificialism (p. 314)

6. class inclusion (p. 314)

7. reversibility; conservation (p. 316)

8. zone of proximal development; Vygotsky (p. 318)

9. discriminate; integrate; visual memory (p. 320)

10. auditory acuity; phonemes (p. 323)

11. syntax; semantics; communicative competence (p. 323)

12. syntax; morphemes; duos (pp. 324–325)

13. undergeneralizations; overgeneralizations (pp. 325–326)

14. reinforcement; imitation; language acquisition device (pp. 329–331)

15. recasting; scaffolding (pp. 333–334)

Multiple-Choice Self-Test

1. Choice (c) is correct. Piaget's second stage of development extends from approximately age two to age seven and is called the preoperational stage. (p. 309)
Choice (a) is Piaget's third stage, characteristic of the school years. Choices (b) and (d) are not terms for Piaget's stages.

2. Choice (a) is correct. The ability to sense variations that normally occur together is an ability that develops during the preoperational stage. (p. 309)

Choices (b) and (d) develop during the sensorimotor stage. Choice (c) develops during the concrete operational stage.

3. Choice (c) is correct. Symbolic thinking is the ability to make one object or action stand for another. This ability opens up the entire area of thinking and is therefore the most significant cognitive achievement of the preoperational period. (pp. 309–310)
   Although identity permanence, choice (a), does emerge during the preoperational period, it does not have such wide-ranging benefits as symbolic thinking. Reversibility of thinking, choice (b), is a concrete skill. Egocentric thinking, choice (d), is more a limitation than an asset.

4. Choice (c) is correct. Egocentrism is the inability to distinguish between one's own point of view and that of another. (p. 311)
   Choice (a) is the belief that nonliving objects are alive or have human characteristics. Choice (b) is a related concept; however, it is the tendency to focus on only one aspect of an object or situation. Choice (d) is the ability to sense variations that normally occur together.

5. Choice (a) is correct. By definition, animism is the belief that nonliving objects are in fact alive and have feelings. (p. 313)
   Choice (b) reflects egocentric thinking; (c) reflects functional relationships; and (d) reflects identity permanence.

6. Choice (a) is correct. Class inclusion involves the notion that an object can be a member of more than one class at a time. (p. 314)
   Choice (b) involves the notion that even though changes are made in appearance, substance and other characteristics do not necessarily change. Choice (c) is the ability to focus on more than one aspect of an object at a time. Choice (d) involves the ability to undo something and get back to the original starting point.

7. Choice (d) is correct. Visual integration refers to the ability to coordinate particular sights with each other and with appropriate actions. Preschoolers do fairly well at visual integration tasks (e.g., catching a ball, drawing a picture); however, distractions can have negative effects. (p. 321)
   Choices (a), (b), and (c) do not accurately describe these abilities and limitations.

8. Choice (c) is correct. The rules of a language are called its syntax. (p. 324)
   Choice (a) refers to a function of language; (b) refers to the meaning of language; and (d) refers to speech that eliminates unnecessary connecting words.

9. Choice (d) is correct. The phrase illustrates a typical two-word sentence that contains no connecting words. (p. 325)
   Choice (a) is speech whose meaning is specific to the child only. Choice (b) is speech that has a particular meaning only to a particular group. Choice (c) refers to the expanded use of a rule or concept.

10. Choice (b) is correct. The usual way to form a plural is to add "s" to the noun; however, *child* represents a special case. Emilio has overgeneralized the use of the rule. (p. 326)
Choice (a) is not true, since "childs" is not used in normal adult speech. Choice (c) involves the elimination of nonessential words. Choice (d) is the lack of application of combinations of words that might normally occur.

11. Choice (d) is correct. Reinforcement predicts that immature utterances will not be reinforced, choice (a), and that correct grammar, choice (b), and close approximations to words, choice (c), will be reinforced in order to shape proper language. (p. 329)

12. Choice (a) is correct. The innate predisposition view hypothesizes a built-in road map, a language acquisition device, to acquire language. (p. 331)
Although choice (b) is consistent with belief in an innate predisposition for language, it is not specifically hypothesized. Choices (c) and (d) are consistent with a reinforcement view of language.

13. Choice (b) is correct. Piaget believed that thought precedes language and that therefore the level of cognitive development places limits on language development. (pp. 335–336)
Skinner, choice (a), viewed reinforcement, not cognitive development, as the primary mechanism of language development. Bruner, choice (c), and Vygotsky, choice (d), tend to view early language and thought as independent.

CHAPTER 10
The Preschool Years: Psychosocial Development

Learning Objectives

1. Describe the general characteristics of preschool social development as seen by Sigmund Freud, Erik Erikson, and Harry Stack Sullivan.

2. Discuss the characteristics of play in the preschool years. Identify and compare the three major theoretical approaches to play.

3. Identify and describe Mildred Parten's levels of play and indicate the developmental patterns for each.

4. Compare and contrast Diana Baumrind's parental styles. Indicate the characteristics and consequences of each style.

5. Describe the nature of the relationship between a child and siblings and the development of other friendships during the preschool period.

6. Define and characterize the changes found in prosocial behavior, empathy, aggression, and assertiveness during the preschool years. Identify the main variables that influence each.

7. Identify and define the various forms of gender development and sex-role stereotypes.

Chapter Outline

I. THEORIES OF EARLY SOCIAL DEVELOPMENT

   A. By the third birthday, most children have achieved a basic sense of trust in others and a sense of autonomy and are firmly convinced of their own personhood.

   B. Psychoanalytic theories have proved particularly helpful in explaining psychological and emotional changes that occur in the preschool years.

   C. According to Freud, the superego and ego ideal that develop during this stage help a child regulate his feelings and actions in socially acceptable ways.

   D. According to Erikson, three important changes during the preschool years contribute to a child's developing sense of self: greater mobility, improved communication skills, and greatly expanded imagination.

   E. Harry Stack Sullivan proposed several additional concepts that are useful for understanding development during the preschool years.

      1. *Egocentric escape* is used by the child to distance herself from unpleasant experiences by acting as if she is unaffected by such experiences or by quickly forgetting them.

      2. *Dramatizations* or "as if" performances are used by the child to try out the role of being someone else, typically her mother or father.

      3. *Malevolent transformation* may occur if a child's attempts to initiate contact and to obtain closeness are rejected. Feelings of anxiety that result may lead to a sense that the world is a harmful and evil place in which it is difficult to achieve closeness with others.

II. PLAY IN EARLY CHILDHOOD

   A. The Nature of Play

      1. Play dominates the preschool years and is usually *intrinsically motivated*.

      2. Children play because doing so is enjoyable. They are generally more interested in the *process* of doing things than in the *product* of what they do.

      3. Play resembles real-life activities but differs from them in that it is not bound by reality.

4. Play tends to be governed by *implicit rules*—that is, rules that can be discovered by observing the activity rather than rules that are formally stated.

B. Theories of Play
There are three main theoretical approaches to play.

1. Psychoanalytic theory

   a. The psychoanalytic theories of Freud and Erikson emphasize the social and emotional importance of play in early childhood.

   b. They note that play provides an opportunity for the child to *gain mastery over problems* by rearranging objects and social situations in ways that allow him to imagine that he is in control.

   c. Through *repetition compulsion*, a child may repeat an experience again and again in symbolic play until she gains control or resolution of it.

2. Learning theory

   a. Learning theorists view play as an opportunity for children to try out new behaviors and social roles safely.

   b. Play is a major way in which children progressively learn adult social skills, either through successive reinforcement of behaviors or through observation.

3. Cognitive theory

   a. Cognitive theorists have identified four major kinds of play that they believe develop sequentially in parallel with the major stages of cognitive development: *functional play* occurs during the sensorimotor period, *constructive play* and *dramatic play* during the preoperational period, and *games with rules* during the concrete operational period.

   b. The basic idea in cognitive views of play is that a child's play abilities depend on her abilities to think and solve problems.

C. Cognitive Levels of Play

1. *Functional play* involves simple, repeated movements and focuses on one's own body. Functional play requires no symbolic activity, and movements tend not to have a purpose other than movement itself. Functional play decreases with age and becomes combined with other playful ends.

2. *Constructive play* involves manipulation of physical objects in order to build or construct something. Constructive play overlaps with functional play.

3. *Dramatic,* or *make-believe, play* is very significant in the years following infancy and probably begins when the child can symbolize or mentally represent objects. Dramatic play grows in complexity and frequency during the preschool years and creates opportunities for new forms of experience to be assimilated into existing schemes and for practice with motor and social skills.

4. *Games with rules* increasingly dominate play as children move into the school years. Games with rules comprise formal types of play such as jump-rope and hide-and-seek. At times, the process of formulating rules takes more time than the play itself and helps children develop a conscious formality.

D. Social Levels of Play

1. Play also varies according to how social it is and to what degree children involve others in their play activities.

2. Mildred Parten (1932) established several categories or levels of sociability in play.

   a. Unoccupied play: A child simply wanders around, not becoming involved in an activity for more than a moment.

   b. Solitary play: A child plays alone with toys and without awareness of other children.

   c. Onlooker play: A child watches others at play without actually entering into the activities herself.

   d. Parallel play: Two or more children play with the same toys in much the same way, in close proximity, and with an awareness of each other.

   e. Associative play: Children engage in a common activity and talk to each other about it.

   f. Cooperative play: Children consciously form into groups to accomplish some activity, often dramatic or make-believe in nature.

E. Other Influences on Play

1. Setting

a. The composition of a child's play is likely to be influenced by the range of play opportunities that her care-givers provide and by the types of play they encourage.

b. Researchers have found that children in centers with high-quality staff and programs engaged in less unoccupied and solitary play than did children in centers of lower quality. Also, preschoolers in the better centers interacted with adults in more positive ways.

2. Siblings

a. The presence of siblings influences play.

b. Older siblings encouraged early dramatic role-playing.

3. Changes with age

a. Social participation in various types of play varies with age. Social involvement also increases with age.

b. All forms of play continue to be important to one degree or another throughout life.

c. Social play takes a variety of forms in later childhood and adulthood.

III. RELATIONSHIPS WITH OTHERS

A. Relationships with Parents

1. Patterns of parental authority: The parents' style of authority is crucial, and three types of child-rearing have been identified.

a. *Authoritarian parents* score high on control but low on nurturance.

b. *Permissive parents* score low on control. They may be *permissive-indulgent* parents, who make few demands and communicate warmth, or *permissive-indifferent* parents, who cop-out on their child-rearing responsibilities.

c. *Authoritative parents* score high on control, clarity of communication, maturity demands, and nurturance. These parents have a very democratic style of parenting.

2. Interviews of families with children have found that parental use of reasoning was related to warmth toward their children and that parental restrictiveness was related to power-assertion techniques, including physical punishment.

3. There is great variation in parenting styles. Ordinary people do not fall neatly into one or another of the categories, so caution should be exercised in interpreting research findings.

B. Relationships with Siblings

1. Studies of children's behavior toward their siblings have shown that most young children are very interested in babies and their behavior and speech are similar to those of adult care-givers (J. Dunn, 1985).

2. Given the social opportunities that siblings make available, one might guess that children growing up with brothers and sisters will develop social skills earlier and more rapidly than will those who have not had this opportunity.

3. For preschoolers, siblings serve as teachers and role models—as well as playmates sharing common pleasures and exciting activities.

C. Friendships in Early Childhood

1. Preschool children seek the security and intimacy of playing with a familiar friend, but they want to participate in the variety of activities possible with many different children.

2. The evolution of friendship

   a. Even infants and toddlers show preferences for particular children and sensitivity to special friends.

   b. By age four, friendships become more involved and durable and are based on shared activities more than on thoughts or feelings.

   c. Preschoolers have enough symbolic skills to know and say who their friends are.

   d. Early friendships are marked by instability; friendship may tend to be a means to other ends.

3. Conceptions of friendship

   a. During the preschool years, children develop ideas about the nature of friendship.

b. As children near school age, more permanent, personal qualities enter into their conceptions and the crucial features of a friend become more often dispositional—that is, related to how the friend is likely to behave in the future.

D. Empathy and Prosocial Behavior
Empathy is a sensitive awareness of the thoughts and feelings of another person; *prosocial behavior* refers to actions that benefit others.

1. The extent of empathy and helpfulness

   a. In many situations, preschool children will respond helpfully to another person's distress.

   b. However, young children are limited in their empathetic and helpful response because of their limited sensitivity to others.

2. Developmental changes

   a. Helpfulness is well established by the time a child reaches the preschool years.

   b. Between ages two and six, children give increasingly complex reasons for helping and are more strongly influenced by nonaltruistic as well as altruistic motives and concerns.

3. Fostering empathy, altruism, and prosocial behavior

   a. Both verbal approval and the opportunity to discover the benefits of cooperation in play situations have proven successful in increasing altruistic and prosocial behavior in preschoolers (Slaby & Crowley, 1977).

   b. Empathy in preschoolers also seems related to parenting styles and parental models.

   c. The influence of adult encouragement is also strong in encouraging prosocial response.

E. Conflict and Aggression

1. The nature of aggression

   a. *Aggression* is an action that is intended to hurt someone or something. It is different from *assertiveness*, which is a more general tendency to communicate clearly and thus fulfill one's needs.

    b. Generally, judgments about a child's aggressiveness are based on her motivations, on her level of knowledge of the effects of her actions, and on whether or not there have been destructive consequences.

2. Changes in aggression during early childhood

    a. Young preschoolers show aggression more physically than older preschoolers do.

    b. As children get older, they shift to more verbal methods of aggression.

    c. When a younger child behaves aggressively, she often has an assertive or practical goal in mind, such as retrieving a toy. This type of aggression is called *instrumental aggression*.

    d. *Hostile aggression* involves the motive of wanting to hurt someone or strike out.

3. Influences on the development of aggression

    a. One important factor is parents' willingness to accept children's hostile-aggressive impulses and help them find nonhostile alternatives.

    b. Biologically based temperamental differences may also be a factor in the development of aggression.

    c. Physical looks may also make a difference.

    d. Gender differences appear in the fact that boys exhibit more aggressive behavior than girls exhibit.

    e. Child-rearing and educational philosophies of parents and teachers also influence overall levels of aggression and gender differences.

    f. A number of child-rearing characteristics have been found to contribute to aggression in preschoolers—for example, lack of acceptance by parents.

    g. Provocation by peers can also be a factor in aggressive behavior by preschoolers. A *dominance hierarchy*, a pattern of status and authority that is influenced by who wins or who loses, can develop among pairs of preschool children.

    h. Viewing of violence on media can *disinhibit* or release violent behavior in children.

    i. Aggression is much less likely to be a problem when adequate adult supervision is available.

4. Responding to aggressive behavior

   a. Structure, predictability, and consistency are important for all preschoolers, and especially for those prone to aggression.

   b. Parents can learn to recognize early signs of aggression and intervene.

   c. Effective parent-child communication can be a key in preventing outbursts of aggression.

   d. Alternative and more constructive ways of dealing with the child's aggression can be learned and taught by therapists.

IV. GENDER DEVELOPMENT
Gender refers to the behaviors and attitudes associated with being male or female. Typically, children develop beliefs about *gender identity*, *gender preference*, and *gender constancy*.

A. Developmental Trends During Early Childhood

   1. Usually even two-year-olds can label themselves correctly as boys or girls. Children tend to learn gender stereotypes very early, especially in terms of appropriate toys and activities.

   2. In contrast to stereotypes about toys and activities, children develop gender stereotypes about personal qualities relatively slowly (Huston, 1983).

B. Influences on Gender Development

   1. Parents tend to treat boys and girls differently.

   2. Peers shape gender differences.

   3. The media tend to present role models that are strongly stereotyped.

C. Androgyny

   1. Androgyny refers to a state of affairs in which sex roles are flexible.

   2. Androgynous individuals are thought to be more flexible and adaptable because they are *gender aschematic*—that is, they are less concerned about what activities are appropriate or inappropriate.

Overview and Key Concepts

Chapter 10 presents key concepts in Erikson's, Freud's, and Sullivan's theories to explain psychosocial growth in preschoolers. The chapter extensively covers the role of play and varieties and levels of play. Relationships with others are explored from the standpoint of relationships with parents and with siblings and friendships in early childhood. The development of empathy and prosocial behavior is contrasted with the emergence of conflict and aggression. The chapter concludes with discussion of issues and influences in the development of gender and androgyny.

Directions: Identify the following concepts introduced in Chapter 10.

1. According to Erik Erikson, three important changes during the preschool years contribute to a child's developing sense of self: _____ , _____ , and _____ .

2. In Erikson's view, the child must master the developmental crisis of _____ .

3. Harry Stack Sullivan proposed several additional concepts. He believed that preschoolers use _____ to distance themselves from unpleasant experiences. He also proposed that _____ may occur if a child's attempts to initiate contact with others are rejected.

4. Children at *play* generally show _____ , which means that they engage in the play because the activity is enjoyable.

5. Psychoanalytic theory emphasizes that play provides an opportunity for a child to _____ by rearranging social situations.

6. Learning theorists view play as an opportunity for children to try out _____ and _____ safely.

7. Cognitive theorists have identified four major kinds of play that they believe develop sequentially along with the major stages of cognitive development. According to their theories, _____ occurs during the sensorimotor period, _____ and _____ during the preoperational period, and _____ during the concrete operational period.

8. Mildred Parten studied social participation among preschool children and proposed that children's play developed according to the following series of six stages or levels of sociability: _____ , _____ , _____ , _____ , _____ , and _____ .

9. _____ score high on control, high on maturity demands, and low on nurturance. Such parents impose their wills by asserting their own power and authority.

10. _____ are just the opposite. They score low on control, high on clarity of communication, low on maturity demands, and high on nurturance. Some of these parents tend to be _____ , making few demands but communicating warmth; others are _____ , tending to cop-out on parental responsibilities.

11. _____ score high on control, clarity of communication, maturity demands, and nurturance. Thus, they differ from the other two types of parents in significant ways. They do set rules and impose limits, but they rely on more democratic techniques.

12. _____ is a sensitive awareness of the thoughts and feelings of another person, and _____ refers to actions that benefit others. _____ or prosocial behavior is well established by the time a child reaches the preschool years.

13. _____ is the general tendency to communicate clearly and effectively and thus fulfill one's needs, but not with the intention of hurting another person. When a youngster behaves assertively to retrieve a toy rather than to inflict pain, her behavior is called _____ ; however, when harm is an important intent, the behavior is referred to as _____ . Children are prone to respond aggressively in the case of _____ , or actions that interfere with their activities.

14. A series of aggressive exchanges among pairs of preschool children sometimes results in a _____ , a pattern of status and authority that is influenced by who wins and who loses but that is also related to leadership and popularity within a group.

15. The term _____ refers to the behaviors and attitudes associated with being male or female. Most children experience it in at least three ways. First, they develop beliefs about _____ , that is, which sex they are. Second, they develop _____ , attitudes about which sex they wish to be. Third, they acquire _____ , a belief that the sex of a person is biologically determined and permanent. _____ refers to a state of affairs in which sex rules are flexible.

Key Terms

Directions: Provide a definition for each of the following key terms. Check your answers against the Glossary or the text page number that follows each term.

Aggression (p. 365) _____

_____

_____

Androgyny (p. 374) _____

_____

_____

Assertiveness (p. 365) _____

_____

_____

Authoritarian (p. 354) _____

_____

_____

Authoritative (p. 355) _____

_____

_____

Blocking behavior (p. 366) _____

_____

_____

Catharsis (p. 346) _____

_____

_____

Constructive play (p. 348) _____

_____

_____

Disinhibit (p. 369) _____

_____

_____

Dominance hierarchy (p. 369) _____

_____

_____

Dramatic, or make-believe, play (p. 348) _____

_____

_____

Dramatization (p. 343) _____

_____

_____

Egocentric escape (p. 343) _____

_____

_____

Empathy (p. 362) _____

_____

_____

Functional play (p. 347) _____

_____

_____

Games with rules (p. 350) _____

_____

_____

Gender (p. 370) _____

_____

_____

Gender constancy (p. 371) _____

_____

_____

Gender identity (p. 371) _____

_____

_____

Gender preference (p. 371) _____

_____

_____

Hostile aggression (p. 366) _____

_____

_____

Initiative versus guilt (p. 343) _____

_____

_____

Instrumental aggression (p. 366) _____

_____

_____

Malevolent transformation (p. 343) _____

_____

_____

Permissive (p. 354) _____

_____

_____

Permissive-indifferent (p. 355) _____

_____

_____

Permissive-indulgent (p. 354) _____

_____

_____

Prosocial behavior (p. 353) _____

_____

_____

Repetition compulsion (p. 346) _____

_____

_____

Study Questions

1. What concepts in Freud's, Erikson's, and Sullivan's theories apply to psychosocial development in the preschool years? (pp. 342–343)

_____

_____

_____

_____

2. Describe the nature of play with reference to at least six major characteristics. (pp. 344–345)

_____

_____

_____

_____

3. From a psychoanalytic point of view, what is the function of play? (pp. 345–346)

_____

_____

_____

_____

4. How do learning theorists view play? (p. 346)

_____

_____

_____

_____

5. How do advancing levels of play match up with cognitive stages of development, according to cognitive theorists? (pp. 346–351)

_____

_____

_____

_____

6. What are the characteristics of Parten's six levels of sociability in play? (pp. 351–352)

_____

_____

_____

_____

7. Identify and briefly describe three other major influences on play. (pp. 352–353)

_____

_____

_____

_____

8. Describe three patterns of parental authority and their likely consequences. (pp. 353–356)

_____

_____

_____

_____

9. How may children's actions influence parenting styles? (p. 357)

_____

_____

_____

_____

10. How do brothers and sisters affect psychosocial development? (pp. 357–358)

_____

_____

_____

_____

11. What is the impact of punishment on psychosocial development in the preschool years? (pp. 354–355)

_____

_____

_____

_____

12. Describe the nature and some of the characteristics of friendship in early childhood. (pp. 359–361)

_____

_____

_____

_____

13. What can parents do to create a climate in which empathy, altruism, and prosocial behavior will be fostered? (pp. 363–365)

_____

_____

_____

_____

14. What is the nature of aggression compared with the nature of assertiveness? (pp. 365–366)

_____

_____

_____

_____

15. What changes occur in aggression during early childhood and what are two types of aggression that children manifest in their behavior? (p. 366)

_____

_____

_____

_____

16. What are some of the factors and circumstances that influence the development of aggression? (pp. 366–369)

_____

_____

_____

_____

17. What are some modes and methods of responding to aggressive behavior in preschoolers? (pp. 369–370)

_____

_____

_____

_____

18. What is meant by *gender, gender identity, gender preference,* and *gender constancy*? (pp. 370–371)

_____

_____

_____

_____

19. How do toys and activities, parents, peers, and the media influence gender development? (pp. 371–374)

_____

_____

_____

_____

20. What is meant by *androgyny* and how does it allow for greater flexibility in social roles? (pp. 374–375)

_____

_____

_____

_____

Multiple-Choice Self-Test

1. Which of Erikson's psychosocial stages most closely corresponds with the preschool period?
   a. autonomy versus shame and doubt
   b. industry versus inferiority
   c. initiative versus guilt
   d. integrity versus despair

2. The notion that play provides an opportunity to release upsetting feelings that cannot otherwise be expressed is consistent with the _____ theory of play.
   a. cognitive
   b. psychoanalytic
   c. social learning
   d. Sullivan

3. Kim jumps up and down in her bed repeatedly. Kim's behavior illustrates
   a. constructive play.
   b. dramatic play.
   c. functional play.
   d. parallel play.

4. Which of the following forms of play tends to decrease across the preschool years?
   a. associative
   b. cooperative
   c. parallel
   d. all of the above

5. Hal and Lisa tend to tell their children what to do, seldom seek their input in family decisions, and generally seem somewhat distant from them. Hal and Lisa's style of parenting would most likely be classified as
   a. authoritarian.
   b. authoritative.
   c. permissive-indifferent.
   d. permissive-indulgent.

6. The most self-reliant and self-controlled children seem to be associated with parents who use the _____ style of parenting.
   a. authoritarian
   b. authoritative
   c. permissive-indifferent
   d. permissive-indulgent

7. In the school years friendships tend to rely more on _____ than they do during the preschool years.
   a. physical similarity
   b. shared activities
   c. shared thoughts and feelings
   d. social status

8. The development of prosocial behavior and empathy in the preschool years is related to
   a. a good parent-child relationship and secure attachment during infancy.
   b. infant temperament and other genetic predispositions.
   c. the level of cognitive and metacognitive awareness in the child.
   d. the number of friendships a child experiences.

9. Aggression in children seems to be associated with
   a. attractiveness.
   b. gender.
   c. frustration.
   d. all of the above.

10. As children get older, aggression seems to shift to _____ forms.
    a. direct
    b. object-oriented
    c. physical
    d. verbal

11. Parents who use excessive permissiveness and inconsistent discipline are likely to produce children who are more _____ than average.
    a. aggressive
    b. androgynous
    c. assertive
    d. empathetic

12. A child's general knowledge of society's expectations about sex roles is referred to as
    a. gender constancy.
    b. gender identity.
    c. gender preference.
    d. sex-role stereotypes.

13. Which of the following concepts seems to emerge during early childhood?
    a. gender constancy
    b. gender stereotypes
    c. gender identity
    d. gender permanence

14. Androgyny refers to individuals who exhibit _____ characteristics and traits.
    a. primarily opposite-sex
    b. both masculine and feminine
    c. primarily same-sex
    d. neither masculine nor feminine

Activities

Activity 10.1

> **Objective:** To be able to distinguish between instrumental and hostile aggression.

Make an appointment to visit a preschool for at least two and a half hours. Explain the assignment, as set forth below, to the director and offer to share your findings before you leave. Reassure the director of the confidentiality of your report.

During your observation, notice as many acts of aggression as you can, including matter-of-fact assertive behavior. Remain in the background, where you can watch without interfering. If the children come to you and ask questions about your presence, answer them briefly and quietly. Do not initiate conversation or activity with the children.

Briefly note each incident and determine whether it was hostile aggression or instrumental aggression. Did one form lead to another?

How many aggressive acts did you observe in what length of time?

Did one form of aggression outnumber the other?

Give two examples of hostile and of instrumental aggression.

Activity 10.2

Objective: To identify the forms and purpose of play.

Make an appointment for a visit to a preschool, either the same one as in Activity 10.1 or another. Explain the assignment to the director and offer to share your findings before you leave. Reaffirm your policy of confidentiality. As before, keep a low profile to allow the children to proceed without self-consciousness.

This time, you are observing the many forms that play takes among young children. Without attempting to verify with the children or adults, make a note of the following varieties of play you observed.

To master a skill

To resolve a conflict or fear

To fulfill a wish

Functional play

To explore the nature of materials and space

Constructive play

Dramatic play

A game with a rule

Note: In some cases, the same incident of play activity will fit under more than one heading.

Activity 10.3

Objective: To note the educational and psychological functions of play.

Parents whose children attend a preschool or a children's center that uses a developmental approach sometimes wonder whether their children's time is well spent. Typical questions and comments follow. What would be your answer to each parent about the educational and psychological value of play? Include specific examples in your answers.

All the children do is play. Don't you teach them anything?

I observed my child riding the trike and playing in the sandbox. He's not learning anything.

My niece is learning her letters and numbers at preschool. Don't you teach the children to read?

What a mess this paint and clay is! Don't they have any workbooks?

Activity 10.4

Objective: To understand the distinction between authoritarian, authoritative, and permissive parenting styles.

You are eavesdropping on parents talking to their children. From the brief remarks below, identify the parenting style.

	Authoritarian	Permissive	Authoritative
Because I said so!			
You may choose one from these three.			
Don't touch that!			
I'm sure you didn't mean to break it.			
Mother and Daddy are so tired; this is the last time.			
We'll set the timer. When the bell rings, it will be your turn.			
Don't eat too much.			
Give him some!			
Well, if you really want to . . .			
If you can't keep your voice down, you'll have to leave.			
It's raining outside; have a cookie instead.			
You need to come down. I don't want you to get hurt.			
Be careful, dear.			
Get off that!			
Your feet belong on the floor, not the table.			
Sister would rather not have you go through her drawers.			
We were saving it for the party, but you can have just a little.			

	Authoritarian	Permissive	Authoritative
How many times have I told you not to talk back?			
Remember? I said we would go when both hands of the clock were . . .			
We'll have to put this away. It's too hard for you to keep . . .			
Keep it up and I'll give you something to cry about.			
You poor dear. I didn't know it would make you so sad. Okay then.			
I know you're unhappy about it, but we don't have time today.			

Activity 10.5

Objective: To gain practice in showing the logical consequences of misbehavior.

Arbitrary punishments are rarely effective in the long run, and many adults see reinforcement of the desired behavior as bribery. A third alternative in helping a young child become self-disciplined is to provide the experience of developmentally appropriate consequences. Since the preschooler lives very much in the here-and-now, the consequence must happen right now.

What consequence do you recommend for the following?

A four-year-old throws blocks instead of building with them.

In preschool, a three-and-one-half-year-old interferes with circle singing by shouting.

A four-year-old has just had a third "accidental" juice spill.

A child tells "tall stories."

At the easel, one child keeps painting on the other's paper.

One child teases by running away from the group during a neighborhood walk.

A child refuses to come indoors when told to.

Children are very noisy in the automobile.

A child kicks other children.

A child bangs on the piano with her fists.

Activity 10.6

Objective: To identify empathy and prosocial behavior in young children.

Young children are said to be highly egocentric. They are. And yet they are also capable of empathy and unselfish acts. Parents and teachers of young children see many instances of this behavior.

Interview a preschool teacher who works with children between the ages of two and five years. First offer a definition of empathy and prosocial behavior, distinguishing them from moral reasoning. Ask for anecdotes or vignettes that exemplify empathy.

Examples

The child who gives another a toy simply because the other child wants it very much

The child who protects another from an aggressor

The child who "translates" when an adult cannot understand a second child's speech

The child who shows sympathy toward a doll or another child during dramatic play

Answer Key

Overview and Key Concepts

1. greater mobility; improved communication skills; greatly expanded imagination (p. 343)

2. initiative versus guilt (p. 343)

3. egocentric escape; malevolent transformation (p. 343)

4. intrinsic motivation (p. 344)

5. gain mastery over problems (p. 345)

6. new behaviors; social roles (p. 346)

7. functional play; constructive play; dramatic play; games with rules (pp. 346–347)

8. unoccupied play; solitary play; onlooker play; parallel play; associative play; cooperative play (p. 351)

9. authoritarian parents (p. 354)

10. permissive parents; permissive-indulgent; permissive-indifferent (pp. 354–355)

11. authoritative parents (p. 355)

12. empathy; prosocial behavior; helpfulness (p. 362)

13. assertiveness; instrumental aggression; hostile aggression; blocking behaviors (pp. 365–366)

14. dominance hierarchy (p. 369)

15. gender; gender identity; gender preference; gender constancy; androgyny (pp. 370–371, 374)

Multiple-Choice Self-Test

1. Choice (c) is correct. Erikson's third stage, which lasts from about three to six years of age, deals with the issues of imagination and self-assertion. (p. 343)
   Choice (a) is Erikson's second stage, which covers late infancy; (b) is his fourth stage, which covers the school years; and (d) is his last stage, which covers individuals over fifty.

2. Choice (b) is correct. The notion that play is an emotional release is consistent with the psychoanalytic view. (p. 375)
   Choice (a) indicates that play is based on problem solving and thinking; (c) indicates that play is used to test new behaviors and social roles. Sullivan, choice (d), does not specifically deal with play.

3. Choice (c) is correct. Functional play involves simple repeated motions that focus on Kim's own body. (p. 347)
   Choice (a) involves the manipulation of objects to build or create something; (b) involves role-playing; and (d) is a form of social play void of true interaction.

4. Choice (c) is correct. Parallel play tends to be characteristic of young preschoolers' play and decreases throughout the preschool period. (p. 351)
   Choices (a) and (b) are considered more social/interactive forms of play and tend to increase across the preschool period.

5. Choice (a) is correct. Authoritarian parents tend not to seek input from their children and are power or punishment oriented. (p. 354)
   Choice (b) tends to involve the children in decision making but maintains the rights of final approval; (c) and (d) tend to be low in control, high in communication, and low in maturity and nurturance.

6. Choice (b) is correct. The authoritative style provides for input by the child and fosters the development of autonomy primarily through the use of reasoning in the parent-child interaction. (p. 355)
   Choice (a) tends to foster distrust, unhappiness, and lower levels of achievement; (c) and (d) tend to foster a lack of self-reliance and self-control.

7. Choice (c) is correct. During the school years, friendships seem to be based more on dispositional factors including shared thoughts and feelings. (p. 361)
   Choices (a) and (b) tend to be characteristics of preschool friendships; (d) does not tend to be a strong factor in determining specific friendships but does have an impact on who is likely to be in one's social network.

8. Choice (a) is correct. Early developments in attachment and other aspects of the parent-child relationship (including parenting style) in infancy set the stage for preschool empathy and prosocial behavior. (pp. 362–364)
   Studies have not found choices (b), (c), or (d) to be related to preschool levels of prosocial behavior and empathy.

9. Choice (d) is correct. Aggressive behavior is associated with children who are less attractive, choice (a); male, choice (b); and in frustrating situations, choice (c). (pp. 365–369)

10. Choice (d) is correct. Younger children are more likely to use physical forms of aggression (such as hitting and pushing), and older preschoolers tend to use more verbal forms (such as insults and demands). (p. 366)
    Choices (a) and (c) tend to decrease with age. Choice (b) has not been studied extensively.

11. Choice (a) is correct. Aggression has been associated with permissive parents, particularly if they are indifferent to the needs of the child with respect to limit setting and emotional support. (p. 368)
    Excessively permissive parents tend to produce children who are less assertive, choice (c), and empathetic, choice (d). Androgyny, choice (b), does not seem to appear until later.

12. Choice (d) is correct. Gender constancy, identity, and preference all contribute to a child's knowledge of society's expectations about sex roles, which is termed sex-role stereotypes. (p. 371)
    Choice (a) is the belief that a person's sex is biologically determined, permanent, and unchanging; (b) is the recognition of which sex a person is and will be; and (c) refers to attitudes about sex.

13. Choice (c) is correct. Gender identity (recognition of one's sex) appears to emerge first by about two years of age. (p. 371)
    Choices (a) and (d) develop around seven years of age, and (b) develops sometime after gender identity is established (around age three).

14. Choice (b) is correct. By definition, androgyny refers to a state in which sex roles are flexible and integrated. Thus choices (a), (c), and (d) are inaccurate. (p. 374)

CHAPTER 11
The Middle Years: Physical Development

Learning Objectives

1. Describe the physical growth characteristics during the middle years and compare these with the preschool years. Discuss the various kinds of normal and abnormal growth and their consequences.

2. Identify the general level of motor development during the middle years and the factors that encourage improvement.

3. Discuss the role of athletics in the development of physical and social skills, noting gender differences in athletics.

4. Describe the general state of health in schoolchildren compared to preschoolers and other groups. Indicate the frequencies and types of illnesses encountered and the variables that influence them.

5. Identify and discuss the characteristics of hyperactivity and attention deficit hyperactivity disorder, their causes, and methods of intervention.

Chapter Outline

I. TRENDS AND VARIATIONS IN HEIGHT AND WEIGHT

    A. Typical six-year-olds are about forty-six inches tall, but individual children vary two or three inches in each direction (Tanner, 1978).

    B. By age ten, children are typically about fifty-four inches tall, and by age twelve, they are about fifty-nine or sixty inches tall.

C. Similar patterns occur for weight. Six-year-olds average about forty-five pounds. By age ten, children average about sixty-six pounds, and by age twelve they may weigh more than one hundred pounds or as little as seventy pounds.

II. PROBLEMS RELATED TO GROWTH AND BODY BUILD

A. Height Variations Because of Puberty

1. Because girls enter puberty earlier than boys, they tend to be taller than boys toward the end of the elementary school years.

2. For boys, a spurt in height tends to follow the other physical changes of adolescence.

3. For girls, a spurt in height happens before the growth of breasts and pubic hair.

4. Inevitably, these changes create temporary embarrassments and emotional adjustments for boys and girls, and the timing of puberty may have a unique effect for each sex.

B. Excess Weight and Obesity

1. At least one American child in ten suffers from *obesity*, meaning that he weighs more than 130 percent of the normal weight for his height and bone size (Walker & Shaw, 1988).

2. If he accepts social stereotypes about weight, he must regard himself as unattractive, and, in the long run, obesity may cause physical problems as well as psychological ones.

3. Children who continue to be obese into adulthood run the risk of a variety of minor illnesses and a few major ones such as heart attacks and diabetes (LeBow, 1986).

4. Unfortunately, it is difficult for children to lose weight permanently and particularly to lose fat cells that have formed as part of the process of gaining weight.

5. In spite of such occasional weight problems, for most children growth is slow and predictable enough that they can afford to ignore it a lot of the time.

III. MOTOR DEVELOPMENT IN THE MIDDLE YEARS

    A. Refinements of Fundamental Skills

        1. During the elementary school years, all basic motor skills improve, but how much each does so depends on whether it relies primarily on strength and size or on coordination and timing.

        2. Skills relying on strength and size improve more or less in proportion to overall bodily growth: around 25 to 35 percent over the middle years.

        3. Much more dramatic improvement—100 percent or more—occurs in skills that depend mostly on coordination and timing.

        4. Such changes probably do not reflect increases in power or size so much as they reflect better use of existing muscles and better timing of reflexes.

        5. As with other physical developments, children vary widely around certain averages. Schoolteachers see these variations especially clearly when they plan group athletic activities.

    B. Influences of Early Athletics

        1. Children in the school years develop the ability to play games with rules. At the same time, children's improvements in coordination and timing make performance better in all kinds of sports; however, the lasting physical and psychological effects of early athletics must be assessed.

        2. Physical effects of early athletics

            a. The most obvious risks are sports-related injuries: bruises, sprains, broken bones, dislocated bones (DeStefano, 1982).

            b. Pessimists point to substantial numbers of injuries received by children. For example, individuals who play a lot of football in childhood may have vulnerable knees before they even begin competitive football in adolescence.

            c. Optimists point out that most children who are injured during sports have relatively minor injuries and the benefits of participation therefore considerably outweigh the risks.

3. Psychological effects of early athletics

   a. The immense popularity of early athletics suggests that psychological benefits are derived from participation. It is thought that sports can provide children with standards that promote the development of achievement motivation.

   b. During the school years, comparing oneself to standards becomes a concern that can be motivational; however, it can also undermine motivation, if a child begins feeling that the standards are arbitrary or too difficult to meet.

   c. Many sports promote teamwork and competition, and certainly learning to cooperate with others is a positive goal. However, when the child's team loses, noticeable stress is produced (Passer, 1982).

   d. Competitiveness seems to lead many children to drop out of sports altogether, not even pursuing recreational uses of sports.

4. Gender and early athletics

   a. In North American society, girls seem especially likely to drop out of athletic activity late in their middle years.

   b. This appears to be due to cultural rather than physiological reasons, since girls compare well with boys in strength, endurance, and motor skill.

   c. Girls' poor performance may result from social expectations about gender.

   d. Fortunately, sex-role standards may be shifting, so that both sexes can enjoy the benefits of physical activity to a greater degree.

IV. HEALTH AND ILLNESS IN MIDDLE CHILDHOOD
In the middle years, children are usually rather healthy: they rarely experience serious illnesses or accidents that have medical consequences.

A. Death Rates Among Schoolchildren

1. One sign of good health in schoolchildren is their very low *mortality*, or the proportion who die at a given age.

2. The decline in mortality has changed the relative importance of different causes of death. The decline of some infectious diseases has made accidents a more prominent cause of death among children.

3. Almost one-half of all childhood deaths in recent years have occurred because of motor vehicle accidents (National Safety Council, 1987).

4. School-age children do sometimes die from other kinds of accidents, such as drowning or fire.

B. Accidents

1. For most school-age children, physical safety poses a serious health problem (Pringle & Ramsey, 1982).

2. Children begin playing in larger territories during the school years. Their curiosity about the wider world has increased since their preschool years.

3. Exploration of larger areas presents an increase in environmental dangers.

4. Most of the time, accidents from environmental sources are relatively minor, but a significant number cause fractures, poisoning, or open wounds that require medical attention.

C. Illnesses

1. On the average, schoolchildren get sick only about one-half as often as preschoolers.

2. Most common childhood diseases are *acute illnesses*, which have a definite beginning, middle, and end.

3. Most acute illnesses, such as colds, flu, and measles, develop from *viruses*, which are complex protein molecules that come alive only when they infect a host tissue.

4. By the school years, about 5 to 10 percent of children develop *chronic illnesses*, or conditions that persist for many months without significant improvement.

5. The most common chronic conditions occur in the lungs and affect breathing (Pless & Satterwhite, 1975).

6. Some children develop *asthma* or persistent congestion in their lungs; others develop chronic coughs or allergies.

7. Social influences on illness can be identified. The seriousness and frequency of illnesses vary a lot according to children's social and economic circumstances.

a. Race and gender matter, too. Black families report fewer illnesses per child than do white families of similar income. All families, black and white, report more illnesses for girls than for boys of the same age (Butler et al., 1984).

b. These trends result partly from families' beliefs about illness, as well as from real differences. Parents, for example, may consider girls physically delicate and therefore keep them home for minor illnesses that they would not consider serious in boys.

D. Dental Health

1. Tooth decay presents the most widespread health problem of middle childhood in spite of recent advances in dental care.

2. Because schoolchildren are beginning to acquire their permanent teeth, their cavities can pose a significant health problem in the long run.

3. Newer techniques of coating teeth with fluorides and painting teeth with a clear acrylic plastic to prevent decay before it begins are very promising; however, access to these treatments is not evenly distributed across society.

E. Hyperactivity and Attention Deficit Hyperactivity Disorder

1. A number of school-age children seem extremely active and have considerable trouble concentrating on any one activity for long (American Psychiatric Association, 1987).

2. The problem is called *hyperactivity* or *attention deficit hyperactivity disorder* (ADHD) and involves behaviors that contribute to emotional problems and conflicts with teachers and other adults, as well as to poor relationships with peers.

3. Reactions to children with ADHD

a. Overly active children cause parents and teachers a lot of worry, and excessive activity is one of the most common reasons for referring children to psychiatrists and other health professionals (Rutter & Garmezy, 1983).

b. About 85 percent of highly active children are reported to be boys. Adults find dealing with highly active children to be very difficult.

4. Causes of hyperactivity and ADHD

a. What causes hyperactivity is not certain, but three possible explanations are that it is genetic, that it is neurological, and that it is related to the child's family and other social environments.

b. Some parents or teachers may accidentally foster hyperactivity in children by setting rules for behavior that are too precise or rigid (N. Lambert & Hartsough, 1984).

5. Helping children with ADHD and their families

   a. There are multiple treatments for ADHD. One of them is feeding highly active children a diet that is free of artificial substances such as food colorings, preservatives, and flavorings (Feingold, 1974). Research, however, has not supported a diet strategy.

   b. Classical psychotherapy also does not work well, probably because active children do not sit still long enough for all the talking involved.

   c. Play therapy, a technique in which child and therapist communicate through play, has shown promise.

   d. With overactive children of all ages, behavior modification often helps.

   e. Behavior modification involves the identification of specific behaviors that need changing as well as straightforward techniques for eliminating or reducing them.

   f. Many ADHD children improve significantly if teachers and parents provide them with a consistent, predictable environment.

   g. Amid much controversy, doctors have sometimes prescribed medication to treat this condition.

Overview and Key Concepts

During the middle years, growth increases more slowly and with much individual variation. Weight and size are important factors in social adjustment. Basic skills, now established, are being refined, and athletics become significant. On the whole, children are quite healthy, and time missed from school may be more a function of parents' perceptions, socioeconomic level, and ethnicity than of the seriousness of the illness. Tooth decay is the most frequent health problem. Hyperactivity and attention deficit hyperactivity disorder become apparent during the middle years.

Directions: Identify the following concepts introduced in Chapter 11.

1. Typical six-year-olds are about _____46_____ inches tall, but individual children vary ____2/3____ inches in each direction from this figure. By age ten, they are typically about ____54____ inches tall, and by age twelve, they are about ____59____ or ____60____ inches tall.

2. Six-year-olds average about _____45_____ pounds. By age ten, children average about _____66_____ pounds, and by age twelve, they are more than _____80_____ pounds. In fact a normal twelve-year-old can weigh more than _____100_____ pounds.

3. Toward the end of the elementary school years, girls tend to become significantly _____taller_____ of the same age. For boys, a spurt in height tends to follow the other _____changes_____ of adolescence.

4. On logical grounds, then, boys who mature _____early_____ and girls who mature _____late_____ should have the easiest time socially regarding their body builds and heights. Nevertheless, research suggests that the timing of puberty may have _____effects_____ for each sex.

5. At least one American child in ten suffers from _____obesity_____ , meaning that he weighs more than 130 percent of his normal weight. This may cause psychological problems and, in the long run, it causes _____physical_____ as well.

6. During the elementary school years, all basic motor skills improve, but how much each does so depends on whether it relies primarily on _____Strength / build_____ or on _____coordination / timing_____

7. The most obvious risks of early athletics are sports-related injuries: _____bruises_____ , _____sprains_____ , and _____breaks_____ .

8. The immense popularity of early athletics probably stems at least in part from the _____ attributed to participation; sports, it is hoped, develops _____ach. motiv._____ , _____teamwork_____ , and a tolerance for or even enjoyment of _____just playing_____ .

9. In North American society, girls seem especially likely to drop out of _____sports_____ late in their middle years. Apparently they do so for _____cultural_____ rather than _____physical_____ .

10. One sign of the good health of schoolchildren is their very low _____mortality rate_____ , or proportion who die at a given age. In recent years, only about three or four children in every _____1,000_____ between the ages of six and thirteen die, compared with twice this number among _____presch._____ and four times this number among _____adol_____ .

11. On the average, schoolchildren get sick only about _____1/2_____ as often as preschoolers. Most common childhood diseases are _____acute_____ ; however, about 5 to 10 percent of schoolchildren develop _____chronic_____ .

12. _____Tooth decay_____ presents the most widespread health problem of middle childhood in spite of recent advances in dental care involving coating teeth with _____flouride_____ and painting teeth with a clear _____ to create a barrier between the teeth and decay-causing bacteria.

13. A small number of school-age children seem extremely active and have trouble concentrating on any one activity for long. Their problem is called _ADHD_ or _____ .

14. Three possible explanations for ADHD exist. The first of these is _genetic_ . The second explanation is _neurological_ . The third explanation concerns children's _____ and _____ .

15. Research has shown that modifying diet and using classical psychotherapy are not particularly helpful in treating hyperactive children; however, _play therapy_ and _behav mod_ offer promising approaches.

Key Terms

Directions: Provide a definition for each of the following key terms. Check your answers against the Glossary or the text page number that follows each term.

Acute illness (p. 400) _____

_____

_____

AIDS (p. 401) _____

_____

_____

Asthma (p. 401) _____

_____

_____

Attention deficit hyperactivity disorder (ADHD) (p. 405) _____

_____

_____

Behavior modification (p. 407) _____

_____

_____

Chronic illness (p. 401) _____

_____

_____

HIV (p. 401) _____

_____

_____

Hyperactivity (p. 405) _____

_____

_____

Mortality (p. 398) _____

_____

_____

Obesity (p. 389) _____

_____

_____

Play therapy (p. 407) _____

_____

_____

Virus (p. 400) _____

_____

_____

Study Questions

1. What are the general trends in height and weight in the middle years? (p. 387)

   _____

   _____

   _____

   _____

2. How do boys' and girls' growth spurts vary in relationship to puberty? (p. 388)

   _____

   _____

   _____

   _____

3. Americans who work with children and are their advocates are also concerned about child-hood obesity. Why? (pp. 389–391)

   _____

   _____

_____

_____

4. Describe refinements in fundamental motor skills in the middle years. (pp. 392–394)

_____

_____

_____

_____

5. What are the physical effects of early athletics? What are the risks and benefits? (p. 395)

_____

_____

_____

_____

6. What are the psychological effects of early athletics? (pp. 395–397)

_____

_____

_____

_____

7. What correlations have been observed between gender and participation and achievement in early athletics? (p. 397)

_____

_____

_____

_____

8. What statistics can be cited regarding death rates among schoolchildren? (p. 398)

_____

_____

_____

_____

9. What are the characteristics and patterns of accidents among schoolchildren? (pp. 398–400)

_____

_____

_____

_____

10. Compare acute illness with chronic illness in school-age children. (pp. 400–402)

_____

_____

_____

_____

11. Why does dental health remain the most widespread health problem among schoolchildren? (pp. 403–404)

_____

_____

_____

_____

12. Describe some recent advances in the treatment of dental problems in children and suggest how these advances can be made available to low-income families. (pp. 404–405)

_____

_____

_____

_____

13. How would a profile of a child who has a true ADHD differ from that of a child who is overly active some of the time? (p. 405)

_____

_____

_____

_____

14. Describe general reactions of parents and teachers to children displaying hyperactivity. (pp. 405–406)

_____

_____

_____

_____

15. What three types of causes of ADHD are hypothesized by researchers? (p. 406)

_____

_____

_____

_____

16. What are two promising avenues of treatment for ADHD? (p. 407)

_____

_____

_____

_____

Multiple-Choice Self-Test

1. During the middle years, physical growth tends to
   a. fluctuate considerably in males as compared with females.
   b. increase sharply.
   c. remain remarkably stable.
   d. slow down as compared with growth in the preschool years.

2. From age five to ten, a child can expect to grow taller at the rate of about
   a. one inch per year.
   b. two inches per year.
   c. four inches per year.
   d. six inches per year.

3. Effects of body size on social relationships during the middle years seem to suggest
   a. boys may be embarrassed about size differences.
   b. small body size is viewed as a sign of immaturity.
   c. overweight children are treated coldly.
   d. all of the above.

4. Girls generally are
   a. shorter than boys throughout the school years.
   b. taller than boys throughout the preschool years and shorter during the school years.
   c. taller than boys toward the end of elementary school.
   d. taller than boys throughout the school years.

5. Billy should weigh seventy pounds given his height and bone size, but he actually weighs one hundred pounds. Billy would most likely be considered
   a. obese.
   b. physically advanced for his developmental level.
   c. slightly overweight.
   d. within the normal weight range.

6. As compared with obese adults, obese children have
   a. larger fat cells.
   b. more fat cells.
   c. larger and more fat cells.
   d. the same size and amount of fat cells.

7. Which of the following increases proportionally more during the middle years than during preschool years?
   a. coordination
   b. height
   c. strength
   d. weight

8. Which of the following is a physical benefit of athletics during the middle years?
   a. earlier development of coordination
   b. earlier development of strength
   c. more efficient heart functioning
   d. all of the above

9. Cooperation tends to increase in teams that
   a. participate in any organized sport.
   b. lose.
   c. win.
   d. are highly competitive.

10. Data from the middle years indicate that
    a. accidental deaths are at their highest level.
    b. chronic illness increases sharply.
    c. it is one of the healthiest times of life.
    d. mortality rates remain relatively stable.

11. Low-income children
    a. get sick more often than upper-income children.
    b. have a mortality rate five times greater than the rate for upper-income children during the school years.
    c. stay sick longer than upper-income children.
    d. all of the above.

12. Attention deficit hyperactivity disorder is most closely associated with
    a. dyslexia.
    b. hyperactivity.
    c. hyposensitivity.
    d. minimal brain damage.

Activities

Activity 11.1

> **Objective:** To become familiar with a few variations in normal growth and weight by plotting them on a graph.

Check with your local health department for height/weight charts. If they do not have any, ask for information about a source.

Plot the lines on the axes of the graphs shown below. Use — (a solid line) to indicate average height or weight. Use - - - (a dashed line) to indicate above-average but normal height or weight.

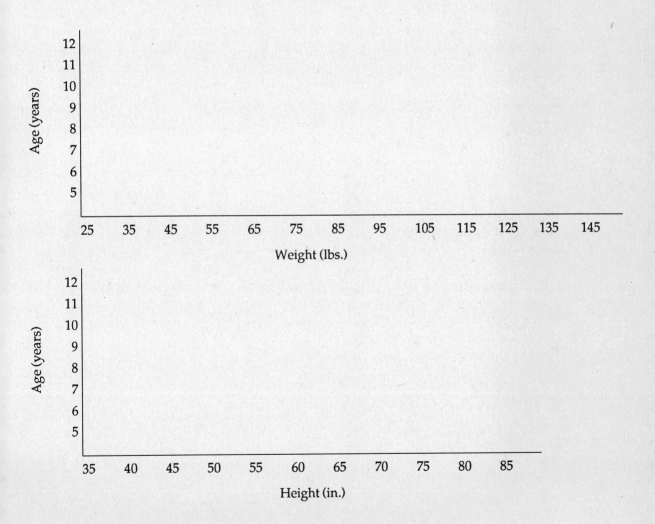

Activity 11.2

Objective: To become familiar with books that reassure children about their bodily proportions and appearance during puberty.

Check public libraries and local bookstores for titles and authors of books that you think would appeal to children who are just entering puberty or are slightly older and may need reassurance.

Borrow at least one book from the library and lend it to a youngster to read and critique. Several days later, ask the following questions.

Did you find this book interesting?

Would you recommend it to a friend?

Could it be helpful to someone about your age?

In what way?

Was it fairly easy to read?

Did you understand all of it?

Do you think the author understands kids?

What did you like about the book?

Was there anything about it that you didn't care for?

Write an annotated bibliography of at least four books that you would recommend to parents or teachers of preadolescent and early adolescent children.

1.

2.

3.

4.

Activity 11.3

Objective: To find out what dentists are doing to help minimize the incidence and severity of tooth decay.

Make an appointment to visit and interview a pediatric dentist or dental hygienist. (Your own dentist or the local chapter of the American Dental Society might be able to recommend someone.) Ask the following questions.

How often do you recommend routine check-ups?

What does a regular check-up include?

What percentage of the school-age children that you see are conscientious about taking care of their teeth?

What do you ask the children to do routinely for their teeth?

How do you try to motivate them?

Do you involve their parents?

If yes, in what way?

In your opinion, what is the status of dental health among the children in your practice?

In the general population of children in your state?

What three recommendations would you make to the general public in the interest of better dental health during childhood?

1.

2.

3.

Activity 11.4

Objective: To recognize that parents of different social and economic statuses perceive and deal differently with their children's illnesses.

Recognizing that a person or family does not necessarily fall into a stereotype that fits the categories listed below, what do you think the following parents would do if their nine-year-old seemed to have a cold?

White, upper income, both parents have jobs

White, lower income, both parents have jobs

Single-parent family, mother leaves home for work each day

Black parents, middle income, mother at home

Black, single-parent family, mother has low-paying job

Newly arrived immigrants from Southeast Asia

White, single-parent family, father leaves daily for office job

What used to be the policy with your family?

Why do you think this was the case?

Activity 11.5

Objective: To follow research developments and advances in the medical treatment for acquired immune deficiency syndrome (AIDS) and consider the implications of such research and treatment for schoolchildren.

Over a period of several weeks watch newspapers (many are available in your campus library) and television news stories for reports on AIDS research as well as reports that relate to children infected with HIV and those manifesting AIDS symptoms. Cite several of these stories and reports below and comment on the implications for treatment in schoolchildren.

Activity 11.6

> **Objective:** To formulate a balanced attitude toward children's participation in sports.

We have two parents with two different kinds of children. Each of them would like to know your thoughts about their youngster's participation in certain sports.

Parent #1: Gentle father of a shy, only slightly undersized ten-year-old. Would like his son to be more successful in sports, especially baseball, than Dad was. The boy is willing; he wants friends and agrees with his parents that the Little League might be enjoyable. He is also keenly interested in his snake collection and loves exploring for new specimens.

What else do you need to know about this child?

If you had the opportunity to observe and chat with him, what would you look for and ask?

What information would you give this parent that might be helpful?

Parent #2: Mother loves sports, as does her ten-year-old daughter, especially swimming. The child learned to swim before she was two years old. Both parents, though, would like her to be a well-rounded person with many interests and a circle of friends. They notice that she is becoming increasingly focused on swimming, and she receives much praise and attention from other children and adults. Mom especially wants to "do the right thing." What do you suggest?

Answer Key

Overview and Key Concepts

1. forty-six; two or three; fifty-four; fifty-nine or sixty (p. 387)

2. forty-five; sixty-six; eighty; one hundred (p. 387)

3. taller than boys; physical changes (p. 388)

4. early; later; unique effects (p. 389)

5. obesity; physical problems (p. 389)

6. strength and size; coordination and timing (p. 392)

7. bruises of various kinds and severity; damage to muscles (sprains); broken or dislocated bones (p. 395)

8. psychological benefits; achievement motivation; teamwork; competition (p. 395)

9. athletic activity; cultural reasons; physiological reasons (p. 397)

10. mortality; ten thousand; preschoolers; adolescents (p. 398)

11. one-half; acute illnesses; chronic illnesses (pp. 400–401)

12. tooth decay; fluorides; acrylic plastic (pp. 403–404)

13. hyperactivity; attention deficit hyperactivity disorder (ADHD) (p. 405)

14. genetic; neurological; family; other social environments (p. 406)

15. play therapy; behavior modification (p. 407)

Multiple-Choice Self-Test

1. Choice (d) is correct. From ages six to twelve, the middle years, physical growth slows down even more than during early childhood. (p. 386)
Although there are greater individual variations, they are not related to sex, choice (a). Choices (b) and (c) are incorrect because a definite decline in growth rate is observed.

2. Choice (b) is correct. The average increase in height during the middle years is just over two inches per year. (p. 387)

3. Choice (d) is correct. Studies suggest that children are concerned about physical stereotypes; thus choices (a), (b), and (c) are all true. (pp. 388–391)

4. Choice (c) is correct. Because girls tend to begin the growth spurt before boys, they tend to be taller toward the end of the elementary school years. (p. 388)
   During the early school years, boys and girls are approximately the same height, choice (a). Toward the end of the elementary school years, when the growth spurt begins, girls temporarily surpass boys in height, choices (b) and (d).

5. Choice (a) is correct. Billy weighs abut 145 percent of the normal weight for his height and bone size. Weights over 130 percent are considered obese; therefore, Billy would be considered obese. (p. 389)
   Excess weight is not viewed as a sign of being physically advanced, choice (b). Billy is considered neither slightly overweight, choice (c), nor within a normal range, choice (d).

6. Choice (b) is correct. Unlike individuals who become obese during adulthood, children gain weight by growing more fat cells. Once formed, these cells are difficult to eliminate. Dieting will make them smaller but not less numerous. (p. 391)
   The key difference is not the size of fat cells, choices (a) and (c). Obese children have more fat cells than obese adults, choice (d).

7. Choice (a) is correct. Coordination and timing improve by more than 100 percent during the middle years as compared with the preschool years. (p. 393)
   Size, choices (b) and (d), and strength, choice (c), show increases of roughly 30 percent during the middle years as compared with the preschool years.

8. Choice (d) is correct. The benefits of athletics during the middle years include better coordination, choice (a); strength, choice (b); and heart functioning, choice (c). (p. 395)

9. Choice (c) is correct. Children tend to practice teamwork better if they win. When a team loses, team members tend to look for someone to blame, be less sociable, and experience stress. (pp. 396–397)
   Simply participating in sports does not promote cooperation, choice (a). Losing, choice (b), tends to have negative effects. Losers actually become more competitive, choice (d).

10. Choice (c) is correct. During the middle years, children rarely experience serious illness, accidents that have medical consequences, or colds and minor viral illnesses. (p. 398)
    Accidental deaths are much more common in adolescence, choice (a). Chronic illness, choice (b), actually decreases. Mortality rates, choice (d), decrease during the school years.

11. Choice (c) is correct. Children from lower-income families stay at home an average of five days per illness. Children from high-income families stay at home an average of one and

one-half days per illness. (p. 402)
Frequency, choice (a), and seriousness, choice (b), of illness do not seem to differ between lower- and upper-class school-age children.

12. Choice (b) is correct. Children who are extremely active and have difficulty concentrating on one activity have been termed ADHD or hyperactive. (p. 405)
Choice (a) refers to reading problems. Choice (c) is actually a low level of sensitivity to stimulation. Choice (d) refers to a possible cause of various learning disabilities or other cognitive-based disorders.

CHAPTER 12
The Middle Years: Cognitive Development

Learning Objectives

1. Name the main characteristics of Jean Piaget's concrete operational stage and contrast it with the preoperational stage.

2. Describe Piaget's concept of conservation and discuss the results of training studies on conservation. Differentiate between the classic Piagetian view and other views.

3. Discuss the research on long-term memory and metamemory processes. Contrast the performance and strategies of children and adults.

4. Identify and describe the different styles of thinking found in children and indicate how these affect other behaviors.

5. Describe learning disabilities, their causes, and means of helping children with learning disabilities.

6. Describe the development of syntax in the middle years and trace the developmental progression in language at this point.

7. Discuss the concept and the measurement of intelligence. Describe how psychologists view intelligence and the characteristics of a good measuring device. Discuss the controversy surrounding test bias.

8. Describe Jean Piaget's, Lawrence Kohlberg's, and Carol Gilligan's views of moral development.

Chapter Outline

I. CONCRETE OPERATIONAL SKILLS

A. During the middle years, children become skilled at *concrete operations*, which are mental activities focused on real, tangible objects and events. Concrete operations involve three interrelated qualities.

1. *Decentration:* attending to more than one feature of a problem at a time

2. *Sensitivity to transformations:* noticing and remembering significant changes in objects

3. *Reversibility of thought:* solving problems by mentally going back to the beginning of them

B. In some ways, concrete operations amount to refinements of the skills that children form in the preoperational period. By about age seven, children have improved their classifying ability and are less confused about *class inclusion*.

C. Conservation in the Middle Years

1. Some cognitive skills make their first real appearance during the middle years. Probably best known is *conservation*, which is the belief that certain properties of an object remain the same in spite of changes in the object's appearance.

2. Several types of conservation can be identified in children's thinking; however, children do not acquire all of the types at the same time, a phenomenon that Piaget called *décallage*.

D. Conservation Training

1. Psychologists have had moderate success in training children to understand and perform the famous Piagetian conservation tasks.

2. Trained conservers often do not stay loyal to conservation in the way that "natural" conservers do, and they often revert to their pretraining performances.

E. Other Concrete Operational Skills
    Piaget described many other forms of knowledge that appear during the middle years.

1. *Seriation* refers to the ability to put items into a series or sequence.

2. *A sense of time:* School-age children understand the nature of time much better than younger children do, and they grasp new aspects of temporal relations.

3. *Spatial relations:* Although preschool children can find their way around their own home, only concrete operational children can reliably navigate in complex and unfamiliar spaces, such as a shopping mall.

F. Piaget's Influence on Education

   1. Style and sequencing of teaching

      a. Educators have borrowed Piaget's idea that true knowledge originates from the active manipulation of materials.

      b. A commitment to active learning leads teachers to add tangible activities to the curriculum.

   2. Curriculum content

      a. Piagetian theory has influenced curriculum content by providing specific ideas about what cognitive competencies to expect from children of particular ages and levels.

      b. Piaget's theory has helped many curriculum planners select and evaluate academic tasks such as the conservation tasks.

   3. Assessment of students' progress

      a. Throughout his work, Piaget emphasized the importance of children's actual thought processes and what these processes help children accomplish.

      b. Many educators feel that interviews offer a better way of assessing students' progress than traditional classroom testing, which tends to promote comparisons among students and to obscure what they have actually learned (Elkind, 1987).

II. INFORMATION-PROCESSING SKILLS

A. Memory Capacity

   1. *Short-term memory,* one component of the child's information-processing ability, is an ability in which schoolchildren perform about as well as adults do.

2. *Long-term memory* (LTM) is the feature of thinking that holds information for long periods. LTM develops slowly because it involves complex methods of storage and retrieval that create *recall memory*, which brings information back into awareness.

B. Influences on Memory Development

1. The effects of logical reasoning on memory: Reasoning skills affect children's memory. Because reasoning often improves with age, memories of specific experiences sometimes actually improve rather than deteriorate.

2. Familiarity and richness of knowledge: Common sense suggests that what a child already knows influences what she can learn and what she can remember. Familiarity matters not only during learning but during recall as well.

C. Metacognition and Learning Strategies

1. As children grow older, they pick up more knowledge about thinking itself, about how learning and memory operate, and about how a person can improve her cognitive performance. Psychologists sometimes call this sort of knowledge *metacognition*, meaning "knowledge about cognition" (Flavell & Wellman, 1977; Flavell, 1985).

2. Types of learning strategies: Some tasks are made easier by the use of broad learning strategies, such as focusing on small details, rehearsing or repeating information, and using organizing tactics or finding structure.

3. Mechanisms for acquiring learning strategies

a. *Trial and error:* Sometimes children happen upon effective strategies more or less by accident.

b. *Logical construction:* A lot of so-called random learning of strategies may really reflect the logical construction of knowledge.

c. *Observational learning:* Siblings often learn by observation, and in many situations children learn by watching others.

4. Helping children to acquire learning strategies

a. The processes described above can all be assisted by adults and often are.

b. Parents, for example, often demonstrate effective ways of remembering the time of an appointment.

c. When interventions are carried out systematically, they constitute various sorts of *strategy training* or coaching.

    d. Strategy training in its simplest form is called *blind training*.

    e. More complex forms are called *informed training* (Palincsar, 1986).

III. STYLES OF THINKING

  A. Convergent and Divergent Thinking

    1. By the middle years, children have begun to develop definite cognitive styles.

    2. One way in which schoolchildren differ is in their use of convergent and divergent thinking.

      a. *Convergent thinking* is focused, deductive reasoning that leads to a solution.

      b. *Divergent thinking* is the production of a variety of ideas.

  B. Field Dependence and Field Independence

    1. Individuals who are *field dependent* see things in relatively large, connected patterns.

    2. *Field-independent* individuals tend to see things more as discrete, independent parts.

  C. Reflectivity and Impulsivity

    1. *Reflectivity* and *impulsivity* refer to cognitive tempo, or speed of thinking.

    2. Reflective children take longer to answer a question; impulsive children respond almost instantly.

IV. LEARNING DISABILITIES
During the middle years, about 5 percent of children develop *learning disabilities*—disorders in basic cognitive processes that interfere with understanding or using language.

  A. Relationships Between Academic and Developmental Disabilities

    1. Academic learning disabilities often result from developmental disabilities.

    2. Symptoms of learning disabilities are complex.

  B. Causes of Learning Disabilities

    1. Some professionals believe learning disabilities may be caused by undetected minimal brain damage.

2. Brain function rather than brain anatomy may account for learning disabilities.

C. Helping Children with Learning Disabilities

1. School professionals have taken the primary role in helping learning-disabled youngsters.

2. Individual diagnosis and tutoring are often used.

V. LANGUAGE DEVELOPMENT IN THE MIDDLE YEARS

A. Word Meanings

1. Language continues to develop in the middle years. Vocabulary grows and children move through various levels or stages in giving meanings to words.

2. Children first define words by associating them with concrete actions; then they use them in sentences; and finally they categorize them.

B. Grammatical Usage

1. Careful observation of children reveals a number of grammatical limitations.

2. Children tend to confuse the subject with the observer; they confuse opinion and fact; and they confuse words that emphasize.

C. Bilingualism and Its Effects

1. Cognitive effects of bilingualism: Balanced bilingual children show more cognitive flexibility than do children who are fluent in one language only.

2. Social effects of bilingualism: If one of the child's languages is lower in prestige, she may be reluctant to use this language in public; there are other social effects as well.

D. Black English

1. In the United States, some black people use a dialect of English called *Black English*.

2. Black English differs from the middle-class dialect that linguists call *Standard English*.

VI. DEFINING AND MEASURING INTELLIGENCE

A. Concepts of Intelligence

1. Intelligence may be, and has been, construed as one specific ability and as multiple or general abilities.

2. Some consider intelligence to be a conglomeration of abilities; others believe the abilities are compounded together and are logically related.

3. Some psychologists believe intelligence develops mainly along quantitative lines. Piaget and others have envisioned qualitative changes in thinking as children progress from one cognitive level to the next.

B. Nature and Purposes of Standardized Tests

1. Tests of general ability or intelligence are one type of standardized test.

2. There are two major groups of standardized tests. *Achievement tests* measure skills or knowledge that individuals have already learned. *Aptitude tests* measure ability or try to estimate future performance in some realm of behavior.

C. Biases of Intelligence and General Ability Tests

1. In spite of trying to measure general qualities, tests of intelligence contain various biases.

2. The biggest problem with intelligence tests, however, comes from their cultural assumptions, which stem entirely from white, middle-class experiences.

D. Common Misinterpretations of Intelligence Tests

1. Intelligence tests have been criticized strongly, principally because of misinterpretation of the results.

2. Many people confuse test scores with true intelligence; they confuse intellectual differences with intelligence; and they assume the tests have more precision than they actually do.

3. Nevertheless, if used properly, tests of intelligence and ability can help parents and teachers understand children.

VII. MORAL DEVELOPMENT

Morality refers to a sense of ethics, or of right and wrong.

A. Piagetian Stages of Moral Thinking

1. In observing children at play, Piaget noted that younger children use *heteronomous morality*, or a "morality of constraint."

2. In later elementary years, they shift to *autonomous morality*, or a "morality of cooperation."

B. Kohlberg's Six Stages of Moral Judgment

1. Kohlberg proposed six stages of moral judgment.

2. The six stages form a progression from egocentric and concrete thinking toward higher levels of cognitive reasoning.

C. Evaluation of Cognitive Theories of Moral Development

1. Piaget's two-stage view is simplistic in some ways, and Kohlberg's theory has been cited for having many limitations.

   a. Kohlberg's stages have been found to accurately reflect levels that children express in their moral opinions; however, these opinions are relatively independent of actual moral development and performance.

   b. It has been shown that children reason at higher levels in familiar situations than in the famous "Kohlberg dilemmas."

   c. Kohlberg did not fully distinguish between social conventions and morality.

2. Studies that distinguish between convention and morality have produced a less stage-like picture of moral development (Nucci, 1978).

D. Gilligan's Ethics of Care in Social Context

1. Kohlberg's theory has been criticized for gender bias and for undervaluing ethical attitudes that may develop more fully in girls and women than in boys and men (Carol Gilligan, 1982, 1987).

2. According to Gilligan, boys and girls view moral problems differently. Girls see ethics as inseparable from the context in which judgments have to be made.

Overview and Key Concepts

During the middle years, children transit from Piaget's preoperational stage to the concrete operational stage, in which they become able to mentally reverse a process, to understand transformations, and to decenter their intellectual activity from only one focal point. Information-processing skills emerge, and long-term memory (LTM) is enhanced through improvements in logical reasoning. Children become aware of their own metacognitive patterns, and their individual learning styles become more fully developed. As language ability grows, children develop more sophisticated definitions of words. Those who are proficient in more than one language have certain cognitive advantages over monolingual children. Even so, the bilingual child must cope with the difference in the status of one language over another. Intelligence as a measure of the ability to utilize experience is tested in a number of ways. The scores from such tests are often confused with actual or true intelligence. Schoolchildren's sense of right and wrong is becoming less dependent on others' approval and more a function of personal reasoning. Kohlberg's six-stage model of moral judgment is built on Piaget's two-stage model and, though offering further insight into children's moral reasoning, has been criticized on a number of points. Carol Gilligan has criticized it for displaying gender bias against girls and women.

Directions: Identify the following concepts introduced in Chapter 12.

1. The stage of concrete operations has three interrelated qualities: _decentration_ , _sens. to transf._ , and _reversibility_ .

2. Schoolchildren are now less confused by _class inclusion_ , or comparing groups of objects with more inclusive groups. _conserv._ , a belief that certain properties of objects remain constant, makes its first real appearance during the middle years.

3. The fact that not all forms of conservation are acquired at the same time was referred to as _decalage_ by Piaget, who was also interested in other concrete operational skills such as _seriation_ , _time_ , and _spatial rel._ .

4. Piaget has exerted a great influence on the field of _educ._ , and particularly in the areas of _teaching style_ , _curriculum_ , and _assessing_ .

5. A different way of looking at children's cognition is through _info. proc._ models in which emphasis is placed on at least four kinds of memory processes: _STM_ memory, _recogn._ memory, _LTM_ memory, and _recall_ memory.

6. Two major influences on memory development are improvement in _logical reas._ and an increase in _familiarity_ and _richness_ .

7. Knowledge about cognition or about thinking itself is called ___Meta cogn___ , an awareness of which produces new learning strategies in the middle years. Such strategies include ___att. to detail___ , ___rehearsal___ , and ___organizing tactics___

8. Mechanisms for acquiring learning strategies include ___stg. training___ , ___blind___ ___log. constr.___ , and ___informed___ ___observ.___ ___tr + err___

9. When interventions are carried out to teach learning strategies, they constitute various sorts of _____ , the simplest form of which might be called _____ and the more complex forms of which might be called _____ .

10. By the middle years, children have begun to develop definite _____ and to perhaps show a preference for _____ or _____ in problem solving.

11. _____ children tend to see things in relatively large, connected patterns; in contrast, _____ children tend to see things more in terms of discrete, independent parts.

12. Still another style of thinking varies along the dimension of _____ , in which a person takes more time to respond to a problem, and the related dimension of _____ , in which a person responds almost instantly and often makes more errors as a result.

13. _____ are disorders in basic cognitive processes that interfere with understanding or using language. Educators often distinguish between _____ and _____ .

14. Some professionals have suggested that many learning disabilities may reflect underlying _____ . A more helpful explanation focuses on _____ rather than on brain anatomy. Helping learning-disabled children requires individual diagnosis. Several researchers have concluded, by studying a phenomenon called _____ , that many disabilities are related to problems with cognitive processing.

15. Among the cognitive effects of bilingualism are greater _____ , skill in detecting multiple meanings of words, and greater degrees of _____ , the knowledge that language can be an object of thought.

16. In the United States, some black people use a dialect or version of English called _____ , which differs from the middle-class dialect that linguists call _____ .

17. _____ refers to adaptability. Tests of general ability or of intelligence are one type of _____ . _____ measure ability or try to estimate future performance in some realm of behavior. _____ measure skills or knowledge that individuals have already learned.

18. _____ refers to a sense of ethics, or of right and wrong. _____ , _____ , and _____ have all proposed stage theories of moral development.

19. Piaget distinguished between _____ in younger children and _____ in children in the later elementary school years.

20. Kohlberg's theory, according to some psychologists, does not fully distinguish between _____ and morality. One especially important criticism of Kohlberg's theory has to do with possible _____ . Gilligan and her associates believe that Kohlberg undervalues _____ that develop more fully in girls and women than in boys and men.

Key Terms

Directions: Provide a definition for each of the following key terms. Check your answers against the Glossary or the text page number that follows each term.

Academic learning disability (p. 433) _____

_____

_____

Achievement test (p. 442) _____

_____

_____

Aptitude test (p. 442) _____

_____

_____

Autonomous morality (p. 445) _____

_____

_____

Bilingual (p. 437) _____

_____

_____

Black English (p. 439) _____

_____

_____

Blind training (p. 426) _____

_____

_____

Class inclusion (p. 413) _____

_____

_____

Cognitive flexibility (p. 437) _____

_____

_____

Cognitive style (p. 428) _____

_____

_____

Concrete operation (p. 412) _____

_____

_____

Conservation (p. 414) _____

_____

_____

Convergent thinking (p. 428) _____

_____

_____

Décallage (p. 415) _____

_____

_____

Decentration (p. 413) _____

_____

_____

Developmental learning disability (p. 433) _____

_____

_____

Divergent thinking (p. 429) _____

_____

_____

Ethics of care (p. 448) _____

_____

_____

Field dependence (p. 430) _____

_____

_____

Field independence (p. 430) _____

_____

_____

Heteronomous morality (p. 445) _____

_____

_____

Impulsivity (p. 431) _____

_____

_____

Informed training (p. 426) _____

_____

_____

Intelligence (p. 440) _____

_____

_____

Learning disability (p. 432) _____

_____

_____

Learning strategy (p. 424) _____

_____

_____

Logical construction (p. 426) _____

_____

_____

Metacognition (p. 424) _____

_____

_____

Metalinguistic awareness (p. 438) _____

_____

_____

Morality (p. 444) _____

_____

_____

Perceptual masking (p. 434) _____

_____

_____

Recall memory (p. 421) _____

_____

_____

Recognition memory (p. 420) _____

_____

_____

Reflectivity (p. 431) _____

_____

_____

Reversibility (p. 413) _____

_____

_____

Sensitivity to transformation (p. 413) _____

_____

_____

Seriation (p. 417) _____

_____

_____

Social convention (p. 447) _____

_____

_____

Standard English (p. 439) _____

_____

_____

Standardized test (p. 441) _____

_____

_____

Strategy training (p. 426) _____

_____

_____

Study Questions

1. Define three interrelated qualities that characterize concrete operational thought. (pp. 412–413)

   _____

   _____

   _____

   _____

2. Describe three types of conservation and Piaget's notion of *décallage*. (pp. 414–415)

   _____

   _____

   _____

   _____

3. What would you say to teachers who want to train their first-graders to conserve? (pp. 416–417)

_____

_____

_____

_____

4. Explain two or three other concrete operational skills that schoolchildren acquire in addition to conservation. (pp. 417–418)

_____

_____

_____

_____

5. How has Piaget influenced education? (pp. 418–420)

_____

_____

_____

_____

6. Describe four categories of memory that are emphasized in information-processing theory. (pp. 420–421)

_____

_____

_____

_____

7. One of the strongest influences on memory is logical reasoning. It is also easier for a child to think about what is known and what has been experienced. How do these factors interact? (pp. 421–423)

_____

_____

_____

_____

8. Metacognition, or thinking about one's own thinking, is an ability that emerges during the middle years. The child then appears to adopt strategies that increase the effectiveness of the learning process. Describe three of these strategies and the actual mechanisms for acquiring them. (pp. 424–426)

_____

_____

_____

_____

9. What formal methods have been developed to help children acquire learning strategies? (pp. 426–428)

_____

_____

_____

_____

10. Define and compare *convergent* thinking with *divergent* thinking. (pp. 428–430)

_____

_____

_____

_____

11. Field dependence and field independence characterize not only learning styles but social relationships as well. Define each of these styles and give examples from the cognitive and social domains. (pp. 430–431)

_____

_____

_____

_____

12. What is meant by *reflectivity* and *impulsivity*? (p. 431)

_____

_____

_____

_____

13. Define *learning disability* and distinguish between developmental learning disabilities and academic learning disabilities. (pp. 432–433)

_____

_____

_____

_____

14. What are possible causes of learning disabilities as well as some ways of helping children with learning disabilities. (pp. 433–435)

_____

_____

_____

_____

15. Describe some predictable levels that schoolchildren go through in giving meanings to words, as well as some grammatical limitations that characterize their use of language. (pp. 436–437)

_____

_____

_____

_____

16. What are the cognitive advantages, as well as the social effects, of bilingualism? (pp. 437–439)

_____

_____

_____

_____

17. Describe at least two concepts of intelligence and comment on the nature and purposes of standardized tests. (pp. 440–442)

_____

_____

_____

_____

18. What biases may exist in tests of ability and intelligence and what are three common sources of misinterpretation of test scores? (pp. 442–444)

_____

_____

_____

_____

19. Describe Piaget's and Kohlberg's theories of moral development. (pp. 444–446)

_____

_____

_____

_____

20. What criticisms, including Gilligan's charge of gender bias, have been made of Kohlberg's theory? (pp. 446–450)

_____

_____

_____

_____

Multiple-Choice Self-Test

1. Roger has just attained the concrete operational stage. His new abilities should include
   a. abstract reasoning.
   b. functional relationships.
   c. identity permanence.
   d. reversibility.

2. The term used by Piaget to describe the fact that not all aspects of a particular concept develop at the same time is
   a. accommodation.
   b. convergence.
   c. décallage.
   d. seriation.

3. Studies that attempt to teach conservation have generally
   a. been successful.
   b. been successful and look exactly like the naturally occurring concept.
   c. been successful although the ability is not identical to one not taught.
   d. been successful only if the child is beyond age twelve.

4. In general, recall memory
   a. is a short-term memory process.
   b. is more difficult to access than recognition memory.
   c. occurs only in adults and adolescents.
   d. stores information temporally.

5. In which of the learning strategies do preschoolers differ from school-age children?
   a. attending to detail
   b. organizing information
   c. rehearsal
   d. all of the above

6. Convergent thinking is the thinking strategy that
   a. involves trial and error response styles.
   b. gathers information from all different areas.
   c. leads to a set of possible solutions to a problem.
   d. leads to one particular solution to a problem.

7. Mothers who tend to teach their children by asking questions and praising appropriate responses tend to be
   a. convergent thinkers.
   b. impulsive thinkers.
   c. field independent.
   d. reflective thinkers.

8. The hypothesis that dyslexia is caused by minimal brain damage is
   a. based on behavioral comparisons of known brain-damaged people.
   b. well documented from neurological tests.
   c. well supported by physiological and behavioral research.
   d. all of the above.

9. When asked what the word "bird" means, Robert said, "You feed the bird." Robert's definition reflects the use of
   a. action.
   b. appropriate sentences.
   c. descriptive categories.
   d. dictionary classifications.

10. In comparison with children who are fluent in one language only, children who learn two languages equally well during childhood tend to
    a. be more aware of language.
    b. be more cognitively flexible.
    c. lack confidence about linguistic skills if there is a social bias against the primary language.
    d. all of the above.

11. Most intelligence tests acknowledge the presence of
    a. cognitive and social factors.
    b. learning and performance factors.
    c. motor and cognitive factors.
    (d.) specific and general factors.

12. An aptitude test measures
    (a.) expected future performance.
    b. intelligence.
    c. learned skills or knowledge.
    d. motor skills.

13. Autonomous morality is characterized by
    a. a lack of rules and lack of understanding of rules.
    b. consideration of intentions when evaluating actions.
    c. highly abstract moral principles.
    d. rigid interpretation of rules.

14. Kohlberg's fourth stage of moral development emphasizes
    a. individual rights.
    b. interpersonal conformity.
    c. law and order.
    d. rewards.

Activities

Activity 12.1

Objective: To consider practical applications of Piaget's theory of cognitive development when teaching arithmetic to first- and second-graders.

According to Piaget, concrete operations emerge at about seven years of age, when children are in the first and second grades. Thus a class of first-graders would include children who are not conservers and do not understand the concept of class inclusion. Even in the second grade there are children who are developing quite normally, yet most of their thinking is preoperational. Their biological maturation may be taking a bit longer, or they have not had enough experience acting on objects in their world. They have not examined and played long enough with the pennies and pebbles and clutter they discover. Yet first- and second-grade arithmetic is an expression of number conservation and class inclusion. We find that children sometimes obligingly memorize number combinations for addition and subtraction without really understanding what they are about.

For example:

$$\begin{array}{r} 5 \text{ girls} \\ +\,3 \text{ boys} \\ \hline 8 \text{ children} \end{array} \qquad \begin{array}{r} 8 \text{ children} \\ -\,5 \text{ girls} \\ \hline 3 \text{ boys} \end{array}$$

The children who "get it" understand, without realizing, the concept of class inclusion.

First- and second-grade teachers are required to teach arithmetic. They must teach children to put the right numbers in the right places. But because they are teachers, they also want the children to understand the underlying concepts.

You are invited by the first- and second-grade teachers in your district to help them become more effective in teaching mathematics. What would you recommend for:

In-service professional growth?

Prearithmetic curriculum?

Materials to assist the children when they are learning math computations?

How could teachers informally check for basic understandings?

What kinds of games and activities would you recommend for those times of the school day when children may choose what to do?

Other recommendations?

Activity 12.2

Objective: To recognize the usefulness of combining several thinking styles in an effort to understand one topic.

The social studies unit in a sixth-grade class will be on the Soviet Union. For the next three months, the students will be required to become knowledgeable about its history, geography, and government. They will also examine the differences in ethnic/cultural backgrounds of the peoples who reside there, as well as current economic, political, and social policies.

What aspects of this topic are best learned by students who prefer convergent thinking styles?

Divergent thinking styles?

Students who enjoy formulating metaphors?

What aspects are best understood and explained by students who are field dependent?

Field independent?

Reflective?

Impulsive?

Do you find that some thinking styles allow for creativity more than others do? If so, identify them.

Activity 12.3

> **Objective:** To gain insight into how it feels to have a learning disability.

Each of us, at some time in our lives, has been unable to become proficient at a skill that seemed important at that time. It may still feel important. Some folks could never learn to play tennis, to sing, to draw, or to sew. Often there was a subject at school that was never really mastered.

Recall your own past or consider the present.

What skill were you unable to master?

How long did you keep trying?

Are you still trying?

What were your feelings as you watched others, apparently without effort, breeze through?

Did you ever become passably proficient or better than that?

Did you give up?

If so, after how long?

At the time, did you discuss this with anyone?

Did you get any psychological support?

Did you get any practical or "technical" help?

What kind?

Is the subject still important to you?

Why?

Activity 12.4

Objective: To clarify arguments for and against using Black English instead of standard English with populations of black children.

Prepare a hypothetical debate. Resolved: In the interests of validating a language and culture that has existed as long as the United States, Black English is to be the language of instruction with children who are growing up in Black English-speaking homes.

Notes for Arguments	Check one	
	Pro	Con
Places where language is used		
Relationships with family and friends		
Complexity of language		
Regularity of syntax		
Social mobility		
Effectiveness of communication		
Aesthetic qualities of language		
Effective communication at home and in neighborhood		
Outside of black communities		
Careers		

Notes for Arguments	Check one	
	Pro	Con
Economic mobility		
Relationships with white population		
Parents' aspirations for their children		
Other arguments		

Debates often polarize. Can you think of a resolution that acknowledges social realities and respects other cultures?

Activity 12.5

Objective: To examine the dimensions of intelligence.

In the text, the authors define intelligence as adaptability or a general ability to learn from experience.

Are these the same?

How would they apply in the case of a fifth-grader from a large East Coast city who is spending the summer in northern Alaska with a community of Eskimos?

Howard Gardner proposes a variety of different kinds of intelligence. Briefly describe someone you know of with the following kinds of intelligence.

Language skill

Musical skill

Logical skill

Spatial skill

Kinesthetic skill

Interpersonal and intrapersonal skills

What kinds of intelligence do you have?

Activity 12.6

> **Objective:** To note the differing levels of moral behavior that may be observed in the same person.

Kohlberg's model of six stages of moral judgment is intriguing, but most of us have problems with it. For example, even adults who are considered to be ethical persons do not consistently behave at the same level of morality. We are at Stage 1 when the thought of a stiff fine causes us to avoid parking illegally. Give an example that would fit each of the remaining five stages and might be observed in the same person of any age.

Stage 2: Ethics of market exchange

Stage 3: Ethics of peer opinion

Stage 4: Ethics of law and order

Stage 5: Ethics of social contract

Stage 6: Ethics of universal principles

Does this mean that our moral standards vary according to convenience? Do we make distinctions? Are there lines we do not cross?

Answer Key

Overview and Key Concepts

1. decentration; sensitivity to transformations; reversibility (p. 413)

2. class inclusion; conservation (pp. 413–414)

3. *décallage;* seriation; sense of time; spatial relations (pp. 415–418)

4. education; style; sequencing of teaching; curriculum content (pp. 418–419)

5. information-processing; short-term; recognition; long-term; recall (pp. 420–421)

6. logical reasoning; familiarity; richness of knowledge (pp. 421–422)

7. metacognition; attention to detail; rehearsal; organizing tactics (p. 424)

8. trial and error; logical construction; observational learning (pp. 425–426)

9. strategy training; blind training; informed training (p. 426)

10. cognitive styles; convergent thinking; divergent thinking (pp. 428–429)

11. field-dependent; field-independent (p. 430)

12. reflectivity; impulsivity (p. 431)

13. learning disabilities; developmental learning disabilities; academic learning disabilities (pp. 432–433)

14. minimal brain damage; brain functions; perceptual masking (pp. 433–434)

15. cognitive flexibility; metalinguistic awareness (pp. 437–438)

16. Black English; Standard English (p. 439)

17. intelligence; standardized test; aptitude tests; achievement tests (pp. 441–442)

18. morality; Piaget; Kohlberg; Gilligan (p. 444)

19. heteronomous morality; autonomous morality (p. 445)

20. social conventions; gender bias; ethical attitudes (pp. 447–448)

Multiple-Choice Self-Test

1. Choice (d) is correct. During the middle years, a child develops the ability to mentally undo something by going back to the beginning. This ability is termed *reversibility*. (p. 413) Choice (a) is a formal operational ability that does not develop until early adolescence. Choices (b) and (c) are preoperational abilities that develop earlier, in the early childhood years.

2. Choice (c) is correct. *Décallage*, which means "gap," occurs when children fail to grasp the general principles underlying a concept and therefore only selectively apply the concept. (p. 415) Choice (a) is a term used to describe the modification of current schemes to deal with new information; (b) is a term used to describe a strategy whereby one centers in on or narrows one's choices to arrive at a solution; and (d) refers to an ability to order items on a certain dimension.

3. Choice (c) is correct. Although it does appear that conservation can be taught, studies have shown that trained conservers are more likely to be swayed from their beliefs than are natural conservers. (p. 417) Thus choices (a), (b), and (d) are inaccurate statements.

4. Choice (b) is correct. Recall memory is more difficult to access than recognition memory because relatively few cues are used to bring information back into awareness. (p. 421) Choice (a): Recall is a long-term memory process. Choice (c): Recall has been observed in school-age children and younger. Choice (d): Recall represents a use of information rather than a store of information.

5. Choice (d) is correct. Preschoolers, in comparison with older children, attend less to detail, choice (a); use less organization, choice (b); and use less rehearsal, choice (c). (p. 424)

6. Choice (d) is correct. Convergent thinking uses focused, deductive reasoning that leads to a particular solution, as in solving a math problem or putting together a model airplane. (p. 428) Convergent thinking could, but generally does not, involve trial and error approaches, choice (a). Divergent thinking uses choices (b) and (c).

7. Choice (c) is correct. Field-independent individuals tend to be rather autonomous in responding to others' opinions. This kind of behavior is fostered by inductive learning techniques such as questioning. (p. 431) Divergent rather than convergent thinking, choice (a), tends to be fostered by questioning styles. There do not seem to be data for choice (b) or (d) with respect to parental behaviors.

8. Choice (a) is correct. The minimal brain damage hypothesis for dyslexia is primarily based on the fact that the symptoms resemble what happens to individuals who suffer injuries in certain parts of their brains. (p. 433)

Minimal brain damage is difficult to detect neurologically; thus choices (b) and (c) are inaccurate.

9. Choice (a) is correct. Robert's response represents a level 1 response for word meaning, which involves describing an action one makes toward the object. (p. 436)
Choice (b) would involve level 2—for example, "The bird flies in the sky." Choice (d) would involve level 3—for example, "A bird has two wings, a beak, and flies." Choice (c) is not a level of word meaning.

10. Choice (d) is correct. Cognitive effects of bilingualism include greater metalinguistic awareness, choice (a), and greater cognitive flexibility, choice (b). If there is a bias against the primary language, children may lack confidence in their linguistic ability, choice (c). (pp. 437–439)

11. Choice (d) is correct. Many intelligence tests are based on the model of intelligence that hypothesizes general and specific abilities. (p. 440)
Although choices (a), (b), and (c) may be factors involved in intelligence, they have not been identified as central factors in the definition of intelligence.

12. Choice (a) is correct. Aptitude tests are used to predict future performance. (p. 442)
An intelligence test, choice (b), is a form of aptitude test, but not all aptitude tests are intelligence tests. Choice (c) would be measured by an achievement test, and (d) would most likely be assessed with an ability test.

13. Choice (b) is correct. Autonomous morality is a morality of cooperation in which both intentions and consequences are considered when a moral judgment is made. (p. 445)
Choice (a) would reflect a premoral level of understanding; (c) would correspond more to Kohlberg's principled level; and (d) would correspond to heteronomous morality.

14. Choice (c) is correct. Kohlberg's fourth stage involves conformity to the social system, including its laws and regulations. (p. 446)
Choice (a) would be stage 5 reasoning; (b) would be stage 3; and (d) would be stage 2.

CHAPTER 13
The Middle Years: Psychosocial Development

Learning Objectives

1. Identify and describe the basic psychosocial challenges of the middle years.

2. Describe how the child develops a sense of self during middle childhood and contrast this sense of self with preschool conceptions.

3. Describe Sigmund Freud's and Erik Erikson's views of middle childhood. Indicate the basic issues of development according to these two theories and show how they differ.

4. Describe the development of achievement motivation during middle childhood. Distinguish between the two forms of achievement motivation and indicate how they develop.

5. Compare and contrast Jean Piaget's and Harry Stack Sullivan's views of the functions of peers.

6. Describe the functioning of peers with respect to age, gender, and race. Indicate the characteristics of a popular and an unpopular child.

7. Examine the role of the child within the family and the changing relationships occurring during middle childhood. Indicate the impact of special circumstances of modern families, including divorce and working mothers.

8. Describe the roles school and teachers play during middle childhood.

9. Describe the unique situation of children with handicaps, particularly in regard to achievement and the definition of the self.

Chapter Outline

I. PSYCHOSOCIAL CHALLENGES OF THE MIDDLE YEARS

    A. The Challenge of Knowing Who You Are

    B. The Challenge to Achieve

    C. The Challenge of Peers

    D. The Challenge of Family Relationships

    E. The Challenge of School

    F. The Challenge of Having a Handicap

II. THE SENSE OF SELF

    A. The Development of Self in Childhood

        1. Self-constancy

            a. Self-constancy, the belief that identity remains permanently fixed, does not become firm until the early school years.

            b. At this time a child becomes convinced that he will remain the same person indefinitely, that he will remain human, and that he will keep his gender forever.

        2. The first beliefs in psychological traits

            a. Around age eight, some children begin to form a more stable sense of self by including psychological traits as part of their self-descriptions.

            b. By the end of the middle years, children begin to integrate contradictory traits as they undergo changes that make a more stable self possible.

    B. Processes in Constructing a Self

        1. Middle-years children construct their identities or self theories by distinguishing their thoughts and feelings from those expressed by others.

        2. A child's emerging sense of self during the middle years is part of a broader process of personality development.

III. THE AGE OF INDUSTRY AND ACHIEVEMENT

   A. Latency and the Crisis of Industry

   1. Freud emphasized the preschooler's disappointment regarding the parent of the opposite sex and the consequent *repression* that occurs from about the time that most children begin school until adolescence. Freud called this a time of *latency*, during which competencies are developed as a *defense*.

   2. Erikson called this process of repression and *identification* the crisis of *industry versus inferiority*, meaning that children of this age concern themselves with *industriousness*.

   B. Achievement Motivation

   1. *Achievement motivation* refers to behavior that enhances competence or judgments of competence (Beck, 1978).

   2. Differences in achievement motivation

      a. Children may be motivated to achieve by a *learning orientation* and by a *performance orientation*.

      b. Some children display an adaptive mastery-oriented pattern of achievement behavior that is characterized by challenge seeking and persistence.

   3. Achievement motivation in the middle years

      a. During the middle years, children become more performance oriented than they were at earlier ages.

      b. Children begin believing that whether they have an ability depends partially on whether others think they do. Generally, achieving successfully becomes more complicated in the middle years.

IV. PEER RELATIONSHIPS

   A. What Theorists Say About Peer Relationships

   1. Piaget: Piaget argued that peers help children overcome their egocentrism.

   2. Sullivan: The most well-developed theory about peers is that of Harry Stack Sullivan (1953). Sullivan believed that peers, in creating a world for children outside their families, filled what he called emotional *warps* created by families.

3. Support for theories about peer relationships

a. Research supports Piaget's and Sullivan's ideas in broad outline but not in certain specifics.

b. Research also supports Sullivan's claim that playmates and peers matter a lot to children.

B. Functions of Peers

1. Peers probably serve a variety of purposes, including some that duplicate the functions of parents.

2. There are also several unique features to peer relationships.

C. Influences on Peer Group Membership

1. Age: Children do mostly play with others of approximately their own age; however, groups of mixed ages have certain special qualities.

2. Gender: Elementary school children tend to favor friends of the same sex. *Sociometric questionnaires* showed that girls' long-term friendships tended more toward exclusive intimacy than did boys' long-term friendships.

3. Race and ethnic background: Preferences based on race and ethnicity can play a significant role in friendship choices and social activity in the middle years. These preferences can also be a mask for *prejudice*.

D. Popularity, Social Acceptance, and Rejection

1. The popular child: Well-liked children are good at initiating and maintaining social interactions and at understanding social situations (Asher, Renshaw, & Hymel, 1982).

2. The unpopular child: Peers describe unpopular children as unpleasant, disruptive, selfish, and aggressive (Coie et al., 1982).

3. Friends: During the early middle years, children base friendships on shared interests and activities; however, by sixth grade they tend to place more emphasis on psychological qualities.

E. Conformity to Peers

1. Because peer groups involve social equals, they give children unique opportunities to develop their own beliefs without having parents or older siblings dominate or dismiss them.

2. Pressures to conform sometimes lead children to violate personal values or needs.

V. FAMILY RELATIONSHIPS

A. How Parents Influence Children

1. Even though children probably do influence their parents to some extent, most of the influence goes the other way, even in the middle years.

2. Parents influence children in at least six ways.

a. Modeling behavior

b. Giving rewards and punishments

c. Direct instruction

d. Stating rules

e. Reasoning

f. Providing materials and settings

B. The Separate Perspectives of Parent and Child

1. In getting along together, children and parents approach their relationship in different ways.

2. Parents already know how social relationships work; children are trying to discover this for the first time. This gap makes misunderstandings almost inevitable (H. Sullivan, 1953).

C. The Quality of Parent-Child Relationships in the Middle Years

1. As middle-years children gradually learn more about their parents' attitudes and motivations, they become more able to control their behavior.

2. Nevertheless, parents do continue to monitor children's efforts to take care of themselves—but in more indirect ways (Maccoby, 1984).

3. By this period, parents and children have a shared history of experiences that make family relations increasingly unique and meaningful.

D. The Changing Nature of Modern Families

1. Until recently, popular stereotypes of so-called typical families existed.

2. However, working mothers, divorce, and reconstituted families have changed stereotypes and raised concerns about children's development.

E. Divorce and Its Effects on Children

1. Increased economic pressures created by divorce affect the children involved.

2. Many psychological pressures also affect divorced parents and their children.

3. Differing effects on boys and girls: Boys often become more aggressive and willful. Girls' responses are less obvious than boys', perhaps because girls are *internalizing*, or holding stress inside.

4. Because the parent with custody may find herself or himself dealing with new economic responsibilities, that parent's relationship to her or his children may be affected and even deteriorate after a divorce. Sometimes these problems are alleviated by *joint custody* of children.

5. Most parents who get divorced remarry within a few years, creating what some call *reconstituted* or *blended families*.

F. The Effects of Work on Families

1. Research suggests that maternal employment as such usually does children no developmental harm.

2. Generally, in fact, maternal employment exerts positive influences on children's development.

3. Society regards paternal unemployment as a serious problem. Unemployed fathers often report being anxious and depressed. Family violence is associated with fathers' being unemployed.

G. Other Sources of Social Support for Schoolchildren

1. Beyond parents and peers, there seems to exist a great network of social support in the lives of most children—especially grandparents.

2. In general, as children move through the middle years, sources of support become more numerous.

VI. SCHOOL INFLUENCES

A. School Culture

1. Each school has its own culture, including values, beliefs, traditions, and customs.

2. The greater the fit between the school's culture and the values of the child's family, the more likely is the school's impact to be positive.

B. The Hidden Curriculum

1. The *explicit curriculum* helps children acquire the academic knowledge and skills thought to be necessary for successful participation in society.

2. The *hidden curriculum* embraces the implicit norms, expectations, and rewards for certain ways of acting and thinking that are conveyed by schools' social and authority relationships. This facet of the curriculum teaches social roles and behaviors expected by society.

C. Teacher Influences

1. Most elementary school children spend more time with their teacher than with any other adult except their parents.

2. Despite considerable variation in teaching styles, effective teachers are able to establish learning environments that are calm, predictable, and engaging.

D. The Student's Experience

1. According to Philip Jackson, students experience delay, denial, interruption, and social distraction in the classroom (Jackson, 1968).

2. However, elementary classrooms can be organized to eliminate these negative characteristics.

3. Schools greatly influence how children experience and interact with others.

VII. PSYCHOSOCIAL CHALLENGES FACING CHILDREN WITH HANDICAPS

A. The Challenge of Knowing Who You Are

1. Children with handicaps face the same task as other children in developing a unique sense of self, but their disabilities may complicate this process in special ways.

2. How quickly children learn about the significance of their handicap depends on their cognitive and emotional capacities.

B. The Challenge to Achieve

1. For children with disabilities, achievement may not be tied to conventional standards of success.

2. Part of learning to achieve, then, consists of selecting appropriate realms of activity.

C. The Challenge of Peers

1. Although children with disabilities want and need the acceptance and affection of other children, their disabilities often interfere with gaining acceptance (Gottlieb et al., 1978).

2. Genuine handicaps can make other children anxious and defensive. In recent years efforts have been made to integrate or *mainstream* children with handicaps into regular classrooms (Turnbull & Turnbull, 1986).

D. The Challenge of Family Relationships

1. Disabilities affect children's relations with their parents and with other family members.

2. Parents often experience a lot of stress as a result of the practical demands that result from their child's handicap, and there are financial as well as emotional burdens.

3. Siblings react in various ways to a disability in the family. They may feel emotionally neglected because parents give so much attention to the disabled child, but they may also develop great tolerance and altruism.

Overview and Key Concepts

During the middle years, children industriously try to become skilled at activities that are admired by society and peers. They are increasingly able to see another person's point of view and try hard to win the approval of their friends and understand the dynamics of their families. Schoolchildren are strongly influenced by peer, family, and school relationships. This is true of both "normal" and disabled children. Societal changes, such as a higher proportion of working mothers and marriages ending in divorce, create challenges that must be met and understood.

Directions: Identify the following concepts introduced in Chapter 13.

1. Throughout infancy, childhood, and adolescence, a child develops a ___sense of self___, which is often called a ___self concept___ and functions more like a theory than like a single concept. ___self constancy___, a belief that identity remains permanently fixed, does not emerge until sometime after age six.

2. Freud believed that ___repression___ resulted from the preschooler's thwarted wish for intimacy with his opposite-sex parent. This occurs at about the time children begin school and precipitates the development of the period of ___latency___, in which the schoolchild focuses on building competencies and skills as a ___defense___, or unconscious self-protective behavior.

3. According to Erikson, children respond to romantic feelings toward their parents by not only repressing their feelings but by consciously trying to be more like their parents. This process of ___identification___ helps them to see themselves as people capable of becoming genuine adults. Erikson called this process the crisis of ___ind. vs inf.___, meaning that children at this age concern themselves with their ___ind.___ so as not to develop poor self-esteem or feelings of ___inf.___.

4. ___Ach. Motiv.___ refers to behavior that enhances competence or that enhances judgments of competence. This definition refers to two different attitudes. One is ___learach orien.___, in which motivation is intrinsic, and the other is ___perf. orien.___, in which motivation is extrinsic.

5. The best developed theory about peers was proposed by Harry Stack Sullivan, who believed that peers create a life for children outside their families and in so doing help correct the emotional biases or ___warps___ that families inevitably give their children. This sort of learning occurs during the ___juvenile per.___.

6. Girls' long-term friendships tend more often toward exclusive intimacy than do boys' long-term friendships. One study tested this idea by using a ___socio. quest.___, or written ballot, which invites children to name their best friends. Compared with boys, the girls more often made mutually exclusive choices: ___dyads___, or two-person relationships, and all-girl triads.

7. Preferences based on race and ethnicity can play a significant role in friendship choices and social activity during the middle years, and these preferences can also be a mask for ___prejudice___, irrational, negative attitudes directed at members of another group.

8. Girls' responses to divorce are less obvious than boys'. Some studies suggest that girls become less aggressive as a result of divorce; boys, more aggressive. Girls tend to worry more about schoolwork, and they often take on more household responsibilities. These changes may mean that they are ___Internalizing___, or holding stress inside.

9. Sometimes problems in the relationship between parents and children following divorce are partially alleviated by ___Jt. custody___ of the children, in which the parents divide their child-rearing responsibilities relatively equally.

10. Most parents who get divorced remarry within a few years, creating what some call reconstituted, or ___blended families___

11. Each school has its own culture, which includes the ___values___, ___beliefs___, ___traditions___, and _____ that make it unique and distinguish it from other schools and institutions.

12. The ___curriculum___ helps children acquire the academic knowledge and skills thought to be necessary for successful participation in society.

13. The ___hidden curr.___ is the implicit norms, expectations, and rewards for certain ways of thinking and acting that are conveyed by a school's social and authority relationships. It teaches students the social roles and behaviors expected by society.

14. Teachers' beliefs and expectations about their students' potential can affect their students' actual performance and overall school adjustment by changing students' behavior in the anticipated direction and thereby serving as a ___self-fulfilling proph___.

15. In an effort to reduce the isolation and possible rejection of disabled and handicapped children, many educators have worked in recent years toward integrating or ___mainstreaming___ these children into regular classrooms.

Key Terms

Directions: Provide a definition for each of the following key terms. Check your answers against the Glossary or the text page number that follows each term.

Achievement motivation (p. 463) _____

_____

_____

Blended family (p. 483) _____

_____

_____

Defense (p. 462) _____

_____

_____

Dyad (p. 470) _____

_____

_____

Explicit curriculum (p. 488) _____

_____

_____

Hidden curriculum (p. 489) _____

_____

_____

_____

Industriousness (p. 462) _____

_____

_____

Industry versus inferiority (p. 462) _____

_____

_____

Inferiority (p. 462) _____

_____

_____

Internalizing (p. 481) _____

_____

_____

Joint custody (p. 483) _____

_____

_____

Juvenile period (p. 466) _____

_____

_____

Latency (p. 462) _____

_____

_____

Learning orientation (p. 463) _____

_____

_____

Mainstreaming (p. 494) _____

_____

_____

Peers (p. 457) _____

_____

_____

Performance orientation (p. 463) _____

_____

_____

Prejudice (p. 471) _____

_____

_____

Repression (p. 462) _____

_____

_____

Self-concept (p. 458) _____

_____

_____

Self-constancy (p. 458) _____

_____

_____

Self-fulfilling prophecy (p. 489) _____

_____

_____

Sense of self (p. 458) _____

_____

_____

Sociometric questionnaire (p. 470) _____

_____

_____

Warp (p. 466) _____

_____

_____

Study Questions

1. What are five major psychosocial challenges that take place in the middle years? (p. 457)

    _____

    _____

    _____

    _____

2. What is meant by sense of self, self-concept, and self-constancy? (p. 458)

_____

_____

_____

_____

3. Explain latency and the crisis of industry from both a Freudian and an Eriksonian standpoint. (pp. 461–462)

_____

_____

_____

_____

4. Define the two kinds of achievement motivation discussed in Chapter 13. How does the emphasis change during the middle years? (pp. 462–465)

_____

_____

_____

_____

5. Briefly explain the importance that both Piaget and Sullivan attached to peer relationships. (pp. 465–466)

_____

_____

_____

_____

6. How do age, gender, and racial/ethnic background influence peer relationships? (pp. 467–471)

_____

_____

_____

_____

7. How did boys and girls differ in their responses to a sociometric questionnaire in Hallinan's and Eder's research? (p. 470)

_____

_____

_____

_____

8. Contrast and compare the traits of popular children with those of unpopular children. (p. 472)

_____

_____

_____

_____

9. How do children's conceptions of friendship change from the early school years to the later school years? (pp. 472–474)

_____

_____

_____

_____

10. Define the terms *peer, peer group,* and *peer conformity;* and briefly enumerate some positive and negative effects of peer pressure. (pp. 474–475)

_____

_____

_____

_____

11. Explain some of the major ways in which parents influence their children. (p. 476)

_____

_____

_____

_____

12. How does the parent's view of social relationships differ from the child's view of social relationships? (pp. 476–477)

_____

_____

_____

_____

13. Describe the quality of the parent-child relationship in the middle years. (pp. 477–478)

_____

_____

_____

_____

14. What are some statistics that support the idea of the changing nature of modern families? (pp. 478–480)

_____

_____

_____

_____

15. What are some of the effects of divorce on children and how do boys and girls respond differently to divorce? (pp. 480–482)

_____

_____

_____

_____

16. Describe different custody arrangements following divorce and indicate what a blended or reconstituted family is. (pp. 482–484)

_____

_____

_____

_____

17. Children of mothers who have jobs away from home feel less stress than do children whose parents are divorced. Even so, there are some sources of stress for them. What are they? (pp. 484–486)

_____

_____

_____

_____

18. Mothers with outside jobs are still rather novel. We take fathers' work for granted; this may be one reason fathers' job losses may be more devastating than mothers'. Explain. (pp. 486–487)

_____

_____

_____

_____

19. Describe the influences of the school in terms of school culture, the explicit curriculum, the hidden curriculum, teacher influences, and the student's experience. (pp. 488–491)

_____

_____

_____

_____

20. Highlight psychological challenges and special dilemmas that must be confronted by children with handicaps. (pp. 491–495)

_____

_____

_____

_____

Multiple-Choice Self-Test

1. Which of the following is considered a major developmental challenge of the middle years?
   a. achievement
   b. peer relationships
   c. family relationships
   d. all of the above

2. The belief that self-identity remains permanently fixed becomes firmly developed
   a. by age two.
   b. between age two and five.
   c. between age six and twelve.
   d. after age twelve.

3. Freud indicated that during the latency stage a child attempts to deal with previous feelings through
   a. direct expression.
   b. regression.
   c. repression.
   d. sublimation.

4. Eric has learned how to play the guitar so that he can impress his friends. Eric's achievement motivation is primarily
   a. learning oriented.
   b. performance oriented.
   c. power oriented.
   d. social oriented.

5. Piaget indicates that peers are more effective in the decline of egocentrism than parents because
   a. parents are formal operational.
   b. parents cannot act as true equals.
   c. parents do not interact with school-age children.
   d. none of the above.

6. Peer relations differ from parental relations in that the child
   a. gets relief from anxiety-provoking situations from parents.
   b. learns social skills from parents.
   c. must act in ways that explicitly support the peer relationship.
   d. all of the above.

7. Compared with same-age groups, mixed-age groups tend to be
   a. dominated by younger children.
   b. less helpful.
   c. less sociable.
   d. more aggressive.

8. Popular children tend to be all of the following *except*
   a. more athletic.
   b. more confident.
   c. more energetic.
   d. more intelligent.

9. During the early middle years, children tend to base their friendships on
   a. mutual support.
   b. physical characteristics.
   c. practical behaviors.
   d. psychological qualities.

10. A parent says, "If you don't share your toys with others, they won't share theirs with you." In this example, the parent is influencing the child's behavior through
    a. direct instruction.
    b. modeling of behavior.
    c. reasoning.
    d. stating rules.

11. In general, a major consequence of divorce is that children
    a. may withdraw from the situation.
    b. often feel guilty about the divorce.
    c. need to adjust to the loss.
    d. all of the above.

12. Which of the following is *not* part of the hidden curriculum within a school?
    a. study habits
    b. conformity to school norms
    c. standard achievement test performance
    d. social interactions

Activities

Activity 13.1

Objective: To highlight necessary versatility in teaching style with various subcultures.

Misunderstandings are common when we do not understand the nonverbal language or child-rearing style of another culture. At the same time, children from Hispanic or Native American families do not understand how to play the game of successful performance in American schools. Understanding these differences can help teachers adjust their styles so that they may gradually accustom children from other cultures to success signals in American schools.

The following table indicates different cultural responses to messages. Fill in the empty spaces, and if you know of other differences, add them.

Behavior	American Children	Native American or Hispanic Children
Eye contact	Looks teacher in the eye to show honesty	Averts eyes to show respect
Answers questions in class	Taken for granted; child is proud when correct	Embarrassed; inhibited; fears risk of public mistake
Rhetorical questions		Puzzled; teacher already knows the answer; feels they are ridiculous
Helping other students	Cheating	
Interrupting other children		
Doing homework together		
Speaking to peers in native language		
Others		

Activity 13.3

> **Objective:** To help children understand and cope with the reality of death.

Despite the prevalence of death in the media, discussing death with youngsters is almost taboo. But people do die: parents of young children and even children. Parents and teachers are often faced with helping children through the shock and bewilderment of the death of a loved public figure, a classmate, the parent or sibling of a friend, or someone in one's own family. Psychologists have taught us not to deny our own or our children's feelings. The reality and permanence of death are difficult to accept, even for adults.

Most adults need help, often quickly and unexpectedly, in explaining to and comforting children when a death occurs. If you had been called in to help teachers immediately after the space shuttle disaster, how would you have proceeded?

With the teachers' own shock?

With the children's shock and fear?

Their questions? (For example, Why did it happen? What about me dying? What if my parents die? Was it my fault? Where are the people in the shuttle? Will they go to heaven? Be careful here. If you send them to heaven, don't emphasize that their families will be joining them. If the subject comes up, and a religious point of view is given, remind the children that God decides when people are to die. Try to keep the explanation secular, about the worldly experience of losing someone through death.)

Find the titles of two books to use as resources. One would be for adults to use. Earl Grollman has written several, and Elizabeth Kübler-Ross's stages of grief has taken death out of the closet.

1.

A second book would be used with children. Most children's books are for preschoolers and the primary grades, but there are a few suited to slightly older children. A good source is Human Sciences Press in New York City. Check with your campus library.

2.

What else would you emphasize to teachers?

Activity 13.4

Objective: To recognize and give examples of sources of psychological support to children.

All of us can remember adults who helped us come through periods of extreme stress during our childhood. Surprisingly, help sometimes came from someone other than parents or teachers. It may have been someone with no experience or formal knowledge of children, who had human compassion and wisdom. It may have been an outsider's objective attitude that helped you put things into perspective or explained the skill you needed. Who, in your childhood, came to your psychological rescue?

A member of the family? a friend? a stranger?

What were the circumstances?

Exactly how did this person help?

Sometimes help comes from a resource within ourselves. In your childhood, how did you get through difficult periods?

Were there any activities or interests that helped you over the hurdles? If so, what were they?

Did you have a special place where you went when in need of comfort?

Have any of these resources remained available to you in adulthood?

Activity 13.5

> **Objective:** To see the disability in ourselves and thereby gain insight into the experience of those who have far more serious disabilities.

No one is perfect, or even adequate, in all facets of life. Everyone regrets some kind of incapacity. Some folks are complete klutzes at playing tennis. Others go to great lengths to hide their phobias. Others could win the Pulitzer Prize, if they only knew how to spell.

What is your disability? How do you cope with it? Do you compensate? If so, how?

Do you know others like you?

How do others respond to your handicap?

What advice do you have for others in the same situation?

Answer Key

Overview and Key Concepts

1. sense of self; self-concept; self-constancy (p. 458)

2. repression; latency; defense (p. 462)

3. identification; industry versus inferiority; industriousness; inferiority (p. 462)

4. achievement motivation; learning orientation; performance orientation (pp. 462–463)

5. warps; juvenile period (p. 466)

6. sociometric questionnaire; dyads (p. 470)

7. prejudice (p. 471)

8. internalizing (p. 481)

9. joint custody (p. 483)

10. blended families (p. 483)

11. values; beliefs; traditions; customary ways of thinking and behaving (p. 488)

12. explicit curriculum (p. 488)

13. hidden curriculum (p. 489)

14. self-fulfilling prophecy (p. 489)

15. mainstreaming (p. 494)

Multiple-Choice Self-Test

1. Choice (d) is correct. The need to achieve, choice (a), and the development of relationships with peers and with the family, choices (b) and (c), present challenges for six- to twelve-year-olds. (pp. 456–457)

2. Choice (c) is correct. Self-constancy becomes firm sometime after the age six but before adolescence. Thus the other age ranges, choices (a), (b), and (d), are inaccurate. (p. 458)

3. Choice (c) is correct. Freud believed that beginning at about age six, children repress feelings of intimacy for the opposite-sex parent and competition with the same-sex parent. (pp. 461–462)
Choice (a) would just create more anxiety; (b) would represent a return to previous immature behaviors; and (d) would involve redirecting the anxieties into socially acceptable activities.

4. Choice (b) is correct. Eric's reason for playing the guitar is to receive external reinforcement from his friends. (p. 463)
Choice (a) would involve an internal source of motivation. Choices (c) and (d) are not forms of achievement motivation.

5. Choice (b) is correct. According to Piaget, children's release from egocentrism comes through interaction on an equal basis because it promotes discussion and negotiation, which allow alternative views to develop. (p. 466)
Choice (a) is not critical; interactions (not cognitive level) are important. Parents do interact with school-age children, choice (b), but not at the same level as peers do.

6. Choice (c) is correct. Peer relationships, unlike parental relationships, are voluntary and involve comparable equals; thus the individual must act in ways to preserve the relationship. (p. 467)
Relief from anxiety, choice (a), can be obtained from either parents or peers. Many social skills, choice (b), are actually learned from peers rather than from parents.

7. Choice (c) is correct. Mixed-age groups tend to have less chatting or friendly conversations than same-age groups. (pp. 467–468)
In mixed-age groups, younger children show more dependency, choice (a); tend to be more helpful and nurturant, choice (b); and actually have fewer fights or arguments, choice (d).

8. Choice (d) is correct. Although popular children may do better academically, they are not necessarily more intelligent than unpopular children. (p. 472)
Popular children tend to be more athletic, choice (a); more confident and good-natured, choice (b); and more energetic, choice (c).

9. Choice (c) is correct. Six- and seven-year-olds tend to base friendships on shared activities, interests, and concrete behaviors. (p. 472)
Older middle-years children (nine-, ten-, and eleven-year-olds) tend to base friendships on choices (a) and (d). For preschoolers, choice (b) may be a factor that influences friendship.

10. The example illustrates the use of reasoning, choice (c). The parent not only gives instruction but also provides an explanation. (p. 476)
Choice (a) would involve the issuance of a specific instruction; (b) would be acting to set an example of the parent's own behavior; and (d) would involve giving a general rule from which the child could deduce appropriate behavior.

11. Choice (d) is correct. Choices (a), (b), and (c) are tasks that children involved in a divorce need to deal with. (pp. 482–483)

12. Choice (c) is correct. Standard test scores are part of the regular curriculum. (p. 490) Study habits, choice (a); the ability to conform to school rules, choice (b); and social skills, choice (d), are all part of the hidden curriculum.

CHAPTER 14
Adolescence: Physical Development

Learning Objectives

1. Describe the concept of adolescence, how it has changed, and the factors that have influenced those changes. Note particularly G. Stanley Hall's view of the adolescent period.

2. Discuss the adolescent growth spurt. Identify the characteristic height and weight changes during adolescence and how they have evolved in the past one hundred years.

3. Describe the physical changes associated with puberty. Identify and describe the primary and secondary sex characteristics.

4. Discuss the role of hormones in puberty. Identify and discuss the functions of the major sex hormones.

5. Describe the effects of early versus late maturing in males and females, including information concerning long-term effects.

6. Characterize the health of the adolescent. Identify the major causes of death in adolescence.

7. Describe the major health problems during adolescence, including sexually transmitted diseases.

8. Discuss drug, alcohol, and mental health problems in adolescence.

Chapter Outline

I. THE CONCEPT OF ADOLESCENCE

Adolescence is the stage of development that leads from childhood to adulthood. Marked by the significant physical changes of puberty and important cognitive and social changes, it is generally considered to begin around age twelve and to end around age twenty.

A. Adolescence: From Idea to Social Fact

1. Although most of us take the idea of adolescence for granted, it is a relatively modern concept. Its "creation" in America was largely a response to the social changes accruing from industrial development in the nineteenth century.

2. State-controlled education was believed to be so essential to ensure law and order that school attendance was made compulsory from age six to eighteen in most states.

3. Children and adolescents had made up a significant part of the work force, but increasing awareness of the harmful effects of factory work spurred the movement toward child-labor laws.

4. Laws restricting child labor defined the end of adolescence.

5. Adolescence as a psychological concept was popularized by psychologist G. Stanley Hall, one of the first developmentalists to study adolescence.

B. Theoretical Views of Adolescence

1. Since the "creation" of adolescence in the United States, there have been two somewhat conflicting views about its basic nature. One view concurs with Hall's: that adolescence is a time of "storm and stress" when major physical, social, intellectual, and emotional changes create tremendous upset and crisis within the individual and conflict between the individual and society.

2. The other view, which has grown out of research, suggests that adolescence contains no more conflict than any other period of life and that most youngsters seem to adapt to it quite well.

II. GROWTH IN HEIGHT AND WEIGHT

A. There is less overall growth in adolescence; however, an unevenness in growth patterns is created by a *growth spurt*.

B. Actually, growth patterns during childhood are better predictors of adult height than are adolescent growth patterns (Faust, 1977).

C. Weight increases during adolescence and is more easily influenced than height by diet, exercise, and life-style; therefore, changes in weight are less predictable than changes in height.

D. Adolescents differ greatly in their rates and patterns of growth.

E. The Secular Trend

1. During the past century children have gradually begun the physical changes of adolescence earlier and ended up taller and heavier than their parents. These tendencies are referred to as the *secular trend*.

2. Improvements in health care, diet, and overall living conditions are thought to be the major reasons for these changes.

3. Because the onset of puberty is related to body weight, improvements in diet have resulted in the achievement of weight increases at earlier ages than in previous generations.

III. PUBERTY

A. Rapid increases in height and weight are one part of the larger pattern of changes called *puberty*, which leads to full physical and sexual maturity.

1. Primary sex characteristics make sexual reproduction possible.

2. Changes in secondary sex characteristics include enlargement of breasts, growth of body hair, and deepening of the voice.

B. Primary Sexual Maturation

1. For boys, the most significant sign of sexual maturation is rapid growth of the penis and scrotum.

2. During adolescence enough live sperm are produced in the testes to make reproduction a real possibility. Around age twelve, boys are likely to experience their first ejaculation of semen as a nocturnal emission.

3. For girls, the appearance of the first menstrual period, which is called *menarche*, signals sexual maturity.

4. For most girls, menstruation involves a certain degree of inconvenience and discomfort but also feelings of happiness about the specialness of their reproductivity and womanhood.

C. Maturation of Secondary Sex Characteristics

1. Breasts

   a. Girls first develop breast "buds" with the beginning of puberty. During the following several years, breasts continue to grow until they reach their full size.

   b. Boys also have a small amount of breast development.

2. Hair

   a. When their genital development is relatively advanced, boys and girls both acquire more body hair.

   b. Although there are considerable differences among individuals, in girls pubic and axillary hair begins to appear and develop from ages eleven to fourteen and in boys from ages twelve to eighteen.

3. Voice

   a. In both sexes the voice deepens near the end of puberty and becomes richer in overtones.

   b. These changes make the adolescent's voice sound more truly adult and less childlike.

D. Hormonal Changes and Their Physical Consequences

1. At puberty boys and girls begin producing substantially more of several sex-related hormones. *Hormones* are chemicals produced by the endocrine glands and released into the bloodstream to be carried to various organs of the body. Both *ovaries* and *testes* contain low levels of hormones that function in sexual maturation.

2. Puberty increases the level of all sex hormones in the blood of both sexes. *Testosterone* (the male sex hormone) and *estrogen* (the female sex hormone) are two of the most important sex hormones.

3. Hormones affect more than just sexual characteristics. For example, they are responsible for the typical differences between boys' and girls' overall body builds.

E. The Extent of Physical Sex Differences

1. Sex differences that develop during puberty are matters of emphasis or degree. Except for eggs, sperm, and form of genitals, every physical structure exists in both sexes.

2. From the biological standpoint, the sexes do not represent physical opposites so much as related but distinct patterns of similar physical elements.

IV. PSYCHOLOGICAL EFFECTS OF PHYSICAL GROWTH IN ADOLESCENCE

A. Body Image and Self-Esteem

1. Almost all adolescents are concerned about their changing bodies and their attractiveness.

2. Conventional standards of attractiveness have considerable influence.

3. Research shows that in terms of *ectomorphic* (slender builds), *mesomorphic* (muscular builds), and *endomorphic* (rounder builds), children and adolescents considered mesomorphic bodies to be the most attractive (Lerner, 1969).

4. Adolescents evaluate themselves and their peers stereotypically and rate mesomorphic peers as the most attractive.

5. Parents who value qualities other than physical attractiveness can best help their teenager cope with the awkwardness of puberty.

6. An adolescent's feeling of attractiveness also depends on how he feels about himself in general.

B. Early- Versus Late-Maturing Adolescents

1. The timing of puberty can make a lasting difference on the psychological development of an adolescent.

2. For example, boys who mature early seem to experience certain advantages because they appear more muscular and mesomorphic.

3. Late-maturing boys may continue to resemble children as late as age sixteen.

4. Achieving puberty may involve considerably more conflict for girls than for boys because stereotypes tend to associate entry into puberty with increased willingness to engage in sexual activity.

5. Early maturation for a girl means that she enters puberty at nine or ten years, an age at which most adults would definitely consider her to be a child.

6. By contrast, girls who mature late, at about age fourteen, experience many social advantages during adolescence.

V. HEALTH IN ADOLESCENCE

   A. Continuity with Health in Childhood

   1. The health and health-care patterns of most individuals show considerable consistency from early childhood through adolescence (Starfield & Pless, 1980).

   2. Health-care availability is of course variable; however, regardless of family situation, adolescents are less likely than other age groups to have consistently positive attitudes toward health care.

   B. Concepts of Illness and Health in Adolescence

   1. Not until adolescence are children able to understand health in terms of multiple causes and to realize that interrelationships among thoughts, feelings, and changes in physical health are significant.

   2. Incomplete understanding of illness reduces an individual's sense of personal responsibility for taking care of herself; however, adolescents can become careful managers of their own health.

   3. Programs to encourage self-care have had significant success in elementary schools and in high schools.

   C. Causes of Death Among Adolescents

   1. Although adolescents are less affected by the health problems that cause death in younger children and adults, the death rate during adolescence is one of the highest of all groups.

   2. Motor vehicle accidents, a high proportion of which involve alcohol, kill more than fifteen thousand teenagers and young adults each year.

   3. More than six thousand teenagers and young adults die from homicide and violence, and five thousand die from suicide and other self-inflicted causes each year. Males are significantly more at risk than females.

D. Adolescent Health Problems

1. Infectious mononucleosis frequently occurs in adolescents whose resistance to illness has been lowered by lack of sleep and poor diet.

2. Sexually transmitted diseases have become a major problem among adolescents because of increased sexual activity throughout our society.

   a. Syphilis and gonorrhea appear frequently among adolescents who are involved with different sexual partners.

   b. Genital warts affect one million individuals each year.

   c. Genital herpes and chlamydia are increasing dramatically in numbers of new cases.

   d. AIDS is perhaps the best known and most feared sexually transmitted disease. Experts are alarmed at the rate at which AIDS is spreading among teenagers (Kolata, 1989).

3. Drug and alcohol abuse occur commonly among adolescents. Smoking and drinking are the most common forms of substance abuse, according to 1985 estimates.

   a. Although recent studies confirm a continuing decline in the use of most drugs, the number of students who used crack at least once has changed very little.

   b. The effects of drug abuse on development are very destructive.

   c. Alcohol, which is the most widely used drug in the United States, takes a staggering toll on teenagers. Chronic alcohol abuse leads to serious health problems and is linked with many accidents.

4. Nutritional problems are most common among adolescents. Girls, especially, often diet and seek to reach unrealistic standards of slenderness, even to the extreme of developing anorexia nervosa, which is often accompanied by bulimia.

5. The most significant factor in adolescents' taking responsibility for their own health is whether they have a clear perception that they really are responsible for it. The achievement of a sense of responsibility signals progress in the transition to young adulthood.

Overview and Key Concepts

Chapter 14 surveys the concept and fact of adolescence. It describes the physical changes that take place, emerging primary and secondary sexual characteristics, changes in appearance, and psychological effects. Health and health problems are discussed as a continuation of childhood health patterns. Causes of death are discussed and so are health problems, particularly the risk of contracting AIDS and other sexually transmitted diseases. The destructive effects of drug and alcohol abuse are stressed to emphasize the need for adolescents to take responsibility for their own health.

Directions: Identify the following concepts introduced in Chapter 14.

1. Although most of us take the idea of adolescence for granted, it is a relatively modern concept. Its emergence in America was a response to social changes that accompanied U.S. _____ in the _____ .

2. Legislation that officially recognized adolescence as a special period before adulthood included _____ laws and _____ as a way of dealing with the newly invented idea of "_____ ."

3. G. Stanley Hall's notion that adolescence is a period of _____ , meaning "storm and stress," is not supported by research.

4. In adolescence, much of the rapid change in height and weight is due to a dramatic _____ that is preceded and followed by years of comparatively little increase.

5. An adolescent girl may think she is too fat even though everyone around her thinks she is quite attractive and not fat at all. A possible reason for her seemingly faulty opinion of herself is _____ , the tendency of adolescents to find it difficult to perceive the world through anyone's eyes but their own.

6. During the past century, children have gradually begun the physical changes of adolescence earlier. This tendency is part of the _____ .

7. Rapid increases in height and weight are only one part of a larger pattern of changes called _____ , which leads to full physical and sexual maturity.

8. Puberty is marked by striking changes in both _____ , which make sexual reproduction possible, and _____ , which include enlargement of breasts and growth of body hair.

9. For boys, the first ejaculation of _____ sometimes occurs during sleep as a _____ . For girls, the appearance of the first menstrual period, which is called _____ , signals sexual maturity.

10. _____ are chemicals produced by the endocrine glands and carried to various organs of the body. Both the female sex glands, or _____ , and the male sex glands, or _____ , contain hormones that play a major role in sexual maturation. _____ (a female sex hormone) and _____ (a male sex hormone) are two very important sex hormones.

11. One researcher documented that children and adolescents judged muscular, _____ body types to be more attractive than slim, _____ body types or rounder, more padded, _____ body types.

12. Boys who physically mature earlier seem to have certain _____ . Boys who mature later still resemble _____ .

13. Very early maturing girls seemed _____ and ill at ease in social situations, and they seemed chronically under stress and _____ .

14. _____ have become a major problem among adolescents, largely because of the increased acceptability of sexual activity throughout our culture.

15. An extreme form of the quest for thinness is _____ , a physical and psychological disturbance in which the afflicted teenager starves herself and develops an unrealistic view of her body. Many of these girls also suffer from _____ .

Key Terms

Directions: Provide a definition for each of the following key terms. Check your answers against the Glossary or the text page number that follows each term.

Adolescence (p. 507) _____

_____

_____

Adolescent egocentrism (p. 511) _____

_____

_____

Anorexia nervosa (p. 535) _____

_____

_____

Axillary hair (p. 514) _____

_____

_____

Bulimia (p. 535) _____

_____

_____

Ectomorphic (p. 518) _____

_____

_____

Endomorphic (p. 518) _____

_____

_____

Estrogen (p. 515) _____

_____

_____

Growth spurt (p. 509) _____

_____

_____

Hormone (p. 515) _____

_____

_____

Menarche (p. 513) _____

_____

_____

Mesomorphic (p. 518) _____

_____

_____

Nocturnal emission (p. 513) _____

_____

_____

Ovary (p. 515) _____

_____

_____

Primary sex characteristic (p. 512) _____

_____

_____

Puberty (p. 512) _____

_____

_____

Pubic hair (p. 513) _____

_____

_____

Secondary sex characteristic (p. 512) _____

_____

_____

Secular trend (p. 512) _____

_____

_____

Testes (p. 515) _____

_____

_____

Testosterone (p. 515) _____

_____

_____

Study Questions

1. How did the notion of adolescence emerge from social changes in the United States in the nineteenth century? (p. 507)

_____

_____

_____

_____

2. What types of legislation passed at the end of the last century and at the beginning of the present century affected adolescence? (pp. 507–508)

_____

_____

_____

_____

3. Who was the developmentalist who popularized the notion of adolescence in psychology? What view of adolescence did he hold? (p. 508)

_____

_____

_____

_____

4. Describe two opposing theoretical views of adolescence. (pp. 508–509)

_____

_____

_____

_____

5. During adolescence, how do boys' typical height and weight differ from girls' and how do height and weight relate to the growth spurt? (pp. 509–510)

_____

_____

_____

_____

6. What is meant by adolescent egocentrism? (p. 511)

_____

_____

_____

_____

7. During the past century, what has been the secular trend for reaching full height and weight? (p. 512)

_____

_____

_____

_____

8. What are the characteristics of primary sexual maturation for boys? (pp. 512–513)

_____

_____

_____

_____

9. What is the pattern of primary sexual maturation for girls? (p. 513)

_____

_____

_____

_____

10. What is the pattern of secondary sexual characteristics for boys and girls? (pp. 513–515)

_____

_____

_____

_____

11. What is the role of hormones in development and what are two important sex hormones? In what ways do sex-related hormones cause differences in body build for boys and girls? (pp. 515–516)

_____

_____

_____

_____

12. What is the extent of physical sex differences? (pp. 516–517)

_____

_____

_____

_____

13. In what ways do conventional standards of attractiveness affect the body image and self-esteem of adolescent boys and girls? (pp. 518–521)

_____

_____

_____

_____

14. In what ways can the timing of puberty affect later development in boys and girls? (pp. 521–526)

_____

_____

_____

_____

15. What concepts of illness and health do adolescents typically have? (pp. 527–528)

_____

_____

_____

_____

16. What are the major causes of death among adolescents? (p. 528)

_____

_____

_____

_____

17. What are some of the major health problems associated with adolescence? (pp. 529–536)

_____

_____

_____

_____

18. What specific and serious problems are related to nutritional patterns in adolescent girls? (pp. 534–535)

_____

_____

_____

_____

19. What seems to be the most significant factor in adolescents' taking responsibility for their own health? (p. 536)

_____

_____

_____

_____

Multiple-Choice Self-Test

1. A rite of passage is
   a. a means of screening out undesirables from a society.
   b. a means of torturing adolescents to impress upon them the fact that adulthood is difficult.
   c. a ritual or ceremony that signifies a change in a person's social standing.
   d. all of the above.

2. G. Stanley Hall viewed the development of the individual as a reflection of
    a. evolutionary change.
    b. structural change.
    c. environmental stimulation.
    d. unconscious conflict.

3. Physical development in height and weight during adolescence can best be characterized as
    a. irregular and uneven.
    b. slow and steady.
    c. dramatically accelerating and increasing.
    d. trivial.

4. Compared with adolescents one hundred years ago, adolescents today
    a. are shorter.
    b. end the growth spurt sooner.
    c. reach puberty later.
    d. weigh less.

5. Physical features that make reproduction possible are termed
    a. gonads.
    b. primary sex characteristics.
    c. secondary sex characteristics.
    d. secular trends.

6. Testosterone is present in
    a. females only.
    b. males only.
    c. males and females.
    d. males and pregnant females only.

7. Josie tends to be slightly overweight and a bit rounded. Her body style is
    a. ectomorphic.
    b. endomorphic.
    c. estromorphic.
    d. mesomorphic.

8. Which group seems to have the most disadvantages during the adolescent period?
    a. early-maturing males and females
    b. early-maturing males and late-maturing females
    c. late-maturing males and early-maturing females
    d. late-maturing males and females

9. Adolescents are likely to visit a physician
   a. if they visited him or her frequently as children.
   b. only if they are in middle- and upper-income families.
   c. only for essential services.
   d. seldom, because they generally rebel against the medical and other kinds of "establishments."

10. The top three causes of death during adolescence are
   a. accidents, cancer, and drowning.
   b. accidents, murder, and suicide.
   c. drug overdose, drowning, and murder.
   d. suicide, murder, and AIDS.

11. Which of the following is a sexually transmitted disease that has no known cure?
   a. genital herpes
   b. gonorrhea
   c. infectious mononucleosis
   d. syphilis

12. Acquired immune deficiency syndrome (AIDS)
   a. has no known cure.
   b. is transmitted through bodily fluids.
   c. destroys the body's ability to maintain its normal immunity to diseases.
   d. all of the above.

13. In recent years, which group has shown the greatest increase in smoking?
   a. adolescent females
   b. adolescent males
   c. adult females
   d. adult males

Activities

Activity 14.1

Objective: To note the almost-universal phenomenon of dissatisfaction with appearance during adolescence.

During your adolescent years, was there something about the way you looked or your bodily proportions that bothered you?

What was it?

Does it still bother you?

Ask those questions of your friends, family, and anyone else. Have you been able to find anyone who was satisfied with his or her appearance during adolescence? (If so, be sure to remember that person so that you may remind yourself that there is no human attribute that is found in 100 percent of humans!)

What encouragement could you give to an adolescent today who confides in you about dissatisfaction with an apparently minor aspect of his or her appearance?

Activity 14.2

> **Objective:** To observe cultural changes in "ideal" body proportions and appearance.

Locate reproductions of paintings or sculptures from the eighteenth century that depict the nude male or female. Such depictions should be those that imply a standard of beauty. If possible, bring these examples to class.

Also locate reproductions of paintings, sculptures, or photographs from the nineteenth and twentieth centuries that depict similar ideals. You may also find these in old snapshots, magazine illustrations, and advertisements.

Pool your findings with those of your classmates.

What similarities do you find in the "body beautiful" from the eighteenth century?

The nineteenth century?

The twentieth century?

Do you or members of your family or friends fit any of these ideals?

From which century?

Do you see any indications in our society today of self-acceptance of what we cannot change?

Activity 14.3

Objective: To become aware of official and unofficial rites of passage during adolescence.

The text mentions a few of our society's official rites of passage, such as graduation and marriage. During adolescence, there are many rather informal, sometimes physiological, rites of passage. These rites, such as the onset of the menarche or getting a driver's license, are signs of growing up.

Consult with your friends as you compose a list of today's rites of passage during adolescence.

Informal personal recognitions

In appearance — start wearing makeup, first bra, beginning of female growth spurt, ~~dating~~

At school   1st date

With your family — being allowed to take the car
curfew moved up

In the work world

In the community   getting confirmed

Within yourself   getting into the college of your choice

Other

Activity 14.4

Objective: To note the risks that adolescents may take as a function of their feeling invulnerable or susceptible to peer pressure.

Adults sometimes recall incidents during their adolescence when they were without the cautionary influence of an older person and took risks that they would never repeat today.

If you are over twenty years old, can you recall such incidents in your own past? What were they?

Physical risks

Social risks

Risks related to your future life-style

Ask your parents and others from their generation whether they can recall such events

Your grandparents or their age mates

Do you find a difference from generation to generation?

Activity 14.5

Objective: To record and observe the maximum height and the age at which it was reached in young men and young women.

To observe this pattern, you need a sample of at least thirty adults. If your class is this size or larger, you may do this as a class activity.

1. On the vertical axis, record the age at which maximum height was attained.

2. On the horizontal axis, record the height in inches.

3. Use an O for women and an X for men.

4. Connect all of the Os; connect all of the Xs.

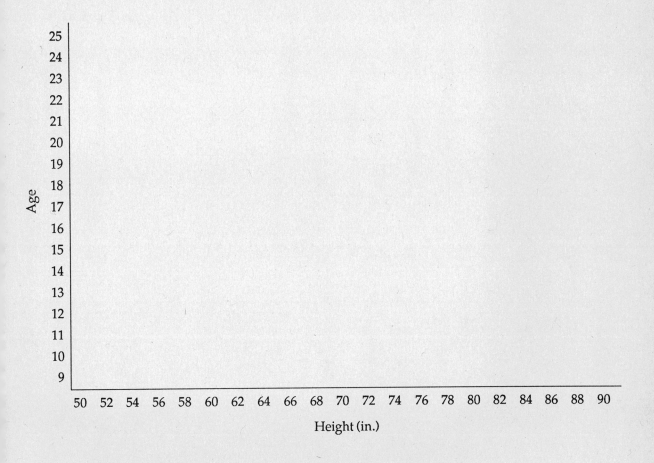

Do you see a pattern? The larger the number in your sample, the more distinct the direction of the lines will be.

Is there a difference in the lines plotted for men and for women? Again, the larger the sample, the more distinct the difference will be.

Activity 14.6

> **Objective:** To observe the secular change in body size.

This activity is best done in a community with a museum that exhibits costumes and furniture.

On a smaller scale, information can be obtained by questioning persons from your parents' and grandparents' generations. Ask them how tall *their* parents were and how much they thought their parents weighed. Naturally, in some cases people will be able to tell you their present height and weight.

Observe the clothing worn by past generations. Would those sizes be the sizes most frequently stocked in today's clothing stores?

Notice the dimensions of the seats and the height of the tables and desks. Are those sizes similar to the furniture you see today?

If you see differences, how might you account for them?

Do you think that humans in Western society will continue to get bigger and bigger?

Why or why not?

Answer Key

Overview and Key Concepts

1. industrial development; nineteenth century (p. 507)

2. child-labor; special legal procedures; juvenile delinquency (p. 508)

3. *Sturm und Drang* (p. 508)

4. growth spurt (p. 509)

5. adolescent egocentrism (p. 511)

6. secular trend (p. 512)

7. puberty (p. 512)

8. primary sex characteristics; secondary sex characteristics (p. 512)

9. semen; nocturnal emission; menarche (p. 513)

10. hormones; ovaries; testes; estrogen; testosterone (p. 515)

11. mesomorphic; ectomorphic; endomorphic (p. 518)

12. social advantages; children (p. 522)

13. relatively awkward; preoccupied with their looks (p. 524)

14. sexually transmitted diseases (p. 529)

15. anorexia nervosa; bulimia (p. 535)

Multiple-Choice Self-Test

1. Choice (c) is correct. A rite of passage indicates a change in status (typically from childhood to adulthood) and serves as a social sign of achievement. (p. 507)
   Choice (a): Although tasks are often involved, the aim of a rite of passage is not to exclude individuals (however, failure would mean they could not advance in status). Choice (b): A rite of passage is not a means of torture.

2. Choice (a) is correct. Hall believed that each stage of a child's physical, biological, and personality growth is predetermined and reflects the evolution of the species. (p. 508)

Structural change, choice (b), occurs only to the extent that it reflects evolutionary change. The environment, choice (c), does have impact, but the primary mechanism remains evolution. Choice (d) is a concept consistent with Freud's view.

3. Choice (a) is correct. Because of variation in the growth spurt, changes in height and weight during adolescence are irregular and uneven. (p. 509)
   Choices (b) and (d) do not describe changes in the growth spurt. Although growth accelerates during part of adolescence, choice (c), it slows as the growth spurt ends.

4. Choice (b) is correct. Adolescents today reach adult height approximately five years earlier than did adolescents one hundred years ago. (p. 512)
   Adolescents today are taller, choice (a); reach puberty a little earlier, choice (c); and weigh more than adolescents in the 1880–1890s, choice (d).

5. Choice (b) is correct. By definition, primary sex characteristics make sexual reproduction possible. (p. 512)
   The gonads, choice (a), are one of the primary sex characteristics. Choice (c) refers to changes that are not directly related to reproduction but are associated with puberty. Choice (d) refers to the trends of increased size and earlier onset of puberty in recent generations.

6. Choice (c) is correct. Testosterone is present in both males and females; however, the concentration in males is higher. (p. 515)
   Choices (a), (b), and (d) are inaccurate.

7. Choice (b) is correct. An endomorph is round and padded. (p. 518)
   Choice (a) describes a very slim shape. Choice (c) is a made-up word. Choice (d) describes a muscular/athletic appearance.

8. Choice (c) is correct. Late-maturing males tend to be regarded as socially inferior and immature, and they tend to lack self-confidence. Early-maturing females appear to be awkward in social situations and more stressed. (p. 522)
   Early-maturing males, choices (a) and (b), and late-maturing females, choice (d), are often viewed quite positively by their peers and teachers.

9. Choice (a) is correct. Regardless of age, early patterns of visiting a physician remain consistent in later years. (p. 526)
   Income, choice (b); need, choice (c); and rebelliousness, choice (d), are either not relevant or not as powerful as previous experiences.

10. Choice (a) is correct. The number-one cause of death in adolescence is motor vehicle accidents. Homicide is second, followed by suicide. (p. 528)
    The other causes listed, choices (b), (c), and (d), rank considerably lower.

11. Choice (a) is correct. Genital herpes causes chronic and painful inflammation of the genitals and other areas of sexual contact. Symptoms can be treated with an antiviral drug but not cured. (p. 530)
Choices (b), (c), and (d) are treatable disorders.

12. Choice (d) is correct. There is no known cure for AIDS, choice (a). The disease is transmitted through contact with the bodily fluids of an infected person, choice (b). It acts on the body's immune system, choice (c). (p. 530)

13. Choice (a) is correct. Smoking among adolescent girls has been increasing, in part because of advertisements targeting them. (p. 533)
Smoking is decreasing among the other groups—choices (b), (c), and (d).

CHAPTER 15
Adolescence: Cognitive Development

Learning Objectives

1. Describe the general characteristics of adolescent thinking.

2. Describe Jean Piaget's view of formal operational thinking. Specify the features of formal thought and contrast them with the concrete operational period.

3. Discuss the information-processing view of adolescent thinking, and indicate how this approach views developmental change.

4. Define and describe adolescent egocentrism, contrasting it with other forms of egocentrism.

5. Discuss the issues surrounding moral, political, and religious development. How does formal reasoning apply in these cases?

Chapter Outline

I. THE COGNITIVE DEVELOPMENTAL VIEWPOINT

    A. General Features of Adolescent Thought

        1. Adolescents are able to speculate about possibilities and to hypothesize.

        2. Adolescents can imagine what situations might be like even though they have not actually experienced them.

        3. In general, the ability to think about the possible creates a new talent for speculating about important events and for guessing about daily experiences (Elkind, 1984). It also stimulates adolescents to daydream.

B. Formal Operational Thinking

1. Because these cognitive skills attend to the logic or form of thinking, adolescent thought is sometimes referred to as *formal thought*, or *formal operational thought*.

2. Formal thought involves attention to possibilities, not just to realities.

3. Scientific reasoning

   a. Formal thought also involves scientific reasoning, the same kind that psychologists use in designing many of their studies of human development.

   b. This quality reveals itself when adolescent students solve problems systematically by designing experiments to test various options, in contrast to concrete operational children, who do not experiment systematically but work by trial and error.

4. Compared with less mature children, formal thinkers can hold several ideas in mind at once and combine or integrate them in logical ways.

C. Concrete Versus Formal Thought: Reasoning About Bending Rods

1. In an experiment designed by Piaget, a set of flexible rods is attached to the side of a basin of water. The rods differ in length, thickness, and material (wood or metal). Small weights are attached to the ends of the rods. A friendly experimenter (or teacher) asks the child to determine what factor or factors control how far the rods bend toward the water.

2. In this experiment, a middle-years child is fascinated by the apparatus itself and enjoys exploring it by trial and error. His haphazard approach probably prevents him from solving the problem.

3. An adolescent, formally thinking child approaches the problem much more systematically by making some guesses or hypotheses to be tested and by drawing reasonable conclusions from observations.

D. Cognitive Development Beyond Formal Thought

1. Piaget and other psychologists have identified formal thought as a major achievement of the adolescent years, but it may not be the final or highest cognitive achievement.

2. Elkind has suggested that teenagers often overrate the importance of logical thinking. They may believe that all problems, even difficult ones such as the matter of world peace, can be solved with proper application of rational principles.

3. Teenagers may fail to notice the limits of logic, that many problems by nature resist the application of general principles.

E. Evaluation of the Cognitive Developmental Viewpoint

1. In reality, the actual cognitive performance of adolescents fails to conform with Piaget's picture of formal operations: a majority of adolescents and adults use formal thinking inconsistently or fail to use it at all.

2. Another difficulty arises in determining when a person has truly attained formal operational thought. The answer depends on the criteria used to define attainment. Most experimental studies have confirmed that cognitive performance depends a lot on how it is observed or measured.

3. Many times a student who can meet one standard for successful formal thinking cannot meet other standards (Linn & Sigel, 1984).

4. Such evidence, however, should not be used as proof that Piaget's theory is wrong. In fact such studies may show only the importance of performance factors. The underlying competencies, related to Piaget's stage of formal operational thought, may indeed exist more or less as Piaget proposed.

II. THE INFORMATION-PROCESSING VIEWPOINT

A. Information-processing theory describes development as if it worked like a computer.

1. According to this view, a *sensory register* receives sensory information and holds it for a few seconds. If any of that information is processed, it is sent to *short-term memory* (STM). It then may be further processed into a form for permanent storage in *long-term memory* (LTM).

2. For adolescents, STM and LTM are the most important parts of the model because they alter or process information in important ways.

3. Actual responses to new information are organized by instructions contained in LTM but carried out in STM. Such instructions are sometimes called *control processes*.

B. An Example of Information Processing: Studying for a Test

1. Imagine how high school students might study for a midterm test in history. Many aspects of their behavior illustrate facets of information-processing theory.

2. Applying expert skills: Adolescents have probably had ample opportunity to become experts in taking multiple choice tests.

3. Selective allocation of attention: Adolescents have probably read enough textbooks to know that authors usually organize material around headings, and they know that test questions will probably summarize these points.

4. Use of domain-specific knowledge: Older students have usually taken several courses in history and in related subjects and thus have a richer store of prior knowledge than younger children.

C. Information-Processing Features of Adolescent Thought

1. Information-processing theory tends not to emphasize qualitative changes or transformations between major stages or periods of life. Instead, it treats each major stage as a continuation or extension of processes begun earlier in childhood.

2. Improved capacity to process information

a. Typically, an adolescent can deal with, or process, more information than a child can.

b. Adolescent differences may result from either of two sources. The first is *structural capacity*, or a person's basic "mental power" or cognitive ability (Case, 1986). The second is *functional capacity*, or the ability to make efficient use of existing mental abilities (Prauat, 1989).

c. When it comes to cognitive development, discriminating between the relative influences of structural and functional capacity is difficult (Siegler, 1983).

3. Expertise in specific domains of knowledge

a. By adolescence, many individuals have become comparative experts in specific domains of knowledge or skill that may or may not be related to school learning. One teenager may favor mathematics, and another may excel in baseball.

b. Much of this expertise may depend not on generalized development of cognitive structures, as Piagetians claim, but on the long, slow acquisition of large amounts of specific knowledge.

D. Evaluation of the Information-Processing Viewpoint

1. By focusing on the detailed features of problem solving, the information-processing viewpoint provides a valuable complement to the broader approach of cognitive developmental theory.

2. By focusing on the fine details of thinking, information-processing theory has more to say about why individuals vary in their thinking performance from one occasion to the next.

III. THE DEVELOPMENT OF SOCIAL COGNITION

A. Social Cognition

1. No matter which approach they take, most developmental psychologists agree that the new cognitive skills of adolescents have important effects on their social cognition, or knowledge and beliefs about interpersonal and social matters.

2. One important form of social cognition is a special form of self-centeredness, or *adolescent egocentrism*, that affects teenagers' reactions to others and their beliefs about themselves.

B. Egocentrism During Adolescence

1. When adolescents first begin reasoning abstractly, they often are overly impressed with their skill and may feel that anything can be solved logically. They wonder why world peace couldn't be achieved simply by logically explaining the dangers of war to the world powers and nations.

2. The development of formal thought leads to a new kind of confusion between an adolescent's own thoughts and those of others, which is a type of egocentrism.

3. Adolescent egocentrism sometimes shows itself in teenagers' preoccupation with the reaction of others. Thirteen-year-olds often fail to differentiate between how they feel about themselves and how others feel about them (Elkind & Bowen, 1979). Instead, they act as if they are performing for an imaginary audience.

4. The personal fable results from their egocentrism. Teenagers often believe that their own lives embody a special story that is heroic and unique.

C. Beliefs About Justice and Care

1. Ethical beliefs about justice emerge more fully in adolescence. Teenagers are less opportunistic than children and less inclined to judge according to immediate rewards or punishments that they personally experience.

2. Ethical beliefs about care are enhanced by teenagers' greater sense of principles of justice. Teenagers develop greater sensitivity to the needs of others (Selman, 1988).

3. Research on ethical development reveals that although teenagers may not always follow their own principles of justice, such principles do represent true convictions.

D. The Development of Political Ideas

1. Because politics involves many ethical problems, the development of political thinking is similar to that of ethical judgment.

2. As in moral development, adolescents show both progress and limitations in political thinking.

3. Teenagers often hold more sophisticated political ideas than children do; they better understand abstract political ideas and opinions and see more relationships among them; they view laws more democratically, seeing that laws are applicable to everybody in society.

E. Religious Beliefs and Orientation

1. During adolescence, cognitive development affects both specific religious beliefs and overall religious orientation. In general, specific beliefs become more sophisticated or complex than they were during childhood.

2. Children's acquisition of specific beliefs often matters less than their development of an overall view of the world, or of a *faith*, a coherent orientation to religious experiences that guides their responses to life.

Overview and Key Concepts

Chapter 15 presents Piaget's final stage, in which adolescents are capable of formal operational thinking. They are able to consider what might be, in contrast to what is. Their thinking is more systematic and logical even though it is bound by many limitations. Information-processing skills increase and enable adolescents to become expert in specific domains of knowledge. They are able to organize information more effectively and to retrieve it more efficiently than youngsters in concrete operations. In the area of social cognition, adolescents are often too preoccupied with the effect they have on others to engage in true formal operational thinking. Their ability to hypothesize influences their attitudes toward justice, politics, and religious beliefs.

Directions: Identify the following concepts introduced in Chapter 15.

1. In Piagetian terms, adolescents are able to engage in _____ or _____ .

2. This level of thinking differs from thinking in the middle years in three major ways: _____ , _____ , and _____ .

3. Another way of viewing cognition in adolescence is from the _____ .

4. According to this view, a _____ receives sensory information and holds it for a brief time. If any of this information is processed, it is transferred to _____ and then may be further processed into a form where it can be stored indefinitely in _____ .

5. Adolescents' improved capacity to process information may result from two sources. The first is _____ , or a person's basic "mental power." The second is _____ , or the ability to make efficient use of mental abilities.

6. _____ is reflection or thought about complex issues, often for the purpose of choosing actions related to the issues.

7. Most developmental psychologists agree that the new cognitive skills of adolescence have important effects on adolescents' _____ , or knowledge and beliefs about interpersonal and social matters. In some respects, adolescents' thinking is marked by a special form of self-centeredness, or _____ .

8. Thirteen-year-olds often fail to differentiate between how they feel about themselves and how others feel about them. Instead, they act as if they are performing for an unseen and _____ . This phenomenon is also revealed through _____ with their peers, encounters that aim either to reveal or to conceal personal information indirectly.

9. As a result of their egocentrism, teenagers often believe in a _____ , or the notion that their own lives embody a special story that is heroic and unique.

10. In imagining their own lives to be so dramatically different from the lives of others, adolescents fail to realize how frequently other individuals feel as they do. Early in adolescence, they still have only limited _____ , or the ability to understand reliably the abstract thoughts and feelings of others.

11. As adolescents gradually overcome egocentrism in their personal relationships, they develop their personal _____ , or sensitivity to and knowledge of what is right and wrong.

12. A few teenagers develop _____ . For the first time, their ethical reasoning goes beyond the judgments that society conventionally makes about right and wrong.

13. Like the ethics of justice, for a few individuals the ethics of care moves beyond the conventional pleasing of others toward _____ as the young person realizes that pleasing everyone is not always possible but that it is important to balance everyone's needs.

14. Although a twelfth-grader's ideas are more abstract and less personal than those of a sixth-grader, neither is really able to express a true political _____ or coherent philosophy about issues such as poverty.

15. Children's acquisition of specific beliefs may matter less than their development of an overall view of the world, or of a _____ , a coherent orientation to religious experiences that guides their responses to life.

Key Terms

Directions: Provide a definition for each of the following key terms. Check your answers against the Glossary or the text page number that follows each term.

Adolescent egocentrism (p. 557) _____

_____

_____

Critical thinking (p. 555) _____

_____

_____

Empathy (p. 558) _____

_____

_____

Ethics (p. 560) _____

_____

_____

Faith (p. 564) _____

_____

_____

Formal operational thought (p. 544) _____

_____

_____

Formal thought (p. 544) _____

_____

_____

Functional capacity (p. 554) _____

_____

_____

Ideology (p. 563) _____

_____

_____

Imaginary audience (p. 558) _____

_____

_____

Integrated care (p. 561) _____

_____

_____

Personal fable (p. 558) _____

_____

_____

Postconventional moral judgment (p. 560) _____

_____

_____

Social cognition (p. 557) _____

_____

_____

Strategic interaction (p. 558) _____

_____

_____

Structural capacity (p. 554) _____

_____

_____

Study Questions

1. What are the general features of adolescent thought? (pp. 543–544)

_____

_____

_____

_____

2. In what three ways does formal thought differ from thinking in the middle years? (pp. 544–545)

_____

_____

_____

_____

3. How would adolescents handle the Piagetian problem about bending rods differently from younger concrete thinkers? (p. 546)

_____

_____

_____

4. What are some of the limitations of Piaget's view of cognition in adolescence? (pp. 548–552)

_____

_____

_____

_____

5. In what ways does the information-processing viewpoint equate the human mind with a computer? (p. 552)

_____

_____

_____

_____

6. How would an information-processing theorist conceptualize the way in which a high school student might study for a multiple-choice history test? (pp. 553–554)

_____

_____

_____

_____

7. What are two sources of the adolescent's improved capacity to process information? (p. 554)

_____

_____

_____

_____

8. What is critical thinking and what are some of the ways that educational psychologists have proposed to classify the elements of critical thinking? (p. 555)

_____

_____

_____

_____

9. Describe adolescents' acquisition of expertise in specific domains of knowledge. (pp. 556–557)

_____

_____

_____

_____

10. What are the major strengths of the information-processing viewpoint? (p. 557)

_____

_____

_____

_____

11. What is social cognition and what is the impact of formal thought on teenagers' social cognition? (p. 557)

_____

_____

_____

_____

12. Describe adolescent egocentrism as a special form of self-centeredness in teenagers. (p. 557)

_____

_____

_____

_____

13. How is the concept of strategic interactions related to the notion of imaginary audience? (p. 558)

_____

_____

_____

_____

14. How does the phenomenon of personal fable reflect the adolescent's limited sense of empathy? (p. 558)

_____

_____

_____

_____

15. In what two major ways does a sense of personal ethics emerge during adolescence? (p. 560)

_____

_____

_____

_____

16. Describe adolescents' ethical beliefs about justice and about care. (pp. 560–561)

_____

_____

_____

_____

17. What progress do adolescents demonstrate toward the formulation of a political ideology? (pp. 562–563)

_____

_____

_____

_____

18. How do adolescents' religious beliefs and orientation differ from those of middle-years youngsters? (pp. 564–565)

_____

_____

_____

_____

Multiple-Choice Self-Test

1. Which of the following is a characteristic of adolescent thinking?
   a. functions primarily in the realm of reality rather than possibility
   b. is incapable of abstract problem solving
   c. increasingly uses imagination
   d. tends to use principled moral reasoning

2. Juan is considered to be a formal operational thinker. He can probably
   a. hold several ideas in his mind at once.
   b. make careful and systematic observations.
   c. go beyond concrete representations of ideas.
   d. all of the above.

3. According to Piaget, formal operations begin to develop
   a. during the preschool years.
   b. in middle childhood.
   c. in early adolescence.
   d. near the conclusion of adolescence.

4. One of the challenges of reasoning beyond the formal operational level is to
   a. view formal reasoning as a tool rather than as a goal in solving problems.
   b. switch thinking from reality to possibility.
   c. eliminate the scientific method.
   d. all of the above.

5. Results from training studies suggest that the less-than-formal operational responses made by adolescents may be due to
   a. competency factors.
   b. genetic factors.
   c. performance factors.
   d. all of the above.

6. Actual responses to new information are organized by instructions contained in the _____ and carried out by the _____ .
   a. short-term memory; long-term memory
   b. long-term memory; sensory register
   c. long-term memory; short-term memory
   d. short-term memory; sensory register

7. In the information-processing model, control processes are
   a. high-order storage of information within long-term memory.
   b. instructions for modifying, classifying, and transferring information.
   c. scanning abilities of short-term memory that screen input.
   d. the use of expert skills to solve problems.

8. The ability to make efficient use of existing mental abilities is referred to as
   a. intelligence.
   b. functional capacity.
   c. structural capacity.
   d. rehearsal.

9. Which of the following is *not* a major component of critical thinking?
   a. domain-specific knowledge
   b. metacognitive knowledge
   c. objective thinking
   d. impulsive thinking

10. Egocentrism in adolescence
    a. results from the confusion of one's thoughts with the thoughts of others.
    b. is identical to egocentrism in childhood.
    c. is a concrete operational skill.
    d. occurs in individuals who had imaginary playmates as a child.

11. Most adolescents function at the _____ level of moral and ethical development.
    a. postconventional
    b. preconventional
    c. conventional
    d. egocentric

12. Most adolescents
    a. frequently contradict themselves when discussing political matters.
    b. have a clearly stated political ideology.
    c. adopt the political ideology of their parents.
    d. none of the above.

Activities

Activity 15.1

> **Objective:** To discern cognitive levels and strategies used in playing chess.

Some children are taught to play chess while they are in the primary grades. More often, the game is played by adolescents and adults.

Fill in the cognitive strategies in the table below. If possible, interview a chess-playing child and adolescent. Many adolescents and adults recall the difference between how they played during childhood and how they played during adolescence. Ask the following questions.

	Concrete Operations	Formal Operations
Why did you want to learn?		
When learning, did you link this game to past experience?		
How did you remember the rules for how each piece could move?		
How did you understand the goal?		
What strategies did you use for playing? For defense? For offense?		
When did you begin to figure out the other player's strategy?		

	Concrete Operations	Formal Operations
At first, how far ahead did you plan your moves? now?		
When did you learn alternative moves?		
Other		

Activity 15.2

> **Objective:** To consider the young person's level of cognition in choosing games to play.

Children and adults have always played games. They are now included in many educational curricula. Some of the games listed below appeal more to adolescents in formal operations than to elementary school children in concrete operations. Place a C (for concrete operations) or an F (for formal operations) next to each of the following games.

Checkers		Charades	
Twenty Questions		Animal, Vegetable, or Mineral	
Hot or Cold		Hangman	
Lotto		Chinese Checkers	
Trivia		Parcheesi	
Poker		Monopoly	
Tic-tac-toe		Diplomacy	
Stone, Scissors, Paper		What's My Line?	
War (cards)		Scrabble	
Black Jack		Solitaire	
Backgammon		Jigsaw puzzles	
Gin Rummy		Bridge	
Go Fish			

Now add six games not mentioned.

Activity 15.3

Objective: To recognize the cognitive element in humor.

All humor has a cognitive element. When you hear a joke and "get it," you have an intellectual understanding of the point, and it is usually a surprise. The point of a riddle, at the concrete operational level, is usually a pun.

- What's black and white and read all over?
  A newspaper.

- Your shoes are on the wrong feet.
  But these are the only feet I have.

- What sting cures hunger?
  Feasting.

The adolescent and the adult in formal operations appreciate a more complex bit of humor such as paradox.

The following were suggested in Martin Gardner's *Aha! Gotcha: Paradoxes to Puzzle and Delight* (New York: W. H. Freeman and Co., 1982).

- The button that says, "Ban Buttons."

- The bumper sticker that says, "Eliminate Bumper Stickers."

- Groucho Marx: "I wouldn't join a club that would have me as a member."

- Many years ago a computer designed for testing the truth of statements was fed the liar paradox: "This sentence is False." According to Theodore Kalin, then an undergraduate at Harvard University, the computer went into an oscillating phase, making "a hell of a racket."

Your assignment is to find a bit of humor that could not be appreciated before the person is in the formal operational stage.

What had to be figured out?

Activity 15.4

Objective: To observe the complexities of moral dilemmas that an adolescent is able to consider.

It is not difficult for teenagers to define their moral principles when faced with the classical moral dilemmas presented by Piaget and Kohlberg. Defining moral principles becomes more complicated when the situation is one that they or their friends could face.

Present three adolescents with a moral dilemma that may well fit into their own experiences. For example:

Your parents are generous and hard working, but you know that they cheat seriously on their income tax.

A couple—friends of yours, who are seniors in high school—have just learned that the girl is two months pregnant. They are about to start college, one on a scholarship, the other on a student loan. They would never allow their baby to be adopted but recognize that they are not ready for parenthood.

Before you realize what is happening, your best friend is about to tell you what the questions on the final exam will be.

Describe a situation to each of three adolescents and ask, "What would you do?" Summarize the comments below.

Anecdote

Responses

Activity 15.5

Objective: To note expressions of political idealism among adolescents.

The ability to hypothesize makes it possible for adolescents to consider how society or the world could be improved. These ideals often find expression through alliance with a political party or a societal movement, such as environmental concerns, nuclear disarmament, anticommunist groups, ERA, pro-life, and gun control.

Check bulletin boards and the student affairs office for groups or clubs that represent such goals. List them below.

Answer Key

Overview and Key Concepts

1. formal thought; formal operational thought (p. 544)

2. in emphasizing the possible versus the real; in using scientific reasoning; in skillfully combining ideas (p. 544)

3. information-processing viewpoint (p. 552)

4. sensory register; short-term memory; long-term memory (p. 552)

5. structural capacity; functional capacity (p. 554)

6. critical thinking (p. 555)

7. social cognition; adolescent egocentrism (p. 557)

8. imaginary audience; strategic interactions (p. 558)

9. personal fable (p. 558)

10. empathy (p. 558)

11. ethics (p. 560)

12. postconventional moral judgment (p. 560)

13. integrated care (p. 561)

14. ideology (p. 563)

15. faith (p. 564)

Multiple-Choice Self-Test

1. Choice (c) is correct. Adolescents are capable of hypothetical reasoning, which, in turn, leads to speculation and imaginative thinking. (p. 543)
   Adolescents are capable of functioning in the realm of possibility, choice (a), and abstract problem solving, choice (b). But they still tend to use conventional moral reasoning, choice (d).

2. Choice (d) is correct. Formal operational thinkers can logically combine ideas, choice (a); use scientific reasoning, choice (b); and deal with the realm of possibility, choice (c). (p. 544)

3. Choice (c) is correct. Although not fully developed, formal operations begin in early adolescence. (p. 544)
Preschoolers, choice (a), are primarily preoperational. Middle-years children, choice (b), are concrete operational. At the end of adolescence, choice (d), formal operations continue to develop.

4. Choice (a) is correct. Teenagers tend to overrate the importance of logical thinking and view it as an end in itself. Thus thinking beyond formal operations involves using logic as a tool. (p. 548)
Choice (b) describes the transition from concrete to formal thinking. Although the limitations of the scientific method are discovered by the post-formal thinker, he does not eliminate the scientific method but uses it as a tool, choice (c).

5. Choice (c) is correct. Studies have found that influences having to do with motivation of momentary variations in situation can change performance. (p. 550)
Choice (a) would suggest that formal operations is not a universal stage. If choice (b) were correct, training studies would have no influence.

6. Choice (c) is correct. Information and strategies are stored in the long-term memory. The execution of that information is carried out by the short-term memory. (p. 552)
The sensory register, choices (b) and (d), holds the information briefly until it is selected to be processed by the short-term memory.

7. Choice (b) is correct. Control processes act like computer programs by supervising the modification, transfer, and classification of information. (p. 552)
Choices (a), (c), and (d) are functions not directly defined by the control processes.

8. Choice (b) is correct. Functional capacity refers to the utilization of various skills or techniques to improve performance. (p. 554)
Although intelligence, choice (a), may include aspects of functional capacity, the term is too broad in this context. Structural capacity, choice (c), refers to the mental power contained within the system. Choice (d) is an example of a technique included within functional capacity.

9. Choice (d) is correct. Critical thinking is viewed as deliberate or reflective, not as impulsive. (p. 555)
Knowing about the topic, choice (a); knowing about one's own thinking, choice (b); and remaining relatively fair and objective, choice (c), are all characteristics of critical thinking.

10. Choice (a) is correct. The adolescent realizes that others can have thoughts about him or her. Thus there is confusion between what the adolescent thinks is occurring and what is actually occurring. (p. 558)
    Egocentrism in childhood, choice (b), involves concrete problems; adolescent egocentrism concerns abstract problems. Adolescent egocentrism represents a formal skill, choice (c), because of the abstract abilities. It is unrelated to imaginary playmates, choice (d).

11. Choice (c) is correct. Adolescents' reasoning is consistent with Kohlberg's third and fourth stages. Adolescents tend to follow personal and social conventions. (p. 560)
    Only a few adolescents tend to use postconventional reasoning, choice (a). Most have advanced beyond preconventional levels, choice (b). Choice (d) is not a level of moral or ethical development.

12. Choice (a) is correct. With respect to political beliefs, most adolescents do not have a fully developed ideology and therefore tend to be inconsistent in their views. (pp. 562–563)
    Studies show that true political ideologies are not found among adolescents, choice (b). Although adolescents' views may be similar to those of their parents, choice (c), the similarity does not represent the simple adoption of the parental viewpoint.

CHAPTER 16
Adolescence: Psychosocial Development

Learning Objectives

1. Discuss the process of identity development from the standpoint of individuation. Describe the four major phases of this process.

2. Compare and contrast Erik Erikson's and James Marcia's theories of identity development. Identify the resolutions of the identity crisis and the four statuses.

3. Discuss the nature of the relationship between parents and adolescents.

4. Describe the nature of adolescent friendships. Indicate the developmental changes in friendships and describe sex differences in peer relations.

5. Describe the development of the peer group throughout the adolescent period. Indicate the relevant variables that determine peer group participation.

6. Discuss the nature of sexuality during adolescence, including dating, sexual behavior, and sexual preferences.

7. Describe the special problems of adolescence, including teenage pregnancy, abuse, delinquency, and suicide.

Chapter Outline

I. INDIVIDUATION AND IDENTITY DEVELOPMENT

    A. The idea that each of us has our own *identity*—a relatively stable sense of our own individual uniqueness and a commitment to an integrated set of goals, values, and beliefs— is not surprising.

B. The process by which an adolescent develops a unique personal identity or sense of self, distinct from all others, is called *individuation*.

C. Individuation has four subphases: differentiation, practice and experimentation, rapprochement, and consolidation (Josselson, 1980).

1. During the *differentiation* subphase, which occurs early in adolescence, the adolescent recognizes that he is psychologically different from his parents.

2. In the *practice and experimentation* subphase, the fourteen- or fifteen-year-old feels that he knows it all and can do no wrong.

3. The *rapprochement* subphase occurs toward the middle of adolescence, when the teenager has achieved a degree of separateness from parents.

4. The final subphase, which lasts until the end of adolescence, is the *consolidation of self*. During this phase, the adolescent develops a sense of personal identity, which continues to be the basis for understanding himself and others.

D. Theories of Identity Development

1. The crisis of identity versus role confusion

   a. Erik Erikson has contributed more than any other theorist to our understanding of identity development during adolescence.

   b. Erikson believes that the psychosocial crisis of *identity versus role confusion* occurs during this stage of development and that to resolve this crisis and achieve a final identity, a person must integrate her many childhood *identifications*, or the ways in which she has come to experience herself as being like her parents and like other important people in her life.

2. The relationship between identity and intimacy

   a. According to Erikson, successful resolution during adolescence of the crisis of identity versus identity confusion prepares the individual to move on to the central crisis of young adulthood—namely, intimacy versus isolation.

   b. A fairly clear and coherent sense of identity is needed to tolerate the loss of self that intense relationships often threaten.

3. Identity status

    a. Guided by Erikson's ideas, researchers have been able to study identity development during adolescence. James Marcia interviewed eighteen- to twenty-two-year-old students about occupation and religion (Marcia, 1967, 1980) and created four categories of *identity status:* identity achievement, identity diffusion, moratorium, and foreclosure.

    b. In general, adolescents seem to progress toward identity achievement. Marcia's categories show that identity achievement is rarest among early adolescents and most likely among older high school students, college students, and young adults.

II. SOCIAL RELATIONSHIPS DURING ADOLESCENCE

A. Relationships with Parents

1. It is a widely held belief that leaving home is an important part of becoming self-reliant.

2. Much of this process occurs during adolescence and highlights what might be called the *generation gap*.

3. The identity confusions that teenagers experience may restimulate similar unresolved feelings in their parents.

4. On the positive side, teenagers and parents generally regard adolescence as the exciting culmination of a long process of development.

5. Parenting styles

    a. Four aspects of parent-adolescent relationships appear to be involved in the adolescent's development of identity: parental interest and involvement, the emotional intensity of family interaction, the degree and nature of family conduct, and the nature of parental authority.

    b. In a study of more than seven thousand adolescents, researchers found that teenagers preferred two parental styles: democratic parenting and equalitarian parenting.

6. Social class differences: In general, differences between the values, child-rearing practices, and expectations of middle-class parents and working- and lower-class parents closely paralleled differences in the nature of their day-to-day work experience.

7. Divorce, remarriage, and single parenthood

   a. The impact of separation and divorce on adolescent development is influenced by a variety of factors, including when the divorce occurs, the nature and length of family conflicts that lead to divorce, the quality of the children's relationship with both parents, and the economic circumstances of the family after the divorce.

   b. Separation from the father early in life has a greater effect on boys and girls than does later separation (Levitin, 1979).

B. Friendship

   1. Friends matter a great deal during adolescence. They offer easier and more immediate acceptance than do most adults.

   2. Qualities of adolescent friendships

      a. Studies of adolescent peer relations reveal a trend toward mutuality.

      b. Unlike younger children's cooperation, adolescent mutuality depends on the understanding that other people share some of one's own abilities, interests, and inner experiences and an appreciation of each person's uniqueness.

   3. Male-female differences

      a. Friendships formed by boys had lower levels of intimacy than those formed by girls (Sharabany et al., 1981). Girls appeared to be better able to express feelings and to be more comfortable with giving emotional support than boys were.

      b. Girls also developed more intimacy with the opposite sex than boys did.

      c. Male-female differences are perhaps best explained as products of traditional sex-role stereotyping.

C. Peer Groups

   1. For most adolescents, social relationships extend beyond family to include peer groups, or age mates who know each other.

   2. For a teenager, peers are a central source of information about himself and others. They provide him with critical information about who he is.

   3. How do peer groups develop?

     a. Early in this period, teenagers form same-sex cliques that have little to do with each other; clique members are still very much like schoolchildren.

     b. With time, boys' and girls' cliques initiate contact with each other through activities.

     c. Parents, teachers, and adolescents all encourage membership in peer groups (Newman, 1982).

  4. Popularity and social acceptance

     a. Peer groups are central to adolescent experience and provide the adolescent with a basis for evaluating who he is and how well he is doing.

     b. In general, boys and girls who are popular are perceived as liking others; they are tolerant, flexible, and sympathetic.

  5. Conformity: Adolescents do pressure each other to conform, although probably not as much as the popular stereotype suggests.

D. The Influence of School

  1. School plays a central role in the development of adolescents in the United States. Students spend most of their days attending school.

  2. In addition to laws that require attendance, social expectations, parental pressures, and vocational requirements are very compelling.

III. SEXUALITY DURING ADOLESCENCE
Developmental changes in sexuality are closely tied to the achievement of physical maturity during puberty. During adolescence, the need for sexual expression is closely related to security needs, freedom from anxiety, and the need for intimacy and close relationships with others.

A. Masturbation

  1. Survey research indicates that 70 percent of boys and 45 percent of girls said they had masturbated by age fifteen.

  2. Sexually experienced adolescents tended to masturbate more than those who were less experienced.

B. Sexual Fantasies: Sexual fantasies about real or imaginary situations often accompany masturbation, although adolescents of all ages report such fantasies.

C. Heterosexuality

1. Sexual experience: During the last thirty years, there has been a significant increase in sexual activity among adolescents, particularly females.

2. Sexual attitudes: The "sexual revolution" of the 1960s and 1970s resulted in greater acceptance of premarital intercourse, masturbation, homosexuality, and lesbianism.

3. Dating: In the United States, dating is the major way in which adolescents begin their sexual activity.

4. Date rape or acquaintance rape is a situation in which a person, usually a female, is forced to have sex with a person she is dating.

D. Homosexuality

1. Largely because of the efforts of the women's liberation and gay rights movements, public acceptance of homosexuality has increased significantly during the past several decades.

2. This acceptance acknowledges the right of individuals to freely choose their own sexual orientations and life-styles.

E. Sex and Everyday Life: Although sex plays an important role in adolescents' feelings, fantasies, and social relationships, it does not necessarily dominate their lives.

IV. SPECIAL PROBLEMS OF ADOLESCENCE

A. Adolescent Pregnancy and Parenthood

1. The great majority of teenage pregnancies are the result of inadequate or no contraception.

2. Approximately 44 percent of all teenage pregnancies end in abortion (more than four hundred thousand in 1984).

3. One of the most helpful ways of understanding teenage pregnancy is in terms of its role in resolving the psychosocial crisis of identity during adolescence.

4. Prevention of teenage pregnancy requires a delay of early sexual activity as well as improved use of contraceptives among teenagers.

B. Abuse of Adolescents

1. Although public attention has recently focused on abuse of young children, violent encounters between adults and adolescents are common.

2. Abuse tends to be greatest for children between three and four and for adolescents between fifteen and seventeen.

C. Homeless and Runaway Adolescents: It is estimated that there are approximately 1.5 million runaways and 500,000 homeless youths living on their own in the United States in a given year (Shane, 1989).

D. Juvenile Delinquency: Juvenile delinquency consists of antisocial and lawbreaking activities that are reported to authorities as well as antisocial behavior that is not reported.

E. Teenage Suicide: Studies of the backgrounds of teens who attempt suicide suggest that they often experience serious family difficulties, personal turmoil, and intense loneliness and isolation and that suicide attempts are almost always cries for help (Shaffer, 1974).

Overview and Key Concepts

Adolescents, on the threshold of adulthood, experience crises of identity that interact with their parents' developmental crises. Career and educational plans tend to vary according to social class and ethnic background. Social relationships intensify, with personal and adult pressures to join certain peer groups. Sexual needs coincide with needs for intimacy as well as autonomy. The risk of pregnancy is high and adds to the burdens of a sometimes overwhelmed young person. The emerging adult is one who has managed to integrate the facets of existence into a cohesive, reasonably healthy personality.

Directions: Identify the following concepts introduced in Chapter 16.

1. The process by which an adolescent develops a unique personal identity is called _____ and is divided into four subphases: _____ , _____ , _____ , and _____ .

2. Erikson believes that the psychosocial crisis of _____ occurs during adolescence.

3. According to Erikson, just as the latency period provides a temporary suspension before puberty, adolescence provides a _____ before young adulthood and its responsibilities.

4. _____ , or a failure to achieve a relatively integrated and stable identity, takes a number of different forms.

5. _____ is a form of identity diffusion that involves rejection and disparagement of the roles offered by one's family or community as proper and desirable and an acceptance of socially undesirable roles, such as that of the delinquent.

6. Guided by Erikson's ideas, James Marcia identified four states of identity development: _____ , _____ , _____ , and _____ .

7. Differences in experiences and understandings between parents and their children account for what is sometimes called the _____ .

8. In a study involving more than seven thousand adolescents, researchers found that teenagers felt most positively about two parental styles: _____ and _____ .

9. Studies of adolescent peer relations reveal a trend toward greater _____ in friendship through increased loyalty and intimacy over the teen years.

10. _____ refers to antisocial and lawbreaking activities that are reported to authorities and to antisocial behavior that is not reported.

Key Terms

Directions: Provide a definition for each of the following key terms. Check your answers against the Glossary or the text page number that follows each term.

Autocratic parenting (p. 581) _____

_____

_____

Clique (p. 587) _____

_____

_____

Consolidation of self (p. 572) _____

_____

_____

Crowd (p. 587) _____

_____

_____

Democratic parenting (p. 581) _____

_____

_____

Differentiation (p. 571) _____

_____

_____

Equalitarian parenting (p. 581) _____

_____

_____

Generation gap (p. 578) _____

_____

_____

Identification (p. 572) _____

_____

_____

Identity (p. 570) _____

_____

_____

Identity diffusion (p. 574) _____

_____

_____

Identity status (p. 576) _____

_____

_____

Identity versus role confusion (p. 572) _____

_____

_____

Individuation (p. 570) _____

_____

_____

Intimacy (p. 586) _____

_____

_____

Juvenile delinquency (p. 603) _____

_____

_____

Mutuality (p. 585) _____

_____

_____

Negative identity (p. 575) _____

_____

_____

Peer group (p. 587) _____

_____

_____

Practice and experimentation (p. 572) _____

_____

_____

Psychosocial moratorium (p. 573) _____

_____

_____

Rapprochement (p. 572) _____

_____

_____

Study Questions

1. Describe each of the four phases of individuation. (pp. 570–572)

   _____

   _____

   _____

   _____

2. How do the concepts of identification and psychosocial moratorium relate to the crisis of identity versus role confusion? (pp. 572–573)

   _____

   _____

   _____

   _____

3. In what ways, according to Elkind, are the markers of adolescence disappearing? (pp. 574–575)

   _____

   _____

   _____

   _____

4. What are the characteristics of Marcia's four categories of identity status? (pp. 576–578)

   _____

   _____

   _____

   _____

5. How do both Erikson and Sullivan view the link between identity and intimacy? (pp. 575–576)

_____

_____

_____

_____

6. How might an adolescent's need to establish a firm identity interact with the parents' developmental tasks? (pp. 578–580)

_____

_____

_____

_____

7. Describe the two parenting styles that are most conducive to rapport between teenagers and their parents. (p. 581)

_____

_____

_____

_____

8. What type of parenting received the lowest ratings from teenagers? (p. 581)

_____

_____

_____

_____

9. What differences in the psychosocial development of adolescents may be attributed to social class? (p. 582)

_____

_____

_____

_____

10. How does the current phenomenon of family changes due to divorce, remarriage, and single-parent families affect an adolescent's psychosocial development? (pp. 582–584)

_____

_____

_____

_____

11. What are the salient qualities of adolescent friendships? (pp. 585–586)

_____

_____

_____

_____

12. What are two common kinds of peer groups and what functions do they serve? (pp. 587–588)

_____

_____

_____

_____

13. In what ways do popular adolescents differ from those who are unpopular? (pp. 588–589)

_____

_____

_____

_____

14. What are some of the factors that produce conformity among adolescents? (pp. 589–590)

_____

_____

_____

_____

15. What are some positive and negative outcomes of the school's influence in the lives of adolescents? (pp. 590–591)

_____

_____

_____

_____

16. How do patterns of heterosexual relationships differ between boys and girls? (pp. 593–595)

_____

_____

_____

_____

17. What are contributing factors to and consequences of teenage pregnancy? (pp. 597–600)

_____

_____

_____

_____

18. Under what circumstances is sexual abuse of adolescents likely to occur and how might the degree of trauma be estimated? (pp. 600–602)

_____

_____

_____

_____

19. What are some factors associated with juvenile delinquency? (pp. 603–604)

_____

_____

_____

_____

20. What type of background is associated with teen suicide? (pp. 604–605)

_____

_____

_____

_____

Multiple-Choice Self-Test

1. In which phase of individuation does the adolescent feel he "knows it all and can do no wrong"?
   a. consolidation
   b. differentiation
   c. practice and experimentation
   d. rapprochement

2. Erikson views the development of identity as
   a. a product of learning experiences during the school years.
   b. the creation of an entirely new self.
   c. the integration of childhood identities.
   d. the loss of egocentric thinking.

3. Isabella has pretty much accepted her parents' values and has not undergone a crisis during adolescence. She would be considered
   a. foreclosed.
   b. identity achieved.
   c. identity diffused.
   d. in moratorium.

4. Recent studies of adolescent gender differences in identity status suggest that
   a. most females are foreclosed and most males are diffused.
   b. most males are foreclosed and most females are achieved.
   c. most males are either achieved or in moratorium and most females are foreclosed or diffused.
   d. there is little or no gender difference in identity status.

5. After leaving home, adolescents often experience
   a. better relations with their parents.
   b. a sense of guilt.
   c. a lessening of parental affection.
   d. all of the above.

6. Parents tend to exert more influence on their adolescent children than do peers in issues concerning
   a. career goals.
   b. dating.
   c. music.
   d. all of the above.

7. Working-class parents
   a. are least likely to be authoritative.
   b. are least likely to support independence.
   c. are extrinsically motivated.
   d. all of the above.

8. What are the two main dimensions of friendship in adolescence?
   a. activities and companionship
   b. independence and flexibility
   c. mutuality and intimacy
   d. socializing and sex

9. The major activity of a clique is _____ ; a crowd involves _____ .
   a. sexual; social activities
   b. small parties; sports
   c. talking; organized social functions
   d. weekend events; weekday events

10. Adolescents who do well in school generally
    a. feel that education is relevant to long-term goals.
    b. meet teachers' expectations.
    c. view educational skills as fitting their life-style.
    d. all of the above.

11. The percentage of teenagers who use contraceptive devices or other birth control methods the first time they have sex is approximately _____ .
    a. 10 percent
    b. 30 percent
    c. 50 percent
    d. 70 percent

12. Parental abuse of adolescents tends to be
    a. about as extensive as abuse of young children.
    b. less common than abuse of young children.
    c. primarily physical rather than sexual.
    d. in the form of neglect.

Activities

Activity 16.1

Objective: To identify examples of adolescents in the differentiation and practicing phases of individuation and identity development.

The adolescent in the differentiation phase seems peculiarly bound to parental wishes. The parent's wish acts as a signal to do something different.

Do you recall acting this way during your early adolescence?

Describe the incident.

Do you know anyone else who got caught in the same kind of trap? What was it?

During the practicing phase, a kind of cognitive conceit may appear. Having found that the parent is not all-knowing and all-wise, the adolescent sometimes concludes that the parent does not know much of anything.

Do you recall actively defying parental standards and admonitions, to proceed with a course of action you had chosen?

What was it?

What was the outcome?

If you are among the fortunate few who did not need to go through this phase, do you know anyone who did? What happened and how did it turn out?

For some people this rejection of parents' wishes continues into adulthood. Do you know of anyone who, as an adult, still fights the old parental rules (e.g., one who might deliberately ignore Mother's Day even though it is an important event to most mothers)?

Activity 16.2

Objective: To recognize the influence of the media on adolescent image makers.

Sociologists and psychologists are concerned about the tendency of the media to push children and adolescents into a premature adulthood, an adulthood for which they are neither cognitively nor intellectually ready.

Do the following films and TV programs realistically portray children and adolescents, or are they "adultified"?

Title	Realistic? Adultified?
Parenthood	
Heathers	
Say Anything	
Pump Up the Volume	
Risky Business	
Leave It to Beaver	
Father Knows Best	
The Cosby Show	
ET	
Family Ties	

Activity 16.3

> **Objective:** To identify the personal stresses that parents may be experiencing during their adolescent children's period of identity crisis.

Interview at least one of your grandparents or another grandparent you may know. Ask them to recall their children's teen years. Ask the following questions.

Do you recall whether your teenager was, at times, hard to parent?

Try to remember what was happening in your own life at that time. What were the challenges?

Were you able to separate your own stresses from those that involved your adolescent?

If so, how did you manage it?

If not, did it make the situation worse?

How did it turn out?

Looking back, would you have wanted a different kind of resolution?

In what way?

Activity 16.4

> **Objective:**   To recall personal examples of peer pressure.

The potential for an unhappy result is high when an adolescent gives in to peer pressure. Recall your own adolescence and the times that you gave in to the pressure of your peers, against your own preference or against your own better judgment.

When it was a matter of opinion, such as whether it was a "good" TV show or movie

When the decision was about which public entertainment all of you would attend

When your parents said it was not safe

When your friends decided to do something that you considered dangerous

When your friends expressed dislike and contempt for someone who struck a sympathetic chord in you

The choice of a school activity

The choice of whom you would date

Opinions about one of your teachers

The brand of clothes to wear

Career choice

When did you take a stand?

Activity 16.5

> **Objective:**   Identifying ways in which an older adolescent can help a younger person.

Suppose that you are nineteen years old, and it looks as if your life is coming together more comfortably than it has for years. You've made a career choice, and you feel good about it. You've decided you look okay for all practical purposes. You have friends of both sexes, including someone special. You're getting along all right with your parents. And now your fourteen-year-old sibling is looking unhappy. How can you help?

If s/he feels unattractive?

Unpopular?

Is furious about being "grounded" for the weekend?

Can't decide which program to choose in high school?

Is afraid to date?

Thinks your parents don't know anything?

Doesn't want to go in a friend's car but is afraid to say so?

Is reluctant to refuse to smoke a joint?

Wants to try the hard stuff?

Answer Key

Overview and Key Concepts

1. individuation; differentiation; practice and experimentation; rapprochement; consolidation (p. 570)

2. identity versus role confusion (p. 572)

3. psychosocial moratorium (p. 573)

4. identity diffusion (p. 574)

5. negative identity (p. 575)

6. identity achievement; identity diffusion; moratorium; foreclosure (p. 577)

7. generation gap (p. 578)

8. democratic parenting; equalitarian parenting (p. 581)

9. mutuality (p. 585)

10. juvenile delinquency (p. 603)

Multiple-Choice Self-Test

1. Choice (c) is correct. During the practice and experimentation phase, the adolescent denies any need for caution or advice and actively challenges his parents. (p. 572)
Choice (a) involves the development of a personal identity of a more realistic nature; (b) involves the realization that the adolescent is different from his or her parents; and (d) involves a cooperative and conciliatory view of others.

2. Choice (c) is correct. Erikson views identity development as the selection of an identity based on previous experiences and thus integrating all the possibilities into a final identity. (p. 573)
Erikson does not limit experience to the school years, choice (a), but rather looks at the entire life span. The child does not form a new self, choice (b), but rather takes aspects of the existing self and integrates them. Erikson does not deal with egocentric thinking, choice (d).

3. Choice (a) is correct. Having no crisis but having made a commitment is what Marcia describes as foreclosed identity. (p. 577)
Choice (b) is a person who has had a crisis and made a commitment; (c) has neither had a crisis nor made a commitment; and (d) is in crisis with no commitment.

4. Choice (d) is correct. Both genders are represented equally among the four identity statuses and seem to develop in similar ways. Thus, choices (a), (b), and (d) are inaccurate. (p. 578)

5. Choice (a) is correct. The quality of the adolescent-parent relationship improves as the adolescent develops a greater sense of independence. (p. 579)
   When the adolescent leaves, there does not appear to be any sense of guilt, choice (b); and parental affection increases, choice (c).

6. Choice (a) is correct. Parents tend to have more influence in issues that have long-range consequences as opposed to issues touching on current social life and behavior. (p. 580)
   Choices (b) and (c) would be considered issues of current social life or behavior over which the parents have less influence.

7. Choice (d) is correct. Working-class families tend to be authoritarian rather than authoritative, choice (a); unlikely to support independence by including adolescents in decision making, choice (b); and extrinsically motivated, choice (c). (p. 582)

8. Choice (c) is correct. Studies have found that mutual understanding and intimacy help foster complementary relationships in adolescence. (p. 585)
   Activities and companionship, choice (a); independence and flexibility, choice (b); and socializing and sex, choice (d), have varying degrees of importance. But they are not the main dimensions of friendship in adolescence.

9. Choice (c) is correct. Cliques tend to be small same-sex groups based on shared purposes and activities. Their major activity tends to be talking. Crowds are larger groups, often made up of several cliques. Their main purpose involves social functions. (p. 587)
   Choices (a), (b), and (d) are not primary functions of cliques and crowds respectively.

10. Choice (d) is correct. Adolescents who generally have positive expectations about school generally adjust and do well as indicated in choices (a), (b), and (c). (p. 591)

11. Choice (c) is correct. About half of all teenagers fail to use any methods of birth control the first time they have sexual intercourse. (p. 597)

12. Choice (a) is correct. The incidence of abuse tends to be highest in young children between ages three and four and in adolescents between ages fifteen and seventeen. (p. 600)
    Rates of abuse are the same for these age groups, choice (b). Abuse of teenagers is both physical and sexual, choice (c). Neglect is more often found among younger children, choice (d).